INTERVIEWING IN A CHANGING WORLD

Interviewing in a Changing World offers students the broadest coverage of interviewing available today by including several unique interview situations. Students begin to develop a better understanding of how to utilize strong interviewing skills in several different settings, as this text demonstrates that interviewing techniques differ in accordance with varying situations and contexts. The Second Edition covers employment contexts such as job interviews, persuasive interviews, performance and appraisal interviews, as well as media interviews on radio, television, newspapers, and political reporting. There are two full chapters on research, including interviewing skills needed for both qualitative and quantitative research. The book covers several unique interviewing situations that are on the cutting edge of communication research with an interview with a professional from the field and multiple sidebars on related theoretical and applied issues within each chapter.

Jonathan Howard Amsbary is a Professor and the Graduate Director in the Department of Communication Studies at the University of Alabama at Birmingham, USA. He serves as the Graduate Director for the Communication Management M.A. program.

Larry Powell is a Professor of Communication Studies who teaches mass communication and communication management courses. He has worked for ten years as a full-time communication consultant and is ranked as one of the top 50 active communication researchers in the nation by *Communication Monographs*.

D1610985

INTERVIEWING IN A CHANGING WORLD

Situations and Contexts

Second Edition

Jonathan Howard Amsbary
and
Larry Powell

Routledge
Taylor & Francis Group

NEW YORK AND LONDON

Second Edition published 2018
by Routledge
711 Third Avenue, New York, NY 10017

and by Routledge
2 Park Square, Milton Park, Abingdon, Oxon OX14 4RN

Routledge is an imprint of the Taylor & Francis Group, an informa business

First edition published by Pearson 2005

Library of Congress Cataloging-in-Publication Data
Names: Amsbary, Jonathan H. (Jonathan Howard), 1956– author. | Powell, Larry, 1948– author.
Title: Interviewing in a changing world : situations and contexts / Jonathan H. Amsbary, Larry Powell.
Description: Second edition. | New York : Routledge / Taylor & Francis Group, [2018]
Identifiers: LCCN 2017037139 | ISBN 9781138080966 (hardback) |
ISBN 9781138080959 (pbk.) | ISBN 9781315113135 (ebk)
Subjects: LCSH: Employment interviewing.
Classification: LCC HF5549.5.I6 A48 2018 | DDC 650.14/4—dc23
LC record available at https://lccn.loc.gov/2017037139

ISBN: 978-1-138-08096-6 (hbk)
ISBN: 978-1-138-08095-9 (pbk)
ISBN: 978-1-315-11313-5 (ebk)

Typeset in Helvetica
by Apex CoVantage, LLC

Visit the companion website: www.routledge.com/cw/amsbary

CONTENTS

CONTENTS

CONTENTS

CONTENTS

Section 1

INTRODUCTION

1

THE BASICS OF INTERVIEWING

John sits nervously in the outer office of a major corporation. Within a few minutes, he will have a job interview that, if successful, could get him a position with the company of his dreams.

June works for a telephone research center. Each night, she places calls to individuals that she has never met with the intent of asking them a series of questions about a new product that will soon be on the market.

Carlos is a reporter for a major newspaper. His job involves gathering information from newsmakers, asking them questions about what is happening that is of importance to the public.

Juanita is a nurse. Part of her job is talking with patients, getting a brief summary of their symptoms and problems, so that the physician can make a thorough diagnosis of their condition.

Each of these people is engaged in the process of interviewing. Indeed, in modern society, the role of interviewing has been increasing as more jobs require some element of interviewing skills. But, what is this skill which is so important in today's career environment? For the purposes of this book, *interviewing is defined as a process of purposeful interaction involving two parties and which involves the asking and answering of questions.* Consider this definition in terms of its component parts.

First, an interview is a **purposeful interaction**. Each person enters the interview with a goal in mind, and each person participates with the intent of increasing his/her chances of achieving that goal. John will enter his employment interview with the intent of impressing the interviewer enough that he will be hired by the company. Across the desk, his interviewer will be working toward a different purpose—seeking to assess the strengths and weaknesses of each applicant for the purpose of hiring the best new employee for the company. As a reporter, Danny will be seeking information that can be used in the writing of an informative news story. Some of the people he interviews, though, may be trying to hide some information that would be useful to that story. The purposes of the participants may vary, but without such a purpose an interview doesn't exist.

In many ways the satisfaction that you will have during various interviews will be determined long before the first question is asked and answered. Interviewing is a goal-driven activity. Each party, the interviewer and interviewee, has an objective they want to accomplish during the interview. Sometimes the goal may be the same; for instance, both you and your doctor will likely have similar goals when he or she takes your medical history: your well-being. On the other hand, there are interviews where the two parties will be at cross-purposes. An employer wants to find the best employee to fill the position he or she is trying to fill, and applicants want the employer to hire them, whether they are the best fit or not. Certainly many people come away from press interviews feeling frustrated because the interviewee has a story to tell, but the reporter may have a very different story to tell.

Second, an interview is **dyadic** when it involves **two parties**. The operative word here is parties, not people. In some instances, the interviewee may be more than one person, i.e., a group of people are brought together and interviewed at the same time. Such interviews are known as *panel interviews* (Hamilton & Parker, 1990, p. 201; Dipboye, Gaugler, Hayes, & Parker, 2001). They are frequently used in research studies in the form of panel studies or focus groups. In other instances, the number of interviewers might outnumber the number of interviewees. Such instances create what is known as a *board interview*. For example, a congressional subcommittee may call for testimony from an expert on terrorism. The expert would then appear before the entire committee, with each committee member allowed to ask questions of the expert.

Third, an interview involves the **asking and answering of questions**. Interviews are not merely an exchange of questions and answers. Sometimes the interviewer simply makes a statement and waits to see how the interviewee responds. Sometimes the interviewer simply remains silent, encouraging the interviewee to provide more information. Still, the asking and answering of questions is the backbone around which the rest of the interaction is organized. The purpose of most interviews involves some element of information exchange or sharing, and the Q&A process is crucial to its success.

Interviewing is often—but not always—a zero-history interaction. The parties in an interview will sometimes have a history of interaction with each other. Counseling, performance interviews, health care interviews, and exit interviews all encompass situations in which the interviewer and the interviewee have had some previous interactions. In many other situations, however, there is likely to have been no previous interaction. Market research interviewers randomly call individuals that they've never met before. College graduates seeking their first job may have never met the people who will be deciding whether to hire them. News reporters may be doing a story on individuals they've never met before. Indeed, one of the purposes in many interviews is for the parties to meet and learn something about each other. Because of this, the interactions in interviews tend to be more formal than in other contexts.

The purpose of this book will be to help the reader understand the various elements of this definition. As a starting point, it is important to understand the basic factors that influence the structure and effectiveness of an interview. Those factors are (1) the different types of interviews, (2) the different phases of the interview process, (3) the various techniques that might be used in many interviews, and (4) an understanding of how the structure of interviews can vary. This chapter will look at these four elements from a basic perspective. Each of the following chapters will explore them in more detail, showing how they pertain to interviews in differing types of situations. It is important to understand that interviewing takes place in many other contexts, but these general contexts cover enough ground that you should be able to generalize the information into many contexts.

Types of Interviews

Workplace Interviews

These interviews include employment, performance review, grievance, exit, and persuasive interviews.

Employment interviews are the poster child of interviewing techniques. Most books that talk about interviews focus on this area. Although it is not the only type of interview, it is easily the most visible and the one that nearly every person will experience at some time in their careers. Employment interviews are a screening technique by which organizations make initial evaluations regarding hiring decisions of new employees. They involve multiple aspects and functions, including information gathering and assessment.

The performance review interview is an interview that is used to assess the work of an individual or group. Devito (2000) calls it an "appraisal" interview (p. 224). Many organizations use annual performance review interviews. Such interviews allow them to (1) identify those workers who are performing at an exceptional level, (2) identify potential weak spots in performances before they become troublesome, (3) create a clear understanding between the employer and employee regarding the employer's level of satisfaction with their work, and (4) allow both parties to focus on future performance.

Hamilton and Parker (1990) define the grievance interview as "any type of one-to-one encounter involving conflict and resolution" (p. 200). Some organizations have a formal grievance procedure in which any employee with a complaint against the company can file for and request a grievance interview. For others, the grievance interview is an informal process in which a dissatisfied worker simply makes a request to their immediate supervisor regarding a complaint that they have. In either instance, though, the grievance interview is a combination of information exchange and persuasive effort.

Some people switch jobs, moving to another that offers better pay, better benefits, or a better work environment. Some people simply burn out from working too long and too hard at one single position. Some people just decide to retire. Organizations, though, may never know why any one person leaves a job with the company unless they ask. That's why many organizations schedule exit interviews with all personnel who decide to quit or retire. Such interviews give the employer a chance to assess what mistakes they might be making that would drive people away from jobs. They give the departing worker one last chance to contribute to the company's success.

Media Interviews

These interviews take place in a variety of contexts and through a growing number of media. Traditionally, these types of interviews were conducted by reporters for newspapers. Although the number of newspapers in America is declining, the variety of press media is expanding—from blogs, to cable news, to traditional broadcast news, to social media. The amount of information being released to the public is staggering. The ability to handle one's self at a press conference or with a reporter with a microphone and/or camera has never been more important for public figures.

Research Interviews

These interviews include information seeking (or research interviews), information giving, and information sharing. A telephone survey represents a type of information-seeking interview; the interviewer asks specific questions designed to provide the researcher with specific information. A telemarketing sales call would be an example of an information-giving interview; the salesperson hopes to speak with the interviewee long enough to give them some information about the product. Three people on a panel, responding to a moderator's questions, would be an example of an information-sharing interview. The questions would spark different responses so that multiple views on the same topic could be obtained.

Informational interviews can also vary in terms of (1) the level of information needed and (2) the expertise required to conduct the interview. A doctor who interviews a patient, for the purpose of diagnosing their condition, might need more information than with some other informational interviews. Similarly, the expertise required for such a medical interview would be higher than the skills needed for a telemarketing interview.

Phases in the Interview Process

Most interviews can be divided into four distinct stages: (1) preparation, (2) opening, (3) Q&A, and (4) closing.

Preparation

Successful interviews start with anticipating and planning. Anticipating the situation allows both the interviewer and interviewee to evaluate and assess their own strengths and weaknesses as it relates to approaching the interview. Planning helps in the identification of the goal for the interview. That latter element is critical. To make the interview more effective and efficient, Edwards and Brilhart (1981) recommend that you use your preparation time to identify the goal of the interview and then be prepared to reveal it to the other person quickly.

Opening

The opening, or first contact, of the interview is often crucial to its success or failure. That initial interaction sets the tone and mood for the interaction that follows, creating a climate for the rest of the interview (Klinzing & Klinzing, 1985, p. 60). Those first few moments can be important in any health-care interview, but it is absolutely critical in therapeutic situations. In those instances, the interviewer's first goal must be to establish a climate that will foster trust and understanding (Northouse & Northouse,1985, p. 182). For that reason, the interviewer cannot rush into some topics. Instead, many interviewers use this time to introduce themselves, to learn the name of the interviewee, and to ask a few questions about the interviewee's interests—looking for common ground that can help establish rapport (Banyard & Fernald, 2002).

For information-oriented interviews, the opening stages of the interview should be used to clarify the purpose of the interview and establish mutual goals with the patient. A common understanding of those goals is a key factor here. If the interviewer and interviewee dance around issues for the remainder of the interview, little will be accomplished. That may seem like a simple concept, but it is easily ignored, particularly if the interviewer rushes through this stage too quickly. False agreement can easily be achieved by speaking in vague terms about the purpose and goal of the interview, and the interviewer may move on to the next stage under the mistaken belief that the interviewee is ready to follow and participate freely in the discussion.

Q&A

Q&A is the exploration, or working phase, of the interview. The interviewer offers questions and seeks responses from the interviewee during this phase. The interviewer must constantly monitor the interviewee's feedback to seek some indication that not all of the necessary information has been provided. The interviewer must also carefully monitor their own communication behavior so that they can maintain an effective relationship with the other person, and thus continue the interview in a productive manner.

One factor affecting the behavior within the interview is the expectation level of each participant. Burgoon's (1993) expectancy violation theory posits that preconceived expectations influence observers' reactions to behaviors and the actors who perform them. Nonconformity to expected norms will either be condoned or condemned, depending on the perceptions of the violator as either rewarding or threatening. Valence is important, with high credible medical personnel allowed to deviate more from the social norm before the behavior is perceived as a violation. Low credibility and female personnel have less freedom in message selection, because—for them—aggressive strategies would be a negative violation of expectations that would inhibit attitude change (Burgoon & Miller, 1985).

Closing

Interviews should not be abruptly ended just because the interviewer has all the information they need. Instead, a successful interview will include an identifiable closing stage in which both participants realize that it's time to close the interview (Sundeen et al., 1981). Unfortunately, that doesn't always happen. Ideally, the closing of the interview should accomplish both of those goals: It should (1) summarize the key points of the interview and (2) ensure that both participants have had an opportunity to say the things they believe should be said. At the very least, the interviewer should ask if the interviewee has any final questions.

Techniques for Interviews

Question Sequence

Stewart and Cash (1982) identified three different sequences that are used in interviews: (1) the funnel sequence, (2) the inverted funnel, and the (3) tunnel sequence. In the *funnel sequence*, the interviewer begins by asking broad questions and then proceeds to more specific questions. This approach gradually focuses the discussion to a specific topic.

The *inverted funnel*, as its name implies, reverses this process. In this approach, the interviewer begins by asking a series of specific questions and gradually broadens the approach to obtain an overall view of the topic being discussed. The inverted funnel is particularly useful in stimulating responses from a reticent and non-talkative interviewee. If someone is reluctant to talk, they will tend to fend off broad, open-ended questions, particularly at the beginning of the interview. But they will respond to short, specific questions, and these can be used as an ice-breaker to get them to talk more freely about all of their symptoms and their emotional responses to their problems.

The *tunnel sequence* is an interview that uses a series of similar questions of the same format. The tunnel sequence is effective when the interviewer needs to cover a number of different topics, but in-depth information on those topics is not necessary.

Verbal Tools

The interviewer's ultimate tools are their personal set of verbal skills. The ability to use language that the interviewee can understand and that will also elicit the desired information is essential to the interview's success. The adept interviewer will learn a variety of techniques that can be used to elicit information from the patient.

The adept interviewer has several different types of questions that can be used to elicit valuable information. These options include open-ended questions, closed-ended questions, probes, third-person questions, and projective questions. *Open-ended questions* are phrased in such a manner as to encourage the interviewee to respond using their own words ("Tell me about yourself"). This open-ended approach allows the interviewee to discuss the topic from their own perspective, with less chance that the interviewee will guide the discussion along a pre-determined path. The broadest form of an open-ended question is simply the process of addressing a topic ("Tell me about the early years of your career"), whereas other forms may direct the interviewee along a slightly more narrow path ("How did your early career influence the success you have today?").

Closed-ended questions offer only limited options for response; such questions would include those that have only a yes/no answer ("Have you ever worked in the fast-food industry before?") or with only limited options ("How would you evaluate your math skills: good, bad, or about average?"). Closed-ended questions are used when the interviewer is seeking clarification or needs to know a specific piece of information. Some interviews will start with a broad, open-ended question and become more closed-ended as the interview progresses. Thus a section of an interview that starts with "Tell me about your early career" may end up with specific, closed-ended questions such as "What year was that?" and "How old were you at the time?"

Follow-up questions are *probes* that seek more information from an initial response. Sometimes, a probe is a simple imperative request ("Tell me more about that"). Other forms of probes include the simple use of question words and phrases such as "Why?" or "What happened next?" Another form of probe is the connective question, i.e., a question created by taking one element of the interviewee's response and building upon it ("You just said you were only 17 when you first worked professionally—how did you get started at such a young age?"). Two nonverbal behaviors—silence and head nods—can also be used as probes. Both of those techniques can be used to encourage a person to continue talking about a subject for a little longer.

Third-person questions are an indirect technique that can be used if the question is one that covers a sensitive topic; in those instances it is usually easier to get the person to talk about the topic in an indirect manner. Thus, if a manager is interviewing a subordinate about the job, they are likely to get little information if he or she asks, "What do you think about the job I'm doing?" In such an instance, an indirect question would work better ("What do most of the other workers think about the job I'm doing?").

Although not appropriate for all interviews, *projective questions* are sometimes used in some interview formats, particularly in therapeutic and market research interviews. The typical projective question asks the interviewee about an unrelated concept ("If you were a car, what would you be?" "If this product were a car, what would it be?"). The responses to such questions can provide insight into an individual's self-esteem ("a Cadillac" vs. "a used car with 150,000 miles") or their image of a product ("one that needs to go to the repair shop"). Furthermore, projective questions frequently trigger responses that can be followed up with other questions that probe for more details.

Phrasing of Questions

One key element in the effective medical interview is the way the medical worker phrases the question. At a basic level, the interviewer has the option of phrasing the question from an open-ended approach ("Tell me about your problem"), which allows for a wide range of responses, or using closed-ended questions ("Does your jaw hurt?"), which have a limited number of possible answers. Interviewers using the funnel sequence, for example, typically start with open-ended questions and switch to closed-ended ones as the interview progresses. Use of the inverted funnel sequence could result in the reversal of that process, with the interviewer starting with closed-ended questions and waiting until they feel the reticent patient is comfortable enough to answer open-ended questions. Open-ended questions encourage a wider range of responses from the interviewee, whereas closed-ended questions allow the interviewer to focus more on specific information needed to make a judgment.

Another important factor is the word choices used in phrasing the question. The skillful medical interviewer learns to ask questions without using professional jargon. Questions should be phrased so that the interviewee can respond to them in their own terms. Care must also be taken not to use words or phrases that will place the interviewee in a psychologically defensive position.

Improper Questions

What is proper and improper to ask during an interview will vary with every situation. Given the variation in what is legally and ethically accepted in each situation, this notion of improper questions will be handled in more detail in each individual chapter. Generally, though, bad questions fall into one of six categories: loaded questions, leading questions, vague questions, double-barreled questions, cross-purpose questions, and illegal questions.

Loaded questions are those to which there is no correct answer. Suppose, for example, that a teacher asks a student, "Do you still cheat on exams?" Notice that either answer, yes or no, hurts the student. Yes admits current guilt, while no is an admission of past guilt. When someone asks you a loaded question, the most effective response is to identify it as such and not limit your answers to the options posed by the interviewer.

Leading questions are biased questions that direct the interviewee toward the response sought by the interviewer. In some instances, such questions are considered both ethical and legal. A lawyer interviewing a hostile witness in court, for example, is often allowed to ask leading questions by the court so that the jury can have a more complete picture of the crime under discussion. Interviewers in the employment setting often betray what they feel is the correct answer. They might ask, "Don't you agree that it's important to stay late and get the work done?" By asking the question in this way, they tip off the interviewee. All interviewees will typically answer with the "correct" answer rather than the truthful one. This leaves the interviewer with no ability to make an informed choice.

Vague questions refer to those that provide few semantic anchors—so few that the interviewee doesn't understand the purpose of the question or the type of information sought by the interviewee. In some highly unstructured interviews, these questions might have some utility purely as conversation starters. In most situations, though, they are ineffective and disruptive to the interview process. When the interviewee doesn't understand the question, they may answer inappropriately. Or, they might be confused and unsure of how to continue. That uncertainty disrupts the flow of conversation.

Double-barreled questions refer to those instances in which the interviewer asks two or more questions in the format of a single question. For example, the interviewer might ask: "Do you support abstinence and safe sex as a means of combating AIDS?" That question is really two different questions: "Do you support abstinence as a means of combating AIDS?" and "Do you support safe sex as a means of combating AIDS?" A person could conceivably answer yes to one part and no to the other. When asked as a single, double-barreled question, it is likely to trigger a limited and perhaps inaccurate response.

Cross-purpose questions refer to those questions in which the nature of the question is counter to the interviewer's goal. One of the most common forms of cross-purpose questions is the asking of a closed question when the interviewer is seeking an open-ended response. This is frequently done as an inappropriate means of identifying a topic while pointing the interviewee toward a desired response. The reader has probably seen dozens of such examples, including the reporter who wants a specific soundbite and asks someone whose home has been destroyed by fire, "Were you upset to learn that your home had been destroyed?" The obvious answer (yes) is the proper response to such closed questions, but what the reporter was probably seeking was an open-ended response ("How did you feel when you learned your home had been destroyed?"). Another example is the sports reporter who approached an athlete who had a minor physical abnormality of having six fingers and six toes. The reporter's question: "How did this happen—were you born this way?" The question was both at cross purposes and inappropriate—an ineffective attempt to address an issue by phrasing the question in a closed-ended format. Using an open-ended question is the more appropriate and effective technique, but reporters often find themselves using a cross-purpose question as an easy way to raise a topic and simultaneously guide the interviewee toward the response the interviewer is seeking. Another variation of a cross-purpose question is the opposite approach, i.e., the person asks an open-ended question when they expected a closed-ended reply. The all-inclusive "How are you doing?" question is typically phrased as an open-ended question that could be answered with a long list of ailments or a recounting of recent successes by the interviewee. Its real purpose, however, is simply to elicit a simple closed-ended response ("I'm fine, thank you") that allows the participants to begin the initial stages of a conversation.

Illegal questions can vary, depending on the situation and type of interview. For that reason, most of these aspects will be discussed in the applicable individual chapters. As an example, though, it is illegal for someone conducting an employment interview to ask questions regarding your marital status, age, or sexual orientation. No questions can be asked to a minor by means of a telephone interview. Part of developing one's skills as an interviewer will include an understanding of the legal limitations of the area in which you will work most often.

Monitoring

Klinzing and Klinzing (1985, pp. 58–60) argue that the cornerstone of effective interviews is the ability of the interviewer to employ empathic listening skills to monitor what the other person is saying. Patients become frustrated if they think the interviewer is not listening to them. Listening is effective, though, only if the interviewer has an accurate assessment of what the person is trying to say. To ensure that their perception is accurate, the interviewer must occasionally employ one of several techniques to assess the accuracy of the information. The most common techniques for doing this are (1) paraphrasing, (2) requesting clarification, and (3) checking perceptions.

Paraphrasing is simply the restatement of the person's response using the interviewer's words rather than theirs. A variation of the paraphrase is the reflective comment, i.e., a statement that provides a verbal mirror for the person's statement. Thus an interviewer may use a reflective statement to summarize their general impression or summary of several of the interviewee's comments ("You seem to be saying that you think you'd enjoy working here").

A less frequently used technique is the *request for clarification*, i.e., the interviewer asks for further explanation of what the interviewee means. Clarification requests seek more details about who, where, and when. A common variation of this approach is to ask the person for an example of what they mean. Asking for the example allows the interviewer to get a clearer view of the response and also encourages the interviewee to look at their answer from a different perspective.

Perception checking is a technique in which the interviewer gives the interviewee a chance to correct any of their previous statements. In this approach, the interviewer interrupts the interview for the moment to ask the other person about the accuracy of their impression.

Feedback

Most of these techniques not only increase the listening skills of the interviewer, but they also provide feedback to the interviewee. That feedback is essential to providing the interviewee with a sense that the interviewer understands. Three other feedback techniques can be used to enhance that perception even further. These are (1) reflection, (2) interpretation, and (3) confirmation. Unlike paraphrasing, which is a restatement of what the person has said, *reflection* focuses on how something was expressed (e.g., "This whole problem seems to be beating you down"). Such statements can increase the interviewee's perception that the interviewer understands their views. *Interpretation* is similar to perception checking, but its purpose is different. In this instance, the interviewer offers an explanation to the person and solicits their reaction. Brammer (1973) noted that the goal of this form of feedback is to encourage the person to provide their own interpretation of the situation. Finally, *confirmation remarks* ("I see what your mean") can be used to acknowledge understanding while encouraging the person to continue talking.

Interview Structure

Devito (2000) noted that interviews generally fall into one of four different interview structures: the open interview (unstructured), the topic interview (moderately structured), the guided interview (highly structured), or the quantitative interview (standardized). These four options are a continuum that reflects the research goals of interview, i.e., whether the interview is part of a qualitative (unstructured) or quantitative (highly structured, standardized) research project. Thus the structure of the interview is related to the interviewer's goals. To the extent that the interviewer wants quantitative explanations of "why," the interview will lean toward the unstructured side of the continuum and also rely heavily on open-ended questions. The unstructured format allows for exploration of areas that were not anticipated by the interviewer—something that's not always possible with a highly structured interview. Conversely, when the interviewer wants quantitative information, i.e., numbers that describe or represents a larger audience, the interview structure moves toward the more highly structured end of the continuum.

The open interview has the least amount of structure and is used in those situations in which the goal is to encourage the interviewee to talk as much as possible about a topic relevant to themselves. This structure is often used in participant-observation research; when done well, the interviewee will often forget that they're being interviewed and respond as if they're participating in a conversation. The interviewer engages the interviewee in a conversation, raises the topic on which they are seeking information, and encourages the interviewee to take that topic along the paths that best reflect their feelings on the subject. Another form of unstructured interview is informal interviews, i.e., those in which the participants gather in an informal situation. Their discussion is also informal, sometimes broaching the topic at hand and sometimes branching off into unrelated areas. Informal interviews are often used after the first round of employment interviews. Assuming that the potential employee has made the first cut, he or she may be invited to have dinner or lunch with one of the current workers. That encounter will provide the interviewer the chance to interact with the applicant on an informal basis, thus learning more about them. In the business world, such informal interviews are a common occurrence—from the golf course to the boardroom.

The topic-sequence interview is a moderately structured interview that represents the type that most people think about when interviews are mentioned. This interview typically uses a lot of open-ended questions and does as much as possible to encourage the interviewee to talk. Still, there are several points that the interviewer considers critical to the success of the interview, and these are inserted into the exchange as some point. Oral history interviews and employment interviews often fall within this structure. An oral historian will encourage the interviewee to speak as freely as possible but will also occasionally bring the discussion back to some key events such as births, marriages, careers, and deaths in the family. Similarly, many employment interviews are dominated by open-ended questions that allow the interviewer to obtain a better understanding of the interviewee as a person; at the same time, though, the interviewer will occasionally refocus the discussion on such topics as employment history and educational background.

The guided interview is one in which the interviewer directs the interviewee to address a pre-determined topic. Journalistic and television interviews often follow such a format. An actor who appears on a talk show to promote a new movie, for example, will likely meet with the interviewer or their representative in advance so that the interviewer will know what questions or topics will be discussed. Journalists often do the same thing when seeking information on a story, particularly from experts. They will call the expert, give them a description of the story they're working on, and then tell them the type of information that they're seeking. Such preliminary discussions serve as a guide for the rest of the interview. Another form of guided interview is a focus group discussion. This group interview employs a trained interviewer who gets the interviewees to discuss a series of specific topics. The questions are open-ended—often no more than the introduction of a topic—but the interviewer works from a discussion guide, which identifies all of the topics that will be discussed within the session.

The most structured form of interviewing is the standardized quantitative interview. The purpose of such interviews is to gather quantitative data from a large sample of people. The data must be gathered in such a manner that it can be assimilated and condensed mathematically to provide some means of summarizing the information. Such interviews are commonly used in survey research. They require a heavy use of closed questions, which limit the interviewee's responses.

Interviewer/Interviewee Relationship

As stated earlier, interviews often reflect information-gathering sessions in which the two participants have had little or no previous interaction with each other. Still, the nature of the relationship can vary tremendously, with at least three different scenarios possible—high individual interest, comparative individual interest, and low individual interest.

High levels of individual interest reflect those situations in which the interviewer directs his/her entire focus on the person that they are interviewing. Such a situation exists in relatively unstructured interviews such as a counseling interview. The interviewer's job is to concentrate solely upon the interviewee and their responses; the goal of the session, after all, is to help that person over some personal crisis. Similarly, a lawyer who is cross-examining a witness in the courtroom will also focus entirely upon the individual being questioned; the goal here is to ensure that the witness's testimony has been thoroughly examined for any weaknesses or indications of deception.

Conversely, some interviews—such as public opinion surveys using quantitative interviewing techniques—have little or no interest in the interviewee as an individual. The interviewee's responses are important, but only to the extent that they reflect or represent the opinions of a group or target audience that is the focus of the survey. Such interviews typically do not even bother to ask the interviewee for their name, since such information could mistakenly lead the interviewee to believe that they were being approached on an individual basis rather than being randomly selected for sample representation.

In the middle is the level of comparative individual interest. In these scenarios, the interviewer is interested in the individual as a person but also needs to compare that individual to others. Employment interviews are the prototype for this type of scenario. Several individuals may be interviewed for a position for which only one person will be hired. The interviewer may be positively impressed with several of the applicants but will only be able to hire one of them. In those instances, the interviewer must gather information that can be used to form an overall and a comparative evaluation.

Nonverbal Issues in the Interview

Interviewing is sometimes viewed as only a verbal communication skill, but nonverbal behaviors also play an important role. One authority has suggested that as much as 65 percent of the total meaning of a message is based on nonverbal behavior (Birdwhistle, 1970). Regardless, one's nonverbal behavior contributes to the total image that the interviewee presents to the interviewer. Sometimes, in fact, one's nonverbal behavior can override one's verbal messages, particularly if the nonverbal behavior is viewed as subconscious "leakage" that conveys one's true feelings (Hybels & Weaver, 2001, p. 136). Suppose, for example, that an interviewee greeted the interviewer and said they were happy to be invited to the interview. At the same time, though, if they expressed those words in a sarcastic tone of voice and while frowning, the interviewer is likely to believe just the opposite. Verbal messages convey what you want the other person to know, but nonverbal messages can show your feelings and emotions (Malandro & Barker, 1983).

Touching

Many employment interviews, for example, often begin with a handshake between the two participants. That initial contact can have a significant impact on the interviewer's impression of the interviewee. It becomes a nonverbal way for the two individuals to acknowledge the presence of the other person while conveying an initial message. Was the handshake the proverbial limp fish, so soft that the individual seems to lack self-confidence? Was it too strong, as if they were trying to assert the power of their personality through the vise-like strength of their hand? Or was it firm and steady—confident without being cocky. The impression created by that first physical touch can endure for much of the entire interview.

Touching behavior can also be used appropriately and effectively in therapeutic interviews. Such interviews often touch on sensitive issues that can trigger emotional responses from the interviewee. If the response is strong, and the interviewee starts to cry, words may not always be adequate in that situation. However, a simple touch on the shoulder may tell the person that you understand and that you're there to help them.

Silence

One underused interview technique is simply to say nothing. Sometimes, by remaining silent, the interviewer can encourage the patient to provide more information. It doesn't always work, though. Baker (1955, p. 161) noted that there was a difference between positive silence and negative silence in an interview. Negative silence makes the participant feel uncomfortable, particularly when tension is high, but positive silence indicates acceptance and satisfied contentment. Silence can be effectively used, particularly during the exploration stage, to encourage the patient to continue talking. It is highly ineffective, though, in both the initiation and termination stages. In the initiation stage, silence creates an awkwardness and sense of uncertainty that can make the person feel uncomfortable. In the termination stage, it can indicate that the interviewer doesn't know how to close the conversation.

Eye Contact

Individuals who are really good at interviewing are also good at maintaining eye contact with the interviewee. Eye contact serves two major purposes for the interviewer: (1) It nonverbally demonstrates to the interviewee that the interviewer is interested in what they are saying, and (2) it allows the interviewer to monitor the interviewee's nonverbal behavior. For example, the interviewee may occasionally let their eyes stray from direct contact with the interviewee. But, when they are finishing a statement and getting ready for the interviewer to talk again, they will often re-establish eye contact with the interviewer. Ekman and Friesen (1969) describe this behavior as a regulation function; the alert interviewer picks up this move and knows that the interviewee has given him a turn-taking cue.

The amount of eye contact will often vary based on the level of interest in the person or topic. Maintaining the proper amount of eye contact can sometimes be difficult. Too little eye contact may convey a lack of attention and too much may make the other person uncomfortable and leave them with the feeling of being stared at. Generally, the person who is in the listening role at any point in the conversation is expected to maintain more eye contact than the speaker. One technique for doing this, without making the person feeling stared at, is to focus your concentration on their nose or at a spot between their eyes.

Smiling

Never underestimate the power of a good smile. The advice is obvious, but—in the pressure of an interview—can be easily forgotten. Like eye contact, smiling is considered as an overt indication of information processing (McCall, 1972; Sroufe & Waters, 1976; Zelazo, 1971; 1972; Zelazo & Komer, 1971) and of interest while also sending a positive affect signal to the interviewer. An interviewee who is almost constantly smiling is indicating high interest in the job, the topic, and the interviewee. The interviewee who rarely smiles is telling the interviewer that they're really not interested in the job. In all likelihood, the interviewer won't be interested in them either.

Body Movements

Two nonverbal body movements can impact the nature of an interview—the *head nod* and *body positioning*. The head nod is a form of nonverbal feedback that encourages the interviewee to continue talking. Interviewers frequently use the head nod—combined with silence—to indicate that they wish for the other person to expand on what they just said. As such, the head nod is essentially a "turn-refusal" cue, i.e., one person comes to an end of a thought, completes their statement, and offers the other person a turn to speak. The other person, however, wants to hear more; rather than speaking, they simply nod to the other person. Thus the nod acknowledges recognition of the turn-taking signal sent from the first person, but politely declines the offer and asks that they continue speaking. It is a simple but effective means for encouraging an interviewee to expand on the topic under discussion.

The head nod can also be used by the interviewee to provide positive feedback to the interviewer. When the interviewer says something that the interviewer likes and wants to address, nodding by the interviewee sends a signal of agreement to the interviewer and also indicates a willingness to address the issue further. Thus the interviewer might say, "We want our employees to be self-starters, someone who can develop their own ideas for improving the company." The interviewee might start nodding when the interviewer says "starters," indicating agreement with the premise of the statement and a willingness to address the issue ("I know what you mean. At my last job, I developed a plan that lowered our overhead while increasing our sales volume.").

Body positioning is another important nonverbal element in the employment interview. Body positioning refers to the general physical orientation of an individual's body in relation to another person. Measurement of body position is usually done along two bipolar dimensions: closed-open and away-forward. You've seen the closed position frequently: an individual who sits with their arms and legs crossed, as if they've erected physical barriers between themselves and those around them. Say something that bothers another person, and they'll frequently cross their arms in a subconscious expression of disagreement. The open position, by contrast, is one in which the individual's arms and legs are not crossed; the individual is telling those around them that they trust the other people and have confidence in themselves.

The second dimension of body position—away-forward—also sends signals related to openness and willingness to communicate. The away body position is one in which the individual leans their body away from the other person. This is most often done while sitting down, with the person letting the upper part of their body shift backward. Such a position can convey an attitude of arrogance or remoteness—either of which can send a negative signal to an interviewer. The forward position, by contrast, can indicate a willingness to communicate. The individual who sits on the edge of their seat, leaning forward while maintaining eye contact, is telling the other person, "What you have to say is important to me."

Artifacts

Nonverbal artifacts refer to those objects associated with an individual that have communicative value. It includes such things as clothing, jewelry, smoking artifacts, or any other objects that another person might use to draw assumptions about a person. McLuhan (1964) called clothing "our extended skin" that is "a means of defining the self socially" (p. 114). Research has indicated, for example, that the way a professor dresses will influence student perceptions of how the professor defines himself or herself as a teacher (Morris, Gorham, Cohen, & Hoffman, 1996). In an interview, "defining the self socially" involves dressing appropriately. In some interview situations, the dress code is prescribed to the point that the clothing is really a uniform (Joseph, 1983). In most business interviews, though, the range of acceptable dress may vary, and the interviewee must hit the proper level. Under-dressing can convey a sense of disrespect for the position. Over-dressing may tell the interviewer that you don't have a good understanding of the group norms. The ideal mark is for the interviewee to be dressed at the same level or slightly higher than that of the interviewer. Jewelry might convey a person's sense of taste or give another person an indication of one's hobbies. Generally, jewelry that represents a specific religious or political affiliation should be avoided, since either could offend the interviewer or their associates (Molloy, 1996). Smoking is also an interview taboo, unless the interviewer indicates it is acceptable. Even then, it may be inappropriate and reduce the credibility of the interviewer. Cigarette smokers are often viewed as less credible, whereas cigar smokers are often considered too verbose (Hickson, Hill, & Powell, 1978, 1979).

Some advisors argue that artifacts are part of one's physical appearance—including one's hair, posture, facial expressions, and physique—all of which can influence the impression presented in an interview (Cerney, 1968). That concept is important, because any artifact is quickly processed by others in image formation, resulting in quick evaluations of both prestige and interpersonal attraction (Powell, Hickson, & Hill, 1977).

Territory and Space

One factor that can have an indirect but critical impact on the interview is the place in which the interview occurs. This can occur along three dimensions: (1) the impact of the location itself, (2) the information that can be learned from artifacts at the location, and (3) the resulting placement of the interviewer and the interviewee. Interviewers usually prefer to conduct the interview on their home territory, i.e., a place in which the interviewer feels comfortable; the interviewee must quickly adjust to this environment. One way to adjust is to look around the room for any artifacts that may tell you something about the interviewer. Are there any family photos? A trophy for a company softball team? Professional journals reporting the latest developments in the field? Books that identify a major topic of interest? Such information can be helpful in the initial conversations of the interview. And, finally, what is the resulting placement of the interviewee in relation to the interviewer. Does the interviewer sit behind a desk, asking questions of the interviewee across the desk? Or does the interviewer move from the desk, so that the conversation can occur with no barrier between them? Such placements can have an indirect impact on the resulting exchange of information. Indeed, individuals sitting across a desk from each other are more likely to be argumentative (Powell, Vickers, Smith, Amsbary, & Hickson, 2002, p. 77), while an open seating arrangement is more conducive to a friendly discussion.

Most interviews occur within a spatial environment that Hall (1959, 1969) called social distance, i.e., a distance of four to twelve feet in which people feel comfortable conducting social interactions. Communication in social space is slightly more formal than personal space (used for informal, one-on-one conversations. Occasionally, group interviews may occur in a space range known as public distance (12 feet or more). That range is more accommodating for a situation in which the interviewee is asked to respond to questions from multiple interviewers, and it is even more formal than those that occur in a social distance climate.

Vocalics

Vocalics refers to the way in which individuals use their voice. One classic consultant in the art of impression management has argued that the interviewee's voice represents their "passport to success" because it represents 15 percent of their "personality appeal" (Cerney, 1968, p. 29). Mehrabian (1981) goes further, estimating that 39 percent of the meaning associated with a message is based on vocal cues. Because success in the workplace is as much a product of how a person is perceived in terms of work ethic and motivation as it is by skills and training, one's voice can play an important role in establishing that attitude. That concept is supported by research indicating that most people can accurately identify the emotions that an individual is feeling based on that person's voice expressions (Malandro & Barker, 1983). It is also, however, a form of nonverbal communication that is difficult to self-monitor, i.e., people often don't realize how they sound to others. That can be partially corrected by listening to recordings of one's own voice and evaluating it in terms of the impression it might be making on others. More importantly, though, is the importance of controlling one's tone of voice during an interview. The interviewee wants to avoid being loud, monotonous, or whining. Asked about something you're proud of reciting? Tell them, but not in a loud or booming voice. Do they ask a routine question that's easy to answer? Answer, but not with a boring or monotonous tone. And if they wonder why you've had bad luck in previous jobs? Tell them, but not in a whining voice that begs for sympathy.

Time

Hybels and Weaver (2001) have noted that time can be used for "psychological effect" and is often connected with status (p. 151). The interviewee should remember that and adhere to one major time-based rule: Don't be late. Tardiness sends an overt message to the interviewer, i.e., that the interviewee didn't consider the interview to be important. Tardiness shows a lack of respect for the interviewer, the organization, and the job under consideration. Unfortunately, the rule regarding tardiness only applies to the interviewee. The interviewer, who is in a stronger status position, can be excused for being a few minutes late, but the interviewee lacks such latitude. Show up late for a job interview, and you have little chance of getting the job.

Summary

Interviewing is a purposeful interaction involving two parties and the asking and answering of questions. It is a purposeful interaction in that each of the participants engages in the interview with a purpose. It involves two parties, but either or both parties may be composed of one or more people. And the asking and answering of questions is the framework in which information is exchanged within the interaction.

Interviews vary by type and purpose. Employment interviews are a screening technique by which organizations make initial evaluations regarding hiring decisions of new employees. Informational interviews are those that place an emphasis on content, and they can include information seeking (or research interviews), information giving, and information sharing. Interrogation interviews are primarily used to gather information from a reluctant source and are frequently used by law enforcement officials. The primary purpose of a therapeutic, or counseling, interview is to establish a supportive relationship that will help individuals identify and work through personal issues, concerns, and problems. The performance review interview is used to assess the work of an individual or group. The grievance interview is one involving conflict and resolution. The exit interview is commonly used when people leave an organization, to get an assessment regarding the reasons for their departure.

Most interviews can be divided into four distinct stages: (1) preparation, (2) opening, (3) Q&A, and (4) closing. Preparation is important, because most successful interviews start with anticipating and planning. The opening, or first contact, of the interview sets the tone and mood for the interaction that follows. Q&A is the exploration, or working phase, of the interview. The interviewer offers questions and seeks responses from the interviewee during this phase. A successful interview will also include an identifiable closing stage that summarizes the key points of the interview and ensures that they have had an opportunity to say the things they believe should be said.

Some of the techniques developed by effective interviewers include question sequences. Three different question sequences are commonly used. In the *funnel sequence*, the interviewer beings by asking broad questions and then proceeds to more specific questions. In the *inverted funnel*, the interviewer begins by asking a series of specific questions and gradually broadens the approach to obtain an overall view of the topic being discussed. The *tunnel sequence* is an interview that uses a series of similar questions of the same format.

The adept interviewer will learn a variety tools that include question-related skills and the effective use of silence. The different types of questions that can be used include open-ended questions, closed-ended questions, probes, and third-person questions. Interviewers must also be aware of improper questions, i.e., loaded questions, leading questions, and illegal questions. And the effective use of silence can increase an interviewer's skill. Sometimes, by remaining silent, the interviewer can encourage the interviewee to provide more information. Other skills are monitoring skills and adeptness at providing feedback to the interviewee.

Nonverbal skills are also important within the interview context. It's important to arrive early, make a good impression with one's clothing and body presence, and speak in a confident voice. The interviewee should use other nonverbal cues—such as eye contact, smiling, and nodding—to indicate that they are paying attention to what the interviewer says. They should also monitor the nonverbal behavior of the interviewer to pick up cues for turn-taking, i.e., when they are expected to speak.

Interviews can vary by structure, ranging from the highly structured (the quantitative interview) to those with loose structures (the informal interview). This chapter has looked at these elements from a basic perspective. Each of the following chapters will go into more detail about these elements as they apply to specific situations.

Discussion Questions

1. Review your interactions with other people over the past week. How many involved situations in which you were interviewed? How many were interactions in which you were asking questions of someone else? What kind of interactions were these?
2. Think of the last major time that you were interviewed by someone else. Were you satisfied with how you handled that interview? What did you like or dislike about what you did during that interview? What did you like or dislike about the questions asked by the other person?
3. Observe a television interview. What interviewing techniques are used by the interviewer? By the interviewee? Were these techniques effective or ineffective?

Please see the companion website for additional resources at [www.routledge.com/cw/amsbary].

References

Baker, S. J. (1955). The theory of silences. *Journal of General Psychology, 53*, 145–167.

Banyard, V. L., & Fernald, P. S. (2002). Simulated family therapy: A classroom demonstration. *Teaching of Psychology, 29*(3), 223–226.

Benjamin, A. (1981). *The helping interview.* Boston, MA: Houghton Mifflin.

Birdwhistle, R. L. (1970). *Kinesics and context.* Philadelphia, PA: University of Pennsylvania Press.

Brammer, L. M. (1973). *The helping relationship: Process and skills.* Englewood Cliffs, NJ: Prentice-Hall.

Burgoon, J. K. (1993). Interpersonal expectations, expectancy violations, and emotional communication. *Journal of Language and Social Psychology, 12*, 30–48.

Burgoon, M., & Miller, G. R. (1985). An expectancy interpretation of language and persuasion. In H. Giles & R. St. Clair (Eds.), *Recent advances in language, communication, and social psychology* (pp. 199–229). London: Lawrence Erlbaum.

Cerney, J. V. (1968). *Talk your way to success with people.* West Nyack, NY: Parker.

Devito, J. A. (2000). *Human communication.* New York: Longman.

Dipboye, R. L., Gaugler, B. B., Hayes, T. L., & Parker, D. (2001). The validity of unstructured panel interviews: More than meets the eye? *Journal of Business & Psychology, 16*(1), 35–50.

Edwards, B.J., & Brilhart, J.K. (1981). *Communication in nursing practice.* St. Louis: C.V. Mosby Co.

Ekman, P., & Friesen, W. V. (1969). The repertoire of nonverbal behavior: Categories, origins, usage, and coding. *Semiotica, 1*, 49–98.

Hall, E. T. (1959). *The silent language.* Greenwich, CT: Fawcett.

Hall, E. T. (1969). *The hidden dimension.* Garden City, NY: Anchor Books.

Hamilton, C., & Parker, C. (1990). *Communicating for results.* Belmont, CA: Wadsworth.

Hickson, M., Hill, S. R., & Powell, L. (1978). Smoking artifacts: Factors of source evaluation. *Perceptual and Motor Skills, 47*, 933–934.

Hickson, M., Hill, S. R., & Powell, L. (1979). Smoking artifacts as indicators of homophily, attraction, and credibility. *Southern Speech Communication Journal, 47*, 191–200.

Hybels, S., & Weaver, R. L., II (2001). *Communicating effectively* (6th ed.). Boston, MA: McGraw-Hill.

Joseph, N. (1983). *Uniforms and nonuniforms.* New York: Greenwood.

Klinzing, D., & Klinzing, D. (1985). *Communication for allied health care professionals.* Dubuque, IA: Wm. C. Brown.

Malandro, L. A., & Barker, L. (1983). *Nonverbal communication.* New York: Random House.

McCall, R. (1972). Smiling and vocalization in infants as indices of perceptual-cognitive processes. *Merrill-Palmer Quarterly, 18*, 341–348.

McLuhan, M. (1964). *Understanding media: The extensions of man.* New York: New American Library.

Mehrabian, A. (1981). *Silent messages: Implicit communication of emotions and attitudes.* Belmont, CA: Wadsworth.

Molloy, J. T. (1996). *New women's dress for success.* New York: Warner.

Morris, T. L., Gorham, J., Cohen, S. H., & Hoffman, D. (1996). Fashion in the classroom: Effects of attire on student perceptions of instructors in college classes. *Communication Education, 45*, 142–148.

Northouse, P. G., & Northouse, L. L. (1985). *Health communication: A handbook for health professionals.* Englewood Cliffs, NJ: Prentice-Hall.

Powell, L., Hickson, M., & Hill, S. R. (1977). Canonical relationships between prestige and interpersonal attraction. *Perceptual and Motor Skills, 44*, 23–29.

Powell, L., Vickers, J. S., Smith, W. S., Amsbary, J., & Hickson, M., III (2002). *Surviving group meetings: Practical tools for working in groups.* Boston, MA: Pearson.

Sroufe, L., & Waters, W. (1976). The ontogenesis of smiling and laughter: A perspective on the organization of development in infancy. *Psychological Review, 83,* 173–189.

Stewart, C. J., & Cash, W. B. (1982). *Interviewing principles and practices.* Dubuque, IA: Wm. C. Brown.

Sundeen, S.J., Stuart, G.W., Rankin, E.D., & Cohen, S.A. (1981). *Nurse-client interaction: Implementing the nursing process.* St. Louis: C.V. Mosby Company.

Zelazo, P. (1971). Smiling to social stimuli: Eliciting and conditioning effects. *Developmental Psychology, 4,* 32–42.

Zelazo, P. (1972). Smiling and vocalizing: A cognitive emphasis. *Merrill-Palmer Quarterly, 18,* 349–365.

Zelazo, P., & Komer, M. (1971). Infant smiling to nonsocial stimuli and the recognition hypothesis. *Child Development, 42,* 1327–1339.

Section 2

INTERVIEWING IN THE
ORGANIZATIONAL SETTING

2

THE EMPLOYMENT INTERVIEW
The Employer's Perspective

Jill, an account executive in a large advertising firm, needs to hire an assistant. She has received more than 100 resumes and has taken the time to narrow the field to two candidates. She brings in the top two for interviews and now must choose one to hire. Candidate one has a lot of experience and presented himself as confident and controlled. He demonstrated a superior command of the concepts and techniques of the field, but he seemed a little set in his ways.

Candidate two was fresh out of school and had no real experience in the field of advertising. He seemed very nervous during the interview and tripped over his words a few times. He got glowing recommendations from his professors, and he seemed eager and able to learn.

Jill is faced with the same problem that all employers face. She has to predict which candidate is most qualified to hire. Not only that, but she has to decide which one will fit into her company's way of doing things, which one will more readily subject themselves to her authority, which one will best "fit" the working circumstance. She may also have to consider which one she can afford, which one helps fits the hiring and recruiting parameters of her organization, or which one will stay with the company for the longest period of time.

Like all employers she wishes she could look into the future and see which of the two would be better employees. Failing that, she wishes that one of them would behave so badly on the interview that her choice will be easy. Unfortunately for Jill, there are no easy answers to her questions, and she walks away from the interviews with a list of plusses and minuses that seem to balance each other out. Rather than clarifying the issues and problems, the interviews seemed to complicate them. Besides, how does one gauge a long-term working relationship based on a one-shot, short-term interview?

Many employers can remember times when they were faced with different types of candidates and one seemed so much better in the interview. The first may have been magnificent during a two-day round of interviews, impressing the committee and the other members of the organization. After he was hired though, he failed to demonstrate the skills needed to perform the job or the temperament to work with other people in the organization on a daily basis. Within a couple of years, he had departed for another position.

The second applicant may have had an impressive resume, one that stood out from all the other applicants for the position. His interview, though, was mundane and unimpressive. His responses to questions were to the point but undynamic. He was calm and composed in informal settings, but he had trouble engaging others in conversation. Despite the less-than-spectacular performance, his resume was still the most impressive. He was hired and did an excellent job. The unspectacular personal skills simply reflected a person who was not encumbered with a large ego; he did his job well, and he worked well with others.

Was the interview misleading? Are all interviews misleading? Can we learn anything by interviewing candidates? At first blush, one may come to the erroneous conclusion that interviews are a waste of time, that one might as well take the top candidates and draw their names randomly out of a hat. But a closer analysis supports the notion that it is not the interviewing process that's to blame but poorly trained interviewers. A glib candidate who may not be able to do the job after all easily fools an interviewer with little or no training. They may miss the proverbial diamond in the rough.

These two examples illustrate the problems associated with the employment interview. Despite the heavy reliance on such interviews, organizations still find that the interview is not a perfect mechanism for making employment decisions. Still, the interview remains the most frequently used element in job hiring decisions. Although it's utility may be questioned, its widespread use demands that workforce participants must be familiar with it and, hopefully, skillful in the use of its techniques.

The Purpose of Job Interviews

Employment interviews can be divided into two separate categories: job interviews and screening interviews. Job interviews are the ones that come to mind first and most frequently. They are those formal sit-downs between a job applicant and a representative of an organization. Yate (1994) describes the job interview as a "measured and ritualistic mating dance . . . that . . . should have all the appearances of a relaxed conversation and produce as much information as an F.B.I. dossier" (p. 16). One misconception about the job interview is that its primary purpose is to assess your qualifications for the jobs. Actually, that's rarely the case. In most instances, the purpose of the interview is to assess (1) your willingness to do the job and (2) your ability to fit in and work within the organization. If you didn't have the qualifications, you probably would never have reached the interview stage.

Screening interviews are often held at job fairs, conventions, or on college campuses by company recruiters. They often have the feel of formal job interviews by the applicants, but they are, in fact, very different. First, they tend to be very short. Formal interviews may literally take days, while screening interviews usually last about 20 minutes to an hour. Second, formal interviews take place after the employer carefully sifts through the applicants' resumes and applications, whereas screening interviews typically take place before formal applications are made. Most large employers use recruiters to screen applicants, but they view this as a method of recruiting promising applicants, not choosing who they will ultimately hire. It is important for applicants to go on screening interviews, but they should understand that they should use this as an opportunity to make initial contact with someone in the company and then to use the interview as a fact-finding tool. Do not expect to be offered a job after a screening interview; it rarely happens.

The Interviewer's Preparation

Preparation to conduct an employment interview begins well before the interview actually occurs. Generally, the interviewer must make the following preparations:

Assessing the Organization's Needs

This is not a solitary assignment, but rather one done through discussion with other members of the organization. What type of personality is needed for the position, particularly in terms of integrity, ambition, motivation, and communication skills of the person? What professional skills and behavioral patterns are necessary? Should they be someone who works well under direct management, or does the position call for a self-starter who will take on added responsibilities? What type of performance will be expected from the applicant? Will they be judged primarily on the basis of the profit they generate, their efficiency in the position, and the process and procedures that they follow? Such parameters need to be established before any formal interviews are started. This preparation is so important to a successful interview that Cohen (2001) recommends that interviewers adopt a "behavioral interviewing" technique in which the focus of the interview is to find employees whose talents and values, rather than their resume, match the job description. In other words, the focus of the interview should be on the talents and values of the applicant, in terms of how those features match the job description. Don't rely upon the resume as a means of making that decision.

Advertising the Position

In some cases, advertising a position may be as simple as putting a help wanted sign in your shop window or taking out an ad in the local paper. In some cases, however, it will be a time- and money-consuming endeavor that will have wide-ranging consequences. It is important to know where your potential employees are. If you are hiring for a highly specialized position, you may have to travel to conferences and conventions that cater to the professionals in question. Many conferences have employment services that are an excellent venue for recruiting candidates and conducting screening interviews. Most universities provide similar services for company recruiters who are interested in hiring recent college graduates.

Word-of-mouth advertising can be very valuable for employers. It is not uncommon for employers to contact friends and colleagues in their profession to find if they can help them identify potential candidates for a position.

Electronic filing, or web-based services, can also be a useful tool, especially if you are hiring someone in the information technology field. One danger with these databases is that they tend to have a "one-size-fits-all" approach, and you may find yourself frustrated with the candidates that your search produces.

Professional employment consultants are also becoming popular. The cost of these services can be prohibitively high—often costing a hundred thousand dollars or more—but some organizations find that when they are hiring high-level or other critical employees, these hiring (headhunter) firms provide excellent candidates for their consideration.

Hickson and Stacks (1998) point out, however, that narrowing your pool of candidates does create a potential legal problem. They claim that "knowing your potential applicant pool certainly helps, but it may also open you to claims of bias against hiring others who may be 'different' or 'more qualified' or older, younger, and so forth" (p. 194). Employers generally have an affirmative responsibility to rectify hiring inequities that have taken place in the past. These obligations extend to any group that has been traditionally targeted for job discrimination in the past (as discussed in detail in a later section). Generally speaking, employers have an obligation to reach beyond tradition or comfortable methods of recruiting and advertise in ways that will be seen by qualified minority candidates.

Filtering the Applicants

Desirable positions generate more applicants than the organization can effectively interview. Some means must be developed to filter out some of the applicants and determine a short list of finalists. A couple of techniques can be used to accomplish this goal, with the most common being the resume review. A review of the applicants' resumes will reveal that many of them lack the educational background or experience to qualify for the position. Another option might be to do a preliminary interview with the applicant—either at a job fair or over the telephone—to get a basic assessment of whether they have the skills and knowledge required for the job. At this point, the questions should be largely limited to those that will expand upon the resume of the applicant, asking about their past experiences, attitudes toward their present job, and areas in which they have been most successful. Yate (1994) recommends asking a few "knockout" questions at this stage, questions that eliminate the applicant from consideration if they cannot answer them. His examples of knockout questions include the following:

"What are the broad responsibilities of your position?"
"What are the major qualities that this job demands?"
"How does your job relate to the overall goals of your department or company?"

Such questions provide an assessment of how involved the applicant is in their current job and provide a barometer of potential ambition in the new position.

Conducting the Interview

As with all interviews, the interviewer should open the session with questions that will make the applicant feel at ease. Early questions should focus on the past—their previous jobs and educational background—for these are less threatening and will help to make the applicant feel comfortable while the interviewer gets some basic information about the person's skills. The specific questions for the interview will vary with the position, but some guidelines can be established. First, the goal of the interview should be to make an assessment of the applicant in terms of three basic categories: capability, work ethic, and interpersonal maturity.

Assessing Capability

Capability refers to the applicant's ability to do the job, and it is the area that should be investigated first. The interview might begin with a review of the applicant's responsibilities with their previous company or their educational experiences (for new graduates). Other questions that can often show up in this assessment stage are:

"Why did you apply for this job?"
"What have you learned from your previous jobs?"
"Have you ever had to make unpopular decisions?"

Assessing Work Ethic

Organizations prefer applicants who demonstrate a willingness to work—both alone and with others. What they don't want are "clock watchers," people who work just enough to keep their jobs but nothing else. Identifying such laggards in advance can be difficult, because "clock watchers" are usually competent people. They will score well on most measures of capability, but they merely lack the ambition and motivation to put their capability to effective use. Questions that might be used for assessing work ethic include:

"Do you set goals for yourself?"
"Did you work much on your own, or do you usually work better with others?"
"How do you plan and organize major projects?"
"Have you ever given a second try at something that didn't work?"
"How would you define a successful career?"

Assessing Interpersonal Maturity

The workplace can be a fragile personal environment. A collection of people is forced into the same environment on a daily basis for an extended period of time. Personality differences will lead to irritation and to the building of conflict. The ideal applicant is someone who can handle such situations with maturity and not add to the volatile mixture of personalities already on the job. To make these assessments, the interview might seek to identify applicants with inflated egos by asking "What have you done that you're proud of?" or "How would you rate your progress in your previous job (or at school)?" Ability to work with others might be ascertained by asking for their opinions of their boss and co-workers; a negative response on either point could indicate trouble getting along with others. Or the interviewer may directly ask, "When was the last time you got really angry?"

Such questions only touch upon those that can be asked in this portion of the interview. What's important is that the interviewer achieve some understanding of how well the person works with others, works with management, and handles criticism. On a personality level, questions should investigate such traits as their self-esteem, integrity, and ability to handle anger and stress.

The Behavioral Interview

As mentioned earlier, one means of assessing interpersonal maturity is a technique known as the behavioral interview. The focus of the behavioral interview is to evaluate the talents and values of the applicant in terms of how those features match the job description. Pincus (1999) describes such an interview as one in which "The interviewer puts the focus on personal conduct, your *modus operandi*" (p. 48). Fry (2000) notes that the form of the questions "stay in the realm of the known" (p. 37) in that they focus almost exclusively on past experiences. Applicants are asked to describe how they have handled a variety of work situations in the past. If leadership skills are needed, the interviewer may ask the applicant to describe a time in which they had to compel others to complete a major project. It's not enough for an applicant to say they're a team player; they have to give an example. Thus the interviewer may ask questions such as: "What happened the last time you had a conflict with a co-worker?" or "How do you respond when a colleague gossips about you?" The focus is always on seeking responses with specific information, with the interviewer using the information as a basis for making extrapolations about behavior in future job situations.

If you're serious about hiring the applicant for a long-term position, a single interview might not suffice. Multiple interviews may be needed (1) to get behind any facades that might be developed and held during a short interview, and (2) to assess the extent to which the candidate will work well with other members of the organization. In such instances, three or more interviews may be employed, with the follow-ups focusing on such areas as judgment, emotional maturity, and manageability. Subsequent interviews—usually in an informal social setting—may be necessary to re-question the applicant on sensitive areas.

Varying by Employment Purpose

One factor that influences the format and structure of the employment interview is the type of position that the organization is seeking to fill and the candidate who is being considered. Different positions require different skills and types of people, and you will have different questions for each type of person you hire. You will not ask someone entering the field the same questions you would ask someone with years of experience. The requirements of each specific job will necessitate some task-specific questions that would not be necessary for some other positions. Exploring every potential variation, based on task, is beyond the scope of this book, but a few examples can be provided.

College Graduates

Employment interviews for people who are just out of college tend to differ from those for other positions. New graduates typically have a broad range of educational skills that would qualify them for several different entry-level positions with the organization. The goal of the interviewer is to decide if each applicant (1) will fit well within one of the slots, (2) will fit well within the organization, and (3) has long-range potential for the organiza-tion. Yate (1994) recommends using three specific questions in this type of interview:

1. "What kind of work interests you, and why?" This question allows for probing of areas of interest that might be mutually beneficial to both the applicant and the organization.
2. "How did you spend your vacations during school?" Some students have summer-time experiences, which demonstrate their ambitions, interests, and work ethic.
3. "Do you plan further education?" On the positive side, an applicant who wants addi-tional education demonstrates a desire to further their career, and that could be good for the organization. On the negative side, if the person is planning to be a full-time student at the graduate level, their tenure with the organization may be short.

Clerical Positions

For most clerical positions, the most important traits are (1) reliability, (2) organizational skills, and (3) flexibility. Those assets are more important than such traits as educational background, intelligence, and experience. Those latter traits are useful only if they can be translated into the first three. Thus, interview questions for clerical hiring often focus on filing techniques and probing on instances in which flexibility was necessary for com-pleting a task.

Sales Positions

Yate (1994) argues that the interviewer must be particularly careful in interviewing appli-cants for a sales position. After all, if the applicant is a good salesperson, they view the interview as a sales opportunity. You're not interviewing them so much as they're try-ing to sell you on themselves. As a result, this may be one of the easiest employment interviews to conduct. Probe questions should focus on such assets as persistence, persuasiveness, ability to handle stress, resilience, and sales maturity.

Management Positions

Employment interviews seeking to fill a management position face a unique situation. In essence, the interviewer has to determine how the applicant would conduct such an interview if their roles were reversed. Why the role reversal? Because the management position is dependent upon the skills of the applicant at working with the organizational personnel. If they were in management, what would their hiring practices be? What would their attitude be toward employee turnover? What is their attitude about discipline and the role of authority? What factors would be required in the orientation of new employees? How would they communicate with and motivate the organizational staff? And what is their record on fiscal responsibility? The goal of such questions is to identify the management philosophy of the applicant, and thus be able to assess whether the applicant's approach would fit with the general approach of the organization.

The Resume Probe

Everybody is a potentially great employee on paper, particularly if they've written the paper. One part of the interviewer's preparation is to review the resumes of those people who've been selected for interviews, looking for gaps that must be probed during the interview. The resume can tell you what an applicant has done in the past, but it is a relatively poor device for telling you what they can do. Thus, the first job of the interviewer is not to be misled by the resume, for there is no necessary connection between the quality of the resume and the quality of the job candidate. As Yate (1994) noted, resumes "are like mirrors in a fun house: They offer a distorted image of reality whose main function is to deceive the eye" (p. 49). Indeed, individuals who have good writing and presentation skills, but not much else, will present some of the best resumes. Some of the worst resumes, including some that get eliminated in the early filtering process, belonged to people who would have made excellent employees.

The employment interviewer has to look beyond the resumes and try to identify those qualities that reflect the usefulness of the applicant to the organization. If a decision is made to interview the applicant, one goal of the interview should be to see behind the resume, filling in gaps of information that have been omitted. Part of the interviewer's job is to identify those gaps and be prepared to ask questions about them. Are there any gaps in the work history or educational history that need to be explained? Why are they leaving their present job? Why leave a position when they have risen in the ranks so quickly? Are there any gaps in productivity in previous jobs that might indicate a potential for burnout at some stage? What elements are missing from their educational background that would be desirable for the company? Such questions will allow the interviewer to obtain a more complete picture of the applicant and their skills as they relate to the organization.

Puzzle-Based Interviews

A popular trend in many organizations today is puzzle-based interviews. These interviews subject the interviewee to high-stress, basically unanswerable questions to see how well they "think on their feet." For example, the interviewer might ask: "Imagine I have a revolver with one loaded chamber. Before I fire it at you, do you want me to spin the chamber?" The interviewer is not attempting to gauge the interviewee's understanding of probability, but rather, how well they cope with bizarre questions.

Poundstone (2003) argues that this type of interview may reveal some important personality characteristics and may be useful with some younger applicants who enjoy this type of approach. He goes on to say, however, that employers run a very big risk of antagonizing older, more experienced applicants and that employers would do better sticking to more traditional questions about experience and abilities.

The Legal Side of Employment Interviews

Personnel who conduct employment interviews must do so under a strict list of rules that limit the type of questions they can ask. They must gather the information necessary for hiring decisions without asking some specific questions. A number of different legal acts apply to what can and cannot be asked in terms of a number of topics (DeLuca, 1997, pp. 151–179). Several areas are of special concern.

Race and National Origin

The Civil Rights Act forbids any action that discriminates against a person on the basis of their race or national origin. To ensure that they meet that requirement, most employers generally follow several guidelines. More specifically, the interviewer cannot ask questions that deal with the following:

- An applicant's skin color or complexion
- The skin color or complexion of the applicant's family
- The candidate's nationality, ancestry, parentage, or next of kin
- The family's birthplace

Sometimes there is a thin line that separates a legal question from an illegal question. For example, it is illegal to ask a candidate how they learned to speak a second language, but it is perfectly acceptable to ask them how many languages they speak. The difference between the two is that the second question deals solely with a skill that could be useful on the job, whereas the first one has the potential to require the applicant to reveal something about their ethnic or racial background. Any question that hints at the second aspect is taboo.

Political Beliefs

The interviewer should not ask the applicant any questions related to political beliefs or political affiliation. They should not ask the applicant to identify for whom they voted in any past election, or which candidate they prefer in an upcoming election. Furthermore, they cannot ask about partisanship or political ideology. Thus "Are you a Democrat or a Republican?" and "Do you consider yourself a liberal or a conservative?" are both taboo within the context of the interview.

Religious Beliefs

The interviewer should not ask any question that would require the applicant to reveal their religious beliefs or affiliations. That means that taboo questions include any that ask about religious denominations, religious organizations, religious activity, or observance of religious holidays. If the nature of the job requires that they be available to work on Saturdays or Sundays, the interviewer can usually ask the applicant about their willingness and availability to work on those days; otherwise, those questions should be avoided, too.

Gender

Hypothetically, gender discrimination could be directed toward either men or women. Realistically, though, most of the gender discrimination in the modern workplace is directed toward women. As a result, most professional employment interviewers take special precautions when interviewing female applicants. The questions that are generally avoided include those about the following:

- Their name, including any change in name or a request to identify their maiden name or original name
- Their preferred form of address, such as Miss, Mrs. or Ms.
- Their marital status, including the name of their spouse
- Their children, particularly questions about number of children and their ages
- Their birth control practices

Again, though, there is sometimes a fine line between legal and illegal questions. As noted previously, the interviewer cannot ask questions about name changes or maiden names, but they can ask if the applicant has ever worked for another company under a different name. The latter question is allowed because it is needed as part of the background check on the applicant.

Age. The Age Discrimination Act prohibits discrimination against candidates between 40 and 70 years of age. Similarly, resumes cannot require that the applicant include their date of birth. The only age-related question that the interviewer is allowed to ask is related to minimal age requirements. For most positions, then, the only legal age question is whether the applicant is at least 18 years old.

Disabilities. The Americans with Disabilities Act prohibits any discrimination on the basis of an applicant's disability or physical handicap. Generally, most interviewers judiciously avoid any questions that might be construed to apply to this area. Still, some problems exist. As consultants Wendleton and Dauten (2000, p. 2G) noted, "that doesn't make doubts go away: Interviewers hate uncertainty. They hire the person with the fewest question marks. Only the interviewee can inoculate against those doubts."

Military Background. Employment interviewers are allowed to ask if the applicant has had military experience, but they cannot ask questions about which branch of service or the type of discharge that the applicant received.

Educational Background. This area is generally safe, because education has a direct bearing on the qualifications for most jobs. As a result, the interviewer can ask questions about educational history and the details of their educational history. One question, though, is taboo. The interviewer cannot directly ask if the applicant has graduated from high school.

Criminal Background. This area varies by state. Still, in some states, the interviewer is not allowed to ask if the applicant has ever been arrested (Tate, 1994).

Exceptions to the Rules. The legality of a question is gauged not only by its subject but also by its context. Any employer may ask questions that are germane to the job for which they are hiring. By sticking to bona fide occupational qualifications, that employer can usually keep out of trouble. For instance, a church committee has every right to question potential ministers about their religious beliefs or knowledge, but they should not ask a custodian the same questions. By the same token, Christian and other religious colleges routinely ask professorial candidates about their religious beliefs and practices, whereas such questions are clearly illegal in public and other non-secular colleges and universities. Firefighters must conform to physical requirements that clearly favor men, but no applicant may be asked about their choice of child care (or if they have children at all).

Summary

The employment interview is the gate through which new employees join an organization. The person conducting the interview serves as a gatekeeper whose function is to identify applicants who will best fit in and be productive for that organization. Their preparation for such interviews should include an identification of the needs of the organization and a filtering process to identify qualified applicants. The interview itself should be intended to gather information that will assist the organization in assessing the capability, work ethic, and interpersonal maturity of the applicant. All of this must be done within some strict legal guidelines that protect the applicant's rights.

The applicant, meanwhile, should also prepare for the interview by preparing an accurate and effective resume, researching the organization, and being prepared for tough questions that could be critical to the interviewer's decision. After all, the employment interview is most effective when information is exchanged so that both the interviewer and the applicant are pleased with the results.

Discussion Questions

1. As a group, decide what characteristics are generally possessed by good employees (i.e., hard working, good listener, etc.) Devise a list of questions that an interview might ask a potential employee to learn these things.
2. Have you ever been asked questions on an interview that you thought were unfair or illegal? What were they and why? Are there ways to not answer such questions that will not anger a potential employer?
3. How do you think employment interviews are fooled by applicants? What can employers do to prevent this from happening?
4. Are the following questions legal or illegal?
   A. Are you a citizen of the United States?
   B. What church do you attend?
   C. Who will watch your children when you work on the weekends?
   D. What school do your children go to?
   E. Where do you live?
   F. What type of boss do you like?
   G. Are you available for night work?
   H. Can you travel out of town with little or no advanced notice?
   I. Who did you vote for in the last election?
   J. What are your hobbies?
   K. How will you get to work?
   L. Jamal? Is that an Islamic name?
   M. Are there any special accommodations you will need to get around on the job?

Answers

A. Legal, while national origin is off-limits, citizenship is okay to ask about.
B. Illegal, goes to religious beliefs and status (unless you are interviewing a minister).
C. Illegal, can be seen as discriminating against those with children and especially women.
D. Illegal, same as letter C.
E. Legal, an employer can ask where you live.
F. Legal, though not a great interviewing question, this is legal.
G. Legal, your availability for work is germane to your hiring.
H. Legal, same as letter G.
I. Illegal, can be used to discriminate based on political belief.
J. Legal
K. Legal
L. Illegal, ethnic origin is off-limits.
M. Illegal, though the employer *will* need to know this information *if* you are hired, they may not base a hiring decision on this, and they may not ask about it.

Please see the companion website for additional resources at [www.routledge.com/cw/ amsbary].

References

Cohen, D. (2001). *The talent edge: A behavioral approach to hiring, developing, and keeping top performers.* New York: Wiley.

DeLuca, M. J. (1997). *Best answers to the 201 most frequently asked interview questions.* New York: McGraw Hill.

Fry, R. (2000). *101 great answers to the toughest interview questions* (4th ed.). Franklin Lakes, NJ: Career Press.

Hickson, M., & Stacks, D. W. (1998). *Organizational Communication in the Personal Context.* Boston, MA: Allyn and Bacon.

Pincus, M. (1999). *Interview strategies that lead to job offers.* Hauppauge, NY: Barrons.

Poundstone, W. (2003). Beware the interview inquisition. High-stress, brain-teasing job interviews are all the rage. But what do they really reveal? *Harvard Business Review, 81*(5), 2.

Wendleton, K., & Dauten, D. (2000, November 5). Networking works best with higher-ups. *Birmingham News*, p. 1G, 2G.

Yate, M. (1994). *Hiring the best: A manager's guide to effective interviewing.* Holbrook, MA: Adams Media.

3

THE EMPLOYMENT INTERVIEW

The Job Applicant's Perspective

Joe shifted in his seat, waiting anxiously until the receptionist called his name. In a few minutes, he would be interviewing with a personnel officer with a major company. If things went well, he could seal his first job out of college and establish himself in a career with a top national company. It all depended on the interview. Would he get the job or not?

Joe's anxiety illustrates the importance of the job interview in modern society. Crucial hiring decisions are made on the basis of the interview, sometimes unfairly so. Some highly qualified people simply don't interview well; if given the chance, they would do a good job. Many don't get the chance, though, because of a poor or mediocre performance in the interview.

Others seem to excel at the job interview. When brought into the interview environment, they turn on performance skills that impress and dazzle the interviewer. Those skills, though, may not always be relevant to the skills needed for the job. Regardless, the job interview is the major means that companies use to assess job applicants. As Gottesman and Mauro (1999) stated, "In a very limited amount of time—probably longer than two minutes, but shorter than an hour—an interviewer needs to find out who you are so she can assess how you'll perform in the future" (p. xiv). And, they add, "It is undeniably true that the job can be won or lost in the time you spend sitting opposite the decision maker" (p. 2). Yeager and Hough (1998) stress the importance of training and preparation, noting "that you had better be better at selling yourself than the competition or you will not win the job" (p. xi). Similarly, while Fry (2000) noted that employers are looking for "self-managing" workers who can get the job done, "you can't get started proving yourself without making it through the interview process" (p. 5).

Starting the Process

The first step, however, is finding out where the jobs are and positioning yourself to get noticed by potential employers. There are a number of things that job seekers can and should do to help their case.

The **informational interview** is a technique used by applicants who are seeking a job interview. An aggressive job applicant may hold informational interviews with people in the company or within the industry. As Yeager and Hough (1998) noted, "Current employees are the best source of information about the inner workings of a company" (p. 25). Such interviews do not directly contribute to a company's hiring decision, but they provide a number of advantages to the job applicant, including the following:

Networking. By interviewing people within the company and industry, you will gradually develop a network of contacts within a company. In essence, if you conduct enough informational interviews, you become an insider and someone with an edge over any outsider being considered for positions within the company. In addition, informational interviews can serve as a source for identifying those at higher levels within an organization—another networking function that can be of value later in the hiring process. Informational interviews can be helpful at any level within the organization. When used to gain a job interview, though, they typically need to be conducted with an individual who is at least two levels above your own.

Informational interviews can also lead to other networking opportunities. You may learn about organizations and associations that most of the employees join. You can find out about conferences and conventions that you can attend. Such networking opportunities allow you to identify job opportunities that most people will not be aware of. Remember that some have estimated that less than 30 percent of jobs are actually advertised. Andrea Bradford (2003), a Vice President at Rights Management Consultants, estimates that 75 percent of all jobs are attained through networking of jobs that are not advertised. Most are filled through informal networking.

Research. Informational interviews are highly effective as a means of researching the individuals and companies with whom you'll later be interviewing. The authors remember one student who had a job interview for a marketing position with a retail company who prepared for the interview with a series of informational interviews in advance. She visited the retail portion of the company prior to the interview, talking with sales associates and observing their dress, behavior, and demeanor. She used that information to select the clothing that she wore to the interview and used information from the visits in her responses to some of the interview questions. Such research can also be supplemented with online research about the company and its policies. Such advance information can be invaluable for discussing topics raised during the employment interview.

Experience. Informational interviews are an effective way of getting interview experience that will be helpful when you get the job interview. You will become more comfortable with the process from the sheer repetition of doing it. Your interview cohorts will also guide you in terms of potential responses that are appropriate or inappropriate, and your increased knowledge of the company will lead to an increased number of appropriate responses presented in a confident manner. Furthermore, you will simply feel more comfortable during the actual interview because you have met and talked with so many people who are already a part of the organization.

Disadvantages. Despite the general belief that informational interviews enhance an applicant's chance of getting a job, there are some dissenters from this view. The major disadvantage of informational interviews is that the organization may have little to gain from engaging in the process. Some argue that the use of informational interviews has, in fact, "died of overexposure" because managers have grown tired of spending time with strangers who use them as "outplacement counselors" (Wendleton & Dauten, 2002). That can be somewhat countered by talking to people in an organization who hold intermediate supervisory positions. If the interviewee approaches people who are too high in the organization, they will consider the interview a waste of time. Talking with those on the same level has limited utility. Mid-level supervisors offer the most efficient targets for informational interviews.

Resumes

Interview skills are relatively unimportant to the job applicant who can't get an interview. That's why the resume is so important. It is the "foot-in-the-door" that determines whether a potential employer is willing to look further at you and your credentials. There is no single best way to construct a resume, but some general guidelines are important.

What to Do

You must provide enough information that the person reviewing your resume could develop some idea of whether your skills would be appropriate for their organization. That will include the following:

- *Your name, address, telephone number, and (for many positions) an e-mail address.* Personnel workers may be reviewing dozens, maybe even hundreds, of resumes. They don't like spending excess time trying to reach you. If they run into a snag when trying to contact you, they will frequently just move on to another applicant. Make it easy for them to reach you.
- *Past employment history.* Identify your past jobs and the work skills that you learned from those jobs. Even relatively minor positions can have implications for future employment.
- *Your educational background.* Some jobs require the completion of specific degrees. Others are more likely to be filled by people with specific types of training.

There are many resume formats available. There doesn't seem to be an overall preference for any specific resume style, but most employers demand that the resume be neat, free from errors, easy to read, and concise. Although some professions may allow a two-page or longer resume, the overwhelming preference is for a resume to be limited to one page (Blackburn-Brockman & Belanger, 2001). Most software packages provide numerous **resume templates** preloaded into the software so that you can experiment and choose a style that best fits your needs.

What Not to Do

Personnel officers often use their first view of resumes for filtering purposes. They eliminate as many of the resumes as possible before taking a closer look at those they will consider interviewing. They look for negative elements, often things that have nothing to do with the job position itself. One employer, for example, once told the authors that he had more than 100 applications for a single position. His first filtering element was to discard everyone whose resume had been sent with a hand-addressed envelope, an approach that cut the pile he had to read by about half. Thus, the first goal of your resume should be to avoid being quickly tossed into the trash as unacceptable. Here are a number of common mistakes that should be avoided:

    Lack of Professionalism. The handwritten envelopes were just one example that falls into the category of unprofessional activities. Your resume is your first contact with the employer, and it must demonstrate a professional mentality. That's not always easy, particularly for new college graduates who've spent four or more years developing highly casual behavioral patterns, but it is essential for consideration by many organizations. Your resume must not do anything that would define you as an amateur in the profession.

Too Cute. One common mistake by new college graduates is to make their resume "too cute." The capability of using computer graphics to "jazz up" your resume will be tempting, but these are usually interpreted by the personnel management for what they are: attempts to cover up a weak resume with an interesting design. Common mistakes in this area include the addition of unusual graphics and the use of eye-catching colors of paper.

Resumania. If you want to do something that will catch a personnel officer's eye, just toss a few typos into your resume or cover letter. They'll notice it and quickly eliminate you from consideration. Robert Hall (2004) coined the term "resumania" to describe such careless resume mistakes. Classic examples of careless resumania include the person who ended their cover letter with the sentence "Hope to hear from you shorty" or the one who listed their skills as "Excellent memory, strong math aptitude, excellent memory." Other resumania can come from people who don't realize that the information they are providing will be viewed negatively by the company. Hall cites two memorable examples of such mistakes. One person explained their frequent address changes with a single line in their cover letter by writing, "Being in trouble with the law, I moved frequently." Another explained their high number of jobs with a simple explanation: "Please don't regard my 14 positions as job-hopping. I never once quit a job."

Perfunctory Preparation. Some people view the resume as a necessary evil, something they must go through the motions of doing before they can get an interview. This attitude dismisses the resume as an inconvenient necessity to getting to the real job application stage in the interview. Such a mentality often produces mundane and blasé resumes that never get noticed. The resume succeeds only in underwhelming the company, and no invitation for an interview is ever offered.

Written Arrogance. Some people are too proud of their resumes. They record all of their achievements with grand flourishes, sometimes scaring off the potential employer. There is a tendency for such people to assume they lost the position because they were overqualified. Sometimes that's the case, but often the reason is simply that the personnel officer could not imagine having to work with such a person on a daily basis. Promote yourself, but don't sound arrogant.

Misrepresentation. Perhaps the worst mistake an applicant can make is to submit a resume that contains factual errors or which overrepresents achievements. In some states, such misdeeds are considered felony crimes. At the very least, though, they represent a fatal mistake that ultimately ruins a person's chances of being hired. Educational background seems to be a common area in which this occurs, with some people listing degrees that they have not earned. Others we have seen include (1) taking a post-graduate night course and inferring that you will soon have a master's degree, (2) obtaining a mail-order degree and implying it came from a legitimate university, and (3) misrepresenting the grades that you received from some key course. Past work experiences sometimes offer chances for exaggeration; the authors remember one person whose management resumes included running a cost-efficient and balanced budget for the three departments they had previously managed. A little research revealed that two of those three budgets had consistently operated at a financial loss during their tenure. The final advice here is simple: Don't lie or exaggerate. In the long run, that will cost you more than you can gain.

Cover Letters

A cover letter tailored to the specific job and company to which you are applying should be included with every application. You may be applying simultaneously to several positions with different job descriptions. A person just graduating with a broadcasting degree, for example, might find themselves applying for a sales position with one station, a production assistant at another, or an assignment desk worker at a third. You may be qualified to handle all three, but your cover letter to each organization should be tailored to their needs.

Many people starting their first job search ask, "Do I have to include a cover letter?" The answer to this question is a resounding "*Yes!*" You should include a cover letter for every application whether the employer asked for one or not. You should not ask "Should I?" but rather "Can I?" The cover letter is a persuasive document that helps to highlight and emphasize things that the employer will find on your resume. With so many people applying for jobs online, a "good cover letter can set a candidate apart from the rest of the pack" (Franzinger, 2001, p. 164).

One of the major complaints that employers make about applicants is that they have poor cover letters. This is not a perfunctory task created to waste your time; it is an invaluable opportunity for you to make a strong case for yourself. The cover letter is a business letter and should be written as such. Unlike the resume, which should only be one page, the cover letter will be as long as it needs to be, though typically they are one to two pages in length. The cover letter should minimally include the following paragraphs:

Paragraph one—The introduction. The first paragraph should introduce you to the employer and precisely identify the job for which you are applying. Many applicants make the mistake of being too general, making statements such as, "I am applying for the position you have open" or "I am writing because I am interested in working for your company." Neither of these statements tells the employer which job you are seeking. Remember that companies may be hiring for multiple positions, and you should not make the reader guess which one is of interest to you. If the reader is not sure what to do with your application, he or she will likely just throw it away. It's also a good idea to mention where you heard about the job. This provides marketing feedback for the employer (which they like) and shows that you are plugged in to the network, especially if you saw an announcement in a trade publication or other "insider" venue. You should end the first paragraph with a strong thesis statement regarding your "fit" for the job.

Paragraph two—Blowing your horn. Remember that the resume is a fact sheet, not a narrative document. It's the cover letter that lets you discuss your greatest strengths for the position for which you are applying. Remember that you compose a new letter for each application and that your strength as a candidate may change from position to position. If, for instance, you are applying for advertising positions, you may apply both to large established firms and to more trendy "hot shops" (small firms that do more cutting-edge work). Your cover letter to the established firms might emphasize your stability, your attention to detail, and your ability to be a team player. On the other hand, your letters to the hot shops might emphasize your knowledge of cutting-edge campaigns, your risk taking, and your aggressiveness. You probably won't change your resume, but the cover letters will guide the reader to the important information for the position in question.

Paragraph three—Why them? An often overlooked but potentially powerful element of the cover letter is some discussion of why you want to work for the company.

Remember that most companies want to develop relationships with their employees and would like to find people who want more than just a paycheck from their job. If you can find something that's attractive about the company to you, it will make you stand out from the other applicants. If there is something that excites you about something special the company does, or if you see this as an opportunity to grow and develop your career, now is the time to discuss it. In short, discuss something that you hope to accomplish other than merely getting paid.

Paragraph four—Your availability. End the cover letter by including times and methods that the employer can contact you with confidence. You may have voice mail, or you may be available at your home number at certain times, or perhaps e-mail is the easiest way for someone to contact you. Most employers will not spend a lot of time trying to track you down. If they try once or twice and can't get you, then they'll likely give up and move on to the next applicant on their list. Make yourself available.

Portfolios

A practice that grew out of the performing arts, more and more job seekers are using portfolios to keep a record of their accomplishments that can be easily given to their potential employers. This is a relatively new practice and is not considered a requirement for most applications, but it certainly can give an applicant an edge in the process.

As with anything that is done during this process, the watchword for preparing a portfolio is professionalism. It should therefore be neat, well organized, and give the appearance that some thought and effort was put into making it. At the very least it should be presented in a three-ring, hard-covered binder, with the pages in plastic protectors, include section tabs, and a table of contents.

What you include in your portfolio will depend on who you are and what types of things will make you look more attractive as a potential employee. At the very least it should contain a copy of your resume, cover letter for that position, an unofficial copy of your college transcripts (you will be required to provide an official copy if you are offered the job), and letters of recommendation. Additionally, you may want to include samples of your writing, videos you have made, speeches you have given, copies of web pages you have designed, and copies of awards you have received. In short, anything that bolsters your standing. This is something you will leave with the interviewers, so make sure you are using copies, not originals.

Preparing for the Interview

Once you get invited for an interview, you have a great deal of preparatory work to do. Preparation is the key to successful interviewing. The first thing you should do when invited for an interview is to gather as much research about the company as you can. You should have done some in preparing your application, but now is the time to really dig. The more you can talk about specific things that the company does and how you can help, the better off you will be.

Go to the company's website and try to learn as much about the company as you can. Pay particular attention to various locations where the company has offices, plans for future growth, and mission statements. Such information can give you insight into the company's culture and help you figure out ways that you fit into it (i.e., "I noticed that you have a branch office in Atlanta. I grew up in Central Georgia and I know the area very well.").

Check back through the local papers for stories about the company. Again, this can provide insight into historical issues that help you understand how the company has grown and evolved and possibly where they want to grow.

If the company is publicly held, you can get an investor's prospectus from them. This is an especially good document for finding out plans for future development.

Set Goals

Often the most important thing an interviewee can do is to make a specific set of goals that he or she wishes to accomplish during the interview. This does not mean saying to yourself "I want to get hired" or to "Look like the best candidate." Rather, the interviewee should make a personal inventory and figure out what strengths they need to push during an interview and what weaknesses need to be addressed.

What are your assets to this particular company? Do you have specific experiences or talents that make you especially qualified for the job? If so, you need to push them during the interview. You need to plan how you are going to communicate these strengths.

As much as you won't want to, you will have to confront your liabilities as a potential employee. Coming out of college, you might not have a lot of, if any, experience. Maybe your educational background is different from the usual employee who gets hired by this firm. You must remember that you cannot hide your weaknesses. The employer will be fully aware of them and will probably want to discuss them at length. There are a few strategies, besides hoping they won't notice, that can help you compensate for weaknesses and even turn them into strengths.

First, **be realistic**. You aren't perfect, but no one is. Everyone has some liability. Good employers know this. What concerns them is how maturely you cope with your weaknesses. Even candidates with years of experience have liabilities.

Second, you can **counter a weakness with a strength**. As noted previously, you may not have any experience in your chosen profession. The inexperienced candidate needs to show some asset that they have that outweighs their lack of experience. Up-to-date knowledge of the field, flexibility of schedule, willingness to learn, ability to learn, and ability to work long hours are often things that younger, less experienced candidates push to make up for their lack of specific job experience. If done correctly, this can even turn a weakness into a strength. The authors know one candidate who, when confronted with his lack of job experience, said, "You bet I don't have any experience. Now you can start training me right away, and you don't have to spend six months untraining me."

Third, you should show how you intend to **overcome your weaknesses**. By detailing a specific plan for overcoming your weaknesses, you demonstrate a great deal of professionalism and maturity. It shows that you may not be a seasoned professional but that you have a plan to become one. No one really expects a recent college graduate to have a long list of professional accomplishments, but they hope that they have a plan.

Dress Appropriately

One of the authors was waiting in an office for an appointment when a young man sat down beside him to fill out an employment interview form. Although he seemed like a nice young man, he wasn't going to get that job. The problem was the way he was dressed. He was wearing dirty jeans and a T-shirt with the sleeves torn out—and he left that day without a job.

The authors also recall another incident in which a student had a job interview for an assistant buyer's position with a department store. The day before the interview, she visited the store as a shopper, made a purchase, and observed what each of the store personnel was wearing—a conservative style of dress and amount of jewelry. She chose her wardrobe for the next day accordingly. Not surprisingly, she got the job.

Such examples illustrate a key principle of job applicants: How you dress for an interview is still important. As Pincus (1999) noted, "Although not everyone is good-looking, everyone can look good. And proper business attire and good grooming helps everyone project a positive image" (p. 33). That means that the expansion of casual dress codes to the modern office applies only to workers who have already been hired. Applicants need to dress better than that. After all, the applicant has only a few seconds at the beginning of the interview to convince the interviewer that they will fit into the company's work environment, and how you're dressed should not detract from that message. As Nicholson (1999) noted, if someone looks as if they'll fit in, they have an edge on getting the job.

While the level of casualness will vary, depending on the type of job under consideration, some basic guidelines should be followed. First, your level of dress should be equal to or slightly above the general dress of the office; "dressing down" sends a negative signal. Second, don't be too flashy; the job interview is no time to experiment with new colors or Hawaiian shirts. Being too conservative is better than being too flashy. Applicants with a number of body piercings, for example, are less likely to be hired by corporate interviewers (Seiter & Sandry, 2003). Third, your clothes should be well-fitting, pressed, and make you "look like someone who could work for the company" (Gottesman & Mauro, 1999, p. 46).

Don't Be Late

Your first impression is an important one. Showing up late for the interview can essentially eliminate you from consideration. Employers expect their employees to be on time; if you can't be on time for the interview, they're not likely to be interested. One Fortune 500 executive (Pincus, 1999) noted that it was "inexcusable" to be late for an interview, but "by the same token, never show up more than five minutes early" (p. 81). Such behavior demonstrates an understanding of how professional organizations value time.

Getting off on the Right Foot

Gill and Lewis (1996, p. 156) compare the employment interview to a blind date in which both parties have to prove their worth to the other. Your first impression should be a positive one, so always start off on a positive note. Don't, for example, complain about how difficult it was to find the office, find a parking space, or find time in your busy schedule to keep the appointment. Instead, look for an easy ice-breaker to get the conversation off to a good start, perhaps commenting on an award or photograph in the interviewer's office, or (if the interview is outside the office) an interesting piece of jewelry they are wearing. Furthermore, be sure you've brought a copy of your resume with you; that shows that you're prepared, and it provides you with a reference copy should the interviewer make a comment about it or its content.

Maintaining Your Composure

Right or wrong, one of the key elements that will influence the hiring decision is the way you communicate during the interview. In fact, research indicates that the communication impression conveyed during the interview is the single-most important factor influencing hiring decisions (Powell, Belcher, Kitchens, & Emerson, 1975). That communication impression will be influenced by both your verbal and your nonverbal behavior. On the verbal level, some applicants seem not to pay attention to the interviewer's questions; they often provide the information they consider relevant instead of the information asked for by the interviewer. On the nonverbal level, nervous applicants often fidget with their clothing or their hair during the interview, something that makes them look both nervous and inattentive. The impression can also be created in non-traditional settings. Companies frequently invite candidates for lunch, where they have a chance to meet and see how they handle themselves. In those situations, the candidate's image can be influenced by a variety of factors, including table manners, treatment of servers, and selections of entrees (nothing extravagant) and drinks (no alcohol) (Collins, 2001).

In responding to questions, two guidelines should be followed: (1) be brief and (2) answer the question. Brevity is important; say what you mean in clean and concise sentences, and answer the question. Don't waffle on questions that bother you; instead, address each subject directly and quickly. Generally avoid the temptation to use the question as a transition to another topic. Most interviewers will find that irritating, since they likely asked the question they did for a specific reason.

Several researchers argue that impression management is a key variable in the interview process (Delrey & Kacmar, 1998). Impression management looks at the applicant's ability to use the interview to address image elements related to one's self (self-focused) and to the interviewer's (other-focused) image (Kacmar, Delrey, & Ferris, 1992). Several researchers have noted that self-focused messages are used more frequently, perhaps because other-focused messages can be problematic if viewed as attempts at ingratiation (Gilmore & Ferris, 1989; Stevens & Kristof, 1995). Six types of verbal impression management tactics can influence the interviewer's evaluation of the applicant (Gardner & Martinko, 1988; Stevens & Kristof, 1995). These include (1) self-enhancement—describing positive or admirable attributes, (2) exemplification—acting as a role model, (3) entitlements—taking responsibility for positive events in one's background, (4) self-promotion—describing knowledge, skill, and ability one possesses, (5) other enhancements—making favorable evaluations of the interviewer's attributes, and (6) opinion conformity—expressions of agreement with the interviewer's comments. Conversely, those verbal behaviors that are most likely to create a negative impression are self-defensive tactics such as providing excuses, claims of innocence, or attempts at justifying past mistakes (Gardner & Martinko, 1988). Researchers have also identified several trait factors that influence the use of such messages (Lamude, Scudder, & Simmons, 2003). Males tend to use self-enhancement more frequently, whereas females are more likely to use self-promotion. Latinos are more likely to use entitlements and less likely to use self-promotion. Blacks are more likely to use accounts and exemplification and less likely to use entitlements, whereas European Americans more frequently use self-promotion.

Handling the Tough Questions

Most interviewers will start with a series of easy and basic questions. If they're serious about hiring you, though, they will eventually move to a series of tough questions that they expect you to handle well (DeLuca, 1997; Fry, 2000). DeLuca argued that answering these tough questions was "the most important aspect of the job search" (p. 1). If you're not sure about a tough question, ask for clarification before you answer. This will help in understanding the question and provide more time to consider your answer.

The nature of those questions will vary by discipline, but some seem to be asked of nearly every job. Six questions that you are likely to be asked include the following:

1. "What are your greatest strengths?" You should respond with specific traits that are relevant to the position. Be as specific as possible, giving examples. You should generally avoid generic responses like "I'm a hard worker" or "I'm a people person" unless you can give specific examples ("Last month we had an unexpected deadline change, and I volunteered to work over the weekend to get the report completed"). Nearly every applicant will give the generic responses; the interviewer will remember the specific ones.

2. "What is your greatest weakness?" The temptation here will be to list an attribute that you can display as an asset, not a weakness. Many people, for example, might say something like "I'm too easy to get along with, and I end up doing too much work that should be done by others." That sounds nice, but it doesn't give the interviewer much useful information. A better approach is to be honest about a past weakness, tell how you overcame that problem, and finish with a strength ("I used to be bad at record keeping, but I took a course at night to improve those skills. Last year, I received a letter of commendation from my supervisor for my improvement in that area").

3. "What is an example of a time you failed?" This is a variation on the "greatest weakness" question, but it asks for a specific example. If you address the previous question with specifics, this one might be skipped entirely by the interviewer. If they ask it anyway, use it as a chance to discuss a time when you learned from a mistake.

4. "Where do you see yourself in five years?" This question, or some similar variation, seems to show up in nearly every job interview. The best response is to mention a realistic position within the organization, usually a title that is two or three steps ahead of the job you're seeking. This not only answers the question but also demonstrates that you have an understanding of the organization. However, whatever goal you mention should be a realistic one, it should not be one that would require you shifting to another organization (that indicates a lack of loyalty), and it should never be the position of the person who is interviewing you.

5. "Why do you want to leave your current job?" A truly tough question with a double bind. You must want to leave it, or you wouldn't be applying for this job. If you didn't get along with the personnel at the other job, then the people at this potential new employer might not like you either. Ultimately, you must answer this question with a positive frame of mind. An overly negative response about your previous employment is viewed as unprofessional behavior that will make you less desirable to a new employer.

6. "Why are you applying for this position?" This is usually a means of identifying long-term goals (Gill & Lewis, 1996, p. 152). Prepare your answer from that perspective.

Focusing on Salary

The general rule is that the applicant should not ask about salary during the first interview at all. If salary is a negotiable element of the position, then the position is likely to be one that will require multiple interviews before it is filled. Thus, there is nothing to be gained by bringing up the topic early, and the only potential impact such an early question might have is to inhibit your chances of being hired.

If the question of money is brought up by the interviewer, that usually is a positive sign that indicates you are still under consideration. Typically the interviewer has two ways of bringing up the topic; they can ask, "What salary are you looking for?" or they might ask, "How much are you making now?" Both questions should generally be answered in the same manner, i.e., giving them an understanding of your current salary and how it compares with what you're seeking. A crucial element here is honesty; be sure you don't exaggerate your current salary. If your current salary is relatively high, it provides them with a sense of your market value. If you feel you're underpaid and looking for an increase, say so and explain why.

Asking the Right Questions

One common misconception about employment interviews is that the potential employer (or their agent) should be asking all the questions. Actually, the person interviewing for a job should be asking questions, too. Marshall and Cooper (2000) noted that asking questions is one of the most effective tools for opening up a healthy relationship with another person. In fact, the person conducting the interview for the company is likely to ask—as one of their final questions—if you have any questions of them. You should be ready to respond by asking questions that (1) demonstrate your understanding of the job and the company, (2) elicit information about the desirability of the job, and (3) express interest in the company.

Business writer Michael Kinsman (2001) recalled the time he first learned the value of asking good questions to the interviewer. As his interview progressed, he asked his interviewer such questions as: "Where is this company headed? Why do you do things this way? Why is this important to you? What makes you feel I can help?" As his questions came out, he recalled, "The chief executive moved to the front of his chair and articulately answered each question that was being thrown his way. When he wasn't sure how to answer, he would lean back in his chair and reflect for a few moments before answering. What I had accomplished . . . was how to engage someone in a discussion that was both stimulating to him and illuminating to me" (p. 1G).

Yeager and Hough (1998) suggest that questions from the interviewee can potentially focus on four different areas: (1) the future of the organization, (2) the future of the position, (3) expectations, and (4) attitudes about change, growth, and organizational development. The first might include questions such as "What opportunities and threats do you see facing this company?" or "What is the company's strongest asset?" Questions about the position might include why it was created and how that position contributes to the company. Questions about expectations should ask about typical work days and criteria for a raise or promotion. Attitudes about the company can be addressed by asking about the chief competition and the factors that will determine the company's future growth.

Practicing Mock Interviews

Some professionals recommend that job applicants enlist their friends or a university placement center to help them prepare by undergoing mock interviews in which they practice the techniques needed for an effective job interview. Yeager and Hough (1998) noted that practicing in front of a mirror or with a friend is essential, because "it is unreasonable to think that you can just do it, and perform well on command" (p. 13). This concept is perhaps articulated best by Gottesman and Mauro (1999), who compare the job interview to that of an actor auditioning for a role as a cast member of a theatrical production. They recommend that the applicant begin by "visualizing yourself in the job" (p. 33), in which you create a mental picture of how you would perform the job. That can then be followed by a practice session with a friend posing as the interviewer. Pincus

(1999) recommends videotaping the session so that you can review it later and evaluate your performance, while Gottesman and Mauro (1999) recommend that each practice session should at least be audio-taped.

Such preparation can make the applicant feel more comfortable with the process and help reduce the anxiety that can be associated with the interview. Excessive anxiety will hinder the applicant's performance and inhibit the chances of getting a job offer (Bartoo & Sias, 2004; Young, Behnke, & Mann, 2004). Still, as Gottesman and Mauro noted, the applicant should remember that "it's easy to communicate with your buddy because you know him well. The same will not be true of your interviewer" (p. 72).

Understanding the Company

The author remembers one job applicant who was interviewed by two members of the department. When his time for questions came, he asked one question immediately: "Where's the third person?"

"What do you mean?" one of the interviewers replied.

"There are three people in your division," the applicant replied. "Why am I being interviewed by only two of them?"

"The third one's in Japan," the interviewers said. "He couldn't be here."

Not surprisingly, that applicant got the job. Although many factors, including his resume, contributed to that decision, both interviewers recounted that story in making their recommendation for hiring. Such a question indicated that the applicant understood the company and its personnel. It also showed a level of initiative that was not demonstrated by any of the other applicants. No wonder he got the job. Your questions may not have to be quite as precise as that one, but you should go prepared to ask at least two questions that are company-focused and show that you have prepared for the interview.

Such preparation does not necessarily require a great deal of advance work. In fact, too much research on a company may make you appear to be an arrogant "know-it-all." Gill and Lewis (1996) recommend that the applicant adopt the mentality of a "ten-minute researcher" and learn enough about the company to demonstrate interest. Spend a few minutes talking to people who might know about the organization or with people who are their competitors. Using that information, plan some of your questions in advance. Relatively "safe" questions that can be used for most interviews include such standards as the following (Gill & Lewis, 1996, p. 150):

1. What resources are available to get my job done?
2. What are the opportunities for growth in this position?
3. How long has this position been open?
4. What makes this position attractive to a candidate?
5. What did the previous person do well and what were some areas of improvement?
6. What is the major reason that the company needs this position?
7. What is the managing style of my supervisor?

Determining Job Desirability

People who are job hunting are often so interested in obtaining a job—any job—that they focus on getting that job instead of evaluating its desirability. Some jobs are better than others, and bad jobs can have a long-term negative impact on your career. In essence, it's better to pass on a really bad job, because it may haunt you for the rest of your career. So, how do you identify a bad job in advance? Yeager and Hough (1998) recommend using your informational interviews for this purpose, noting that "Nobody knows better what working in a place is like than someone who works there" (p. 25). Still, the job interview itself offers the applicant a chance to gather some additional information. There's no sure-fire technique, but some indication can be gleaned by the questions that the prospective job hunter asks of their interviewer. Although the specific types of questions you will need to ask will vary, depending on the job, Kennedy (1980, pp. 180–184) recommends four questions that apply to most jobs:

1. "What kind of performance-appraisal system does the organization use?" For some jobs, this may be a two-part question—one to look at the appraisal form and one to ask about the evaluation system. This question should provide you with an idea of what is expected of you for advancement within the organization and what bias might be present in the system. Any appraisal system will have some built-in biases, but you need to know if those biases will play to your strengths or your weaknesses. Furthermore, this question sometimes brings to light other potential problems; if the interviewer has a negative opinion of the company's appraisal process, you need to know about it and why.
2. "What has the turnover been in the department and the position?" If there's a heavy turnover, there's likely a reason. Perhaps the department has a hostile work environment. Perhaps the actual duties of the position are more detailed than those described in the job description. Whatever the reason, a high turnover rate makes the position a high risk for a new employee. Even an evasive response to this question should be viewed negatively.
3. "Why is the job vacant and what happened to the person who held the job previously?" The goal here is to learn something about the upward mobility offered by the position. Is this position a stepping stone, either within the organization or within the industry? Or is it a dead-end job that burns people out until they eventually quit?
4. "Will I have a chance to meet the people with whom I will work?" If you take the position, you're going to be working with these people on a daily basis. You should at least have the chance to see if there are going to be any major personality clashes. After all, one possible reason that the job is open is that the previous employer was unable to work with another co-worker or supervisor. That's why Kennedy (1980) argued that, "Anything less than enthusiasm for this request on the part of the interviewer is a cause for alarm" (p. 184).

Expressing an Interest in the Company

The informational goal of the interviewee's questions should be to learn more about the company and the desirability of the job, but the questions that the applicant asks can also leave an impression with the interviewer that may influence the job decision. The general rule here is that while it helps to demonstrate knowledge about the company, it's even better to express interest. Don't try to impress the interviewer with how much you know, but with your interest in what the company will be doing in the future.

Closing the Interview

The request on the part of the interviewer for questions from the applicant is usually a signal that the interview is approaching its conclusion. The applicant's questions will play a significant role in the final impression that they will leave, but other factors are also important. The most important factor is politeness; the applicant should be sure to thank the interviewer before they depart, and a nonverbal indicator (such as a parting handshake) can also provide positive closure to the meeting. Just getting up and leaving is simply not an acceptable alternative here. Something must be said or done to leave the interviewer with a final positive impression.

Post-Interview Behavior

Yeager and Hough (1998) noted that "The people who get the important interviews, and the important jobs, are the ones who understand the importance of follow-up" (p. 12). Once the interview is over, the applicant should write and mail a thank-you note "within 24 hours of your interview" (Pincus, 1999, p. 110). Depending on the organization, the thank-you note can be typed, handwritten, or sent by e-mail. Regardless, it should come across as if it was individually written for that specific person. Indeed, if more than one thank-you letter is needed, each person should be given a customized response.

Even with such follow-up, though, one common occurrence in interviews is that the applicant leaves the interview with the impression that they will receive a job offer. Weeks may go by, though, with no offer forthcoming. Eventually, the applicant finds that somebody else has been hired for the position. How does this occur? First, the *recency effect* comes into play. The recency effect says that those applicants who have the last interview are the ones with the best advantage. Those individuals who are interviewed first often leave with a positive impression, and the company representatives are often nice to them, often with positive opinions. But they have little or no means of comparing early applicants with those who will be interviewed later. The first applicant is often used as a standard by which others are judged, and any positive evaluation for the latter applicant moves the position to their favor. Furthermore, as time passes, the company's interviewers' memories will fade; after two weeks, they may forget the specific things about the first interview that left them with a positive impression.

Second, some companies adopt a *string-along strategy* in dealing with applicants. After interviewing all applicants for the position, four or five may be deemed acceptable and then ranked according to preference. While the negotiations are then pursued with the top-ranked applicant, the company delays telling the others that they probably will not receive the job. Should the top-ranked applicant accept a position elsewhere, they may need one of those other applicants as a fallback strategy. If this process is repeated two or three times, the applicants who are ranked fourth or fifth may be held in limbo for weeks without knowing their position.

When this happens to you, the most effective technique is to use it to your advantage rather than wondering what is happening. Specifically, your first job interview is likely to be unsuccessful, simply because you'll be a little nervous or rusty at the process. Once it is completed, then, simply use it as a means of obtaining other job interviews. In this process, any decisional delay on the part of the first company works to your advantage, not to your detriment. You can legitimately call other potential employers and say, "I'm interviewing at Company A, but I wanted to talk with you before accepting anything from anybody else." If they then agree to interview you, you can then use the same approach with another prospective job: "I have interviews scheduled with A and B, but I was really interested in working with you."

Dealing with Rejection

Unfortunately, not all interviews end on a positive note. Even if you do an excellent job during the interview, you still might not get hired. A number of other factors—including budgets, internal conflicts, and the nature of your competition—will ultimately play a factor in influencing the hiring decision. One common scenario is for a person to have a great interview and leave expecting to get an offer, but the hiring manager still has other interviews to conduct, and one of those also is a great one. Furthermore, the new candidate may bring up different issues and attributes—things that the interviewer had forgotten to mention to you. You may call back to see how things are going; typically, you'll be told that the organization is still interviewing. You might then sit back and wait awhile longer, but—unless they give you more specifics than the "still interviewing" answer—you're already out of the loop. They're likely to hire somebody else. What happens is that as they interview a number of different applicants, they learn something about the potential skills of all the applicants. As a result, toward the end of those rounds of interviews, the image of the ideal candidate has shifted. You may have met that image early on, but you're unlikely to do so later. That's another reason why the first person interviewed has the least chance of getting the job and why the last person interviewed has the best chance. For an early interviewee to have a good chance at such a job, they typically have to do some type of follow-up work to remain competitive. That may include a telephone call during which you have an in-depth conversation with the hiring manager, or a letter that provides them with additional information to consider.

When the interview doesn't lead to a job, you should not take the rejection personally. As Yeager and Hough (1998) noted, "Keep in mind that the interview process is a flawed one and that often the reasons for your rejection have nothing to do with you or your performance" (p. 29). Furthermore, the interview can still be valuable if you can learn something from the experience. Review the interview, thinking of "what went well and what didn't" (Gottesman & Mauro, 1999, p. 104). What would you do differently the next time? What do you think worked well? Pincus (1999) recommends keeping a notebook so that you can record key points immediately. The goal should be to make each interview a learning experience.

Summary

Employee interviews—employment interviews from the perspective of the job seeker—are the job applicant's means of entry into the employment world. They represent a particularly important form of interviews for college students who are approaching graduation and seeking their first major job in their profession. Those applicants who are prepared and perform well in these interviews enhance their chances of getting job offers. However, preparation for such an interview is often more complex than it might seem at first.

Effective employee interviews usually begin with a series of pre-interviews known as informational interviews. Informational interviews are a series of systematic interviews with people in the company or within the industry. The purpose of these interviews is to assist the job applicant in researching the company/profession and in building a network of contacts within that industry. Such interviews provide the applicant with information about the company, the profession, and the personnel of a company that can provide important insight into the needs of that company. Furthermore, they can provide the applicant with news about job opportunities that might not be available to the general public.

To be considered for a job interview, the applicant must be able to do something that brings them to the attention of the person or persons conducting the interview. The networks developed through the informational interviews will contribute to this, but two other elements are also needed—a resume and a cover letter.

The resume is the "foot-in-the-door" that determines whether a potential employer is willing to look further at you and your credentials; generally, the resume must provide enough information that the person reviewing your resume could develop some idea of whether your skills would be appropriate for their organization. It should include contact information (your name, address, telephone number, e-mail address), past employment history, and your educational background. Resumes should be void of mistakes, carefully prepared, and emphasize the applicant's strengths without sounding arrogant or exaggerating one's accomplishments. Templates for developing your resume are available from a number of online sites and/or software manufacturers.

A cover letter tailored to the specific job and company to which you are applying should be included with every application. The first paragraph should introduce yourself to the employer and identify the job for which you are applying. That should be followed by a discussion of your greatest strengths in relation to that position and why you want to work for the company. End the cover letter by including times and methods that the employer can contact you.

Preparing for the interview itself will include (1) researching the company, (2) identifying your own strengths and weaknesses, (3) establishing goals that you hope to achieve during the interview, (4) learning the appropriate dress, (5) arriving on time, and (6) being prepared to start the interview on a positive note. Advance preparation for the interview should also include identifying tough questions in advance and preparing answers for those questions. Furthermore, the applicant should also be prepared to ask questions of the interviewer. Such questions allow the applicant to engage the interviewer in a dialogue, learn more about the company, and demonstrate their level of preparation for the interview.

Interview follow-up is often necessary, and even positive performances in an interview will not necessarily lead to the applicant receiving a job offer. Still, those applicants who feel comfortable during the interview, and those who have prepared for such interviews, have a better chance of making a positive impression and a better chance of receiving a job offer.

Discussion Questions

1. As a group, discuss what you each think your greatest weaknesses as potential employees are. Discuss different ways to talk about these weaknesses and how you might best compensate for them.
2. How would you deal with someone who asked you an illegal question during an interview?
3. What are your career goals, and what types of things might you want to include in your portfolio?
4. What type of things should you be doing now to prepare yourself for job hunting?

Please see the companion website for additional resources at [www.routledge.com/cw/amsbary].

References

Bartoo, H., & Sias, P. M. (2004). When enough is too much: Communication apprehension and employee information experiences. *Communication Quarterly, 52*, 15–26.

Blackburn-Brockman, E., & Belanger, K. (2001). One page or two? A national study of CPA recruiters' preferences for resume length. *The Journal of Business Communication, 3*(1), 29–69.

Bradford, A. (2003). The resume, the pitch, the close. *Black Enterprise, 33*(7), 78–80.

Collins, K. (2001, April 8). Mind your manners at lunch-time interviews. *The (Knoxville) News-Sentinel*, p. 1J.

Delrey, J. E., & Kacmar, K. M. (1998). The influence of applicant and interviewer characteristics on the use of impression management. *Journal of Applied Social Psychology, 28*, 1649–1669.

DeLuca, M. J. (1997). *Best answers to the 201 most frequently asked interview questions*. New York: McGraw Hill.

Franzinger, K. (2001). Covering the cover letter. *Machine Design, 73*(1), 164.

Fry, R. (2000). *101 great answers to the toughest interview questions* (4th ed.). Franklin Lakes, NJ: Career Press.

Gardner, W. L., & Martinko, M. J. (1988). Impression management in organizations. *Journal of Management, 14*, 321–340.

Gill, A. M., & Lewis, S. M. (1996). *Help wanted*. Prospects Heights, IL: Waveland.

Gilmore, D. C., & Ferris, G. R. (1989). The effects of applicant impression management tactics on interviewer judgments. *Journal of Management, 15*, 557–564.

Gottesman, D., & Mauro, B. (1999). *The interview rehearsal book: 7 steps to job-winning interviews using acting skills you never knew you had*. New York and Berkeley, CA: Berkeley Trade.

Hall, R. (2004). *Welcome to Resumania*. Retrieved from www.resumania.com/roberthalfindex.html

Kacmar, K. M., Delrey, J. E., & Ferris, G. R. (1992). Differential effectiveness of applicant impression management tactics on employment interview decisions. *Journal of Applied Social Psychology, 22*, 1250–1272.

Kennedy, M. M. (1980). *Office politics*. New York: Warner.

Kinsman, M. (2001, September 2). Asking questions is important means of making connections. *Birmingham News*, pp. 1G–2G.

Lamude, K. G., Scudder, J., & Simmons, D. (2003). The influence of applicant characteristics on use of verbal impression management tactics in the employment selection interview. *Communication Research Reports, 20*, 299–307.

Marshall, S., & Cooper, R. K. (2000). *How to grow a backbone: 10 strategies for gaining power and influence at work*. New York: McGraw-Hill.

Nicholson, J. (1999). *Dressing smart in the new millennium*. Manassas Park, VA: Impact Publications.

Pincus, M. (1999). *Interview strategies that lead to job offers*. Hauppauge, NY: Barrons.

Powell, J. L., Belcher, D. V., Kitchens, J. T., & Emerson, L. C. (1975). The influence of selected variables on the employment interview Situation. *Journal of Applied Communication Research, 3*, 33–53.

Seiter, J. S., & Sandry, A. (2003). Pierced for success? The effects of ear and nose piercing on perceptions of job candidates' credibility, attractiveness, and hirability. *Communication Research Reports, 20*, 287–298.

Stevens, C. K., & Kristof, A. L. (1995). Making the right impression: A field study of applicant impression management during job interviews. *Journal of Applied Psychology, 80*, 587–606.

Wendleton, K., & Dauten, D. (2002, August 4). Small raise, overtime make: Squeaky wheel. *Birmingham News*, pp. 1G–2G.

Yeager, N., & Hough, L. (1998). *Power interviews: Job-winning tactics from Fortune 500 recruiters*. New York: John Wiley and Sons.

Young, M. J., Behnke, R. R., & Mann, Y. M. (2004). Anxiety patterns in employment interviews. *Communication Reports, 17*, 49–57.

4

ONLINE EMPLOYMENT INTERVIEWS

Changing the Game

By Jacquelyn S. Shaia

The scenario is more common every day: The candidate gets "the interview," but the interview is not a traditional, face-to-face interview. Instead, the employer wants the candidate to first go through a telephone interview, maybe interact through instant messaging or e-mail, and then, perhaps, participate in an online interview. With new and ever-changing technology, the process of interviewing for a job has undergone major changes in recent years. Online interviews have become a crucial part of the hiring process and can move the candidate to the next stage of the recruitment process—perhaps that one-on-one time with the employer or even a job offer if the employer handles all of its interviewing online (Doyle, 2015). However, and just as common, these interviews can quickly eliminate a candidate when handled improperly.

The online interview process is widely used by employers as a vital part of the selection of candidates for jobs and is quickly gaining popularity in virtually every field. These kinds of interviews allow for the screening, recruiting, or hiring of potential employees—all done through the aid of technology. Anyone who is a candidate should anticipate that he/she will most likely be asked to participate in an online interview, usually early on in the process. The use of telephone, instant messaging, and e-mail are common; more than 63 percent of human resources managers report using videos or webcams in the interview process (Carniol, 2015).

The marketplace is increasingly competitive, and the composition of the workforce is of key concern. Success in a global economy is dependent upon a workforce that is diverse and possesses the talent to achieve the organization's goals and objectives. A workforce that is multicultural allows the organization to connect with its customers or clients, no matter what culture or region. The online interview process is particularly helpful to employers who wish to find a diverse pool of applicants who can offer key advantages such as language skills and cultural insight. Diversity increases an organization's chances of success in the marketplace; more than 85 percent of respondents in one survey felt that diversity was essential to creativity and innovation in the organization, producing fresh perspectives and ideas (McGrory-Dixon, 2011).

Online interviews are extremely efficient with the use of time and technology, adding to their popularity with potential employers. There is no awkward period of introductions and small talk: Rather, this process allows the employer to quickly assess the candidate in a number of areas and make a decision of whether or not to proceed to the next stage, which might include a secondary interview or job offer. It also allows employers to initiate contact with a candidate at very little financial cost to the employer. These interviews can occur anytime, anywhere, without the expense of travel or meals or lodging. Depending on the choice of technology, which may or may not be mainstream, this kind of interview offers the employer a simple, consistent, and effective way to screen and interview candidates. An employer who uses this method can ask the same questions of every candidate. These interviews can occur in locations specified by the employer or, as is most often the case, at the candidate's choice of location (such as their own home), using webcams or even the candidate's own cell phone (Doyle, 2015). These interviews are every bit as critical as one-on-one interviews and can, when properly handled, be a very valuable tool to both the employer and candidate. They can also be disastrous.

The Online Process: First the Ad and Then the Interview

Estimates indicate that only 20–25 percent of job openings are posted online; this means that close to 80 percent of jobs are not advertised online (Mayhew, n.d.; Luckwaldt, 2013). However, that number is rapidly decreasing, and posting or advertising for jobs online is becoming more and more commonplace and gaining in popularity for several reasons. Online posts can be far-reaching outside of the employer's immediate locus, allowing the employer to cast a wide net and quickly reach qualified applicants from a greater population of candidates. In addition, online posting can effectively promote the organization's brand, not only attracting interested applicants, but also reaching passive candidates. Online posting through company websites, job boards, blogs, and other forms of social media is inexpensive, replacing, or in some cases supplementing, the more traditional methods of recruitment such as newspaper ads, career fairs, and recruitment agencies or headhunters, which are costly and time-consuming. Online posting via social media is growing in frequency today, and most newspapers, trade journals, and other kinds of recruitment tools also offer the convenience of online services. Response time to these ads is greatly shortened and no longer limited to business hours or snail mail. Instead, the web allows candidates to review the posting and respond anytime, uploading and transmitting their applications in seconds.

Online posting allows the employer to target a large (think huge!) audience, and digital technology also allows the employer to easily review and summarize large amounts of data for the initial screening of candidates and determine whether or not the candidate should proceed to whatever the next step is in the hiring process for that employer. The same technology also allows the employer to add filter screening to narrow responses (i.e., include special questions designed to identify relevant applications). A quick search of the Internet finds dozens of companies that completely manage the online posting process should the employer wish to outsource: developing the ad, posting the ad, collecting responses, sorting and classifying the responses, and even making recommendations to the employer of top candidates. These companies range from small organizations, which recruit for very specific and targeted jobs, to much larger organizations, which handle hundreds of thousands of job searches in a single day.

Online posting does have its negatives for the employer and the candidate. The employer is often inundated with responses from candidates who are neither seriously interested nor qualified. In addition, even though the online process allows the employer to quickly assemble data using a common standardized response form, that standardized format can make it difficult for candidates to include additional or nontraditional information, particularly for those jobs that involve a high level of creativity (such as graphics, art, and photography). The constraints of the technology can force a candidate to include only items that are supported in file size and formats specified by the employer. This kind of information could well be of interest to the employer as it makes its decision on whom to select for the next stage of the interview process. In addition, candidates do not have the opportunity to build any kind of relationship with the employer using this kind of format. In any case, the wide reach and cost-efficiency advantages available to the employer and the convenience to the candidate pretty much ensures that the practice of online job postings is here to stay.

Online Interviews

The employer's goal in using this kind of an interview process is to screen multiple candidates from numerous locations with as efficient use of time and money as possible. The candidate's goal for these kinds of interviews is the same as in traditional one-on-one interviews: getting the job. But because these interviews are virtual, they present a set of unique challenges to both employer and recruiter—and there is more than one kind of online interview.

The differences in online interviews can be divided up by the type of communication the employer and candidate engage in: asynchronous (non-real-time) or synchronous (real-time). Typically, questions are developed by the employer and may be provided to the candidate in advance or only during the interview itself. The employer may request that the candidate video him/herself responding to the questions and upload the video to the employer, or respond to the questions via e-mail or text. In this case, no conversation or true communication occurs between the two—the candidate is simply providing responses to written questions back to the employer. The employer does not see those responses in real time and, as a result, the candidate never gets any feedback from the employer. Other employers may choose to communicate with the candidate via live chat and will provide the questions to the candidate in real time, allowing the employer and the candidate to engage in conversation and receive feedback. In some cases, the interaction will be verbal and in some cases the interaction will be via e-mail and even text. In any event, a dialogue can be started between the two and relationship building can begin.

The most typical online interview is conducted via webcam. Some employers actually send the candidate a set of questions and a webcam, or arrange for a webcam to be available at a location determined by the employer. However, most employers will e-mail the candidate a video link and expect the candidate to use his/her own webcam—another example of how employers are choosing technology in this interview process which is mainstream, readily available, inexpensive, and relatively easy to operate (Doyle, 2015). Web-based systems are frequently used for interviewing and, depending on the employer, sometimes the questions are provided in advance and the candidate is given a period of time to respond. Just as likely, however, the candidate may not have been provided the opportunity to review the questions. In this type of online interview, the question appears on a screen and the candidate is given a certain amount of time to respond. Employers may also choose to conduct more in-depth interviews online using a split screen and engaging the candidate in the interview.

Like online job postings, online interviews are also frequently conducted using technology companies that manage the entire process. These services automate the process, resulting in a manageable number of applications presented for review to the employer. At this point, the employer can elect to complete the interview process or instruct the technology company to conduct additional, targeted, and focused interviews, perhaps to probe the candidates on particular issues of interest to the employee or designed to narrow the candidate pool. Depending on the type of job, it is common for the employer to work closely with the technology company in the design and conduct—and sometimes actual evaluation—of these additional interviews.

The advantages to the employer of the online interview process are numerous. First, the employer can ensure it exercises complete consistency in the questions presented in the interview, in how the questions are framed or posed, and in the amount of time each candidate is given to respond. If the interview has been recorded, the employer can watch the interview over and over again, compare the responses among all the candidates, and rate the responses. The online process is less expensive and time consuming than one-on-one interviews and brings great efficiency where an employer is particularly interested in ensuring that it has cast as wide a net as possible to screen potential employees.

Online interviews present significant challenges, however, to the candidate. The very nature of the process minimizes, if not eliminates, the ability to establish any kind of rapport or relationship between the candidate and prospective employer. Nonverbal communication becomes more important than ever and even then is one-sided, because only the employer can read the nonverbal cues of the candidate; the candidate usually has no such opportunity unless the interview is live. Eye contact, posture, hand gestures, and facial expressions are all vital aids in communication. The employer can observe these things, but the candidate cannot and therefore does not have the chance to modify or reinforce his/her presentation based on any kind of feedback. Communication between the two never takes place in this example. Given that anywhere from 60 to 70 percent of how we communicate with each other is nonverbal, the inability to read any of these kinds of cues will always place the candidate at a disadvantage, particularly in a world where communication begins with perception (Moore, Hickson, & Stacks, 2014).

Some companies make all arrangements for the interview and even provide a location where the candidate can be interviewed. However, the candidate is usually primarily responsible for arranging the technology for the interview. That includes providing not only the webcam but also a background setting that will simulate a professional environment, free of distraction and clutter. An individual who has a background in photography, the framing of subjects, and the need for stability of the equipment will operate at a greater advantage than an individual who does not. This process can be very challenging to the novice and greatly add to the stress involved in the interview process itself. Several companies offer interview simulations, and most are now offering those simulations online. This kind of practice is immensely valuable before the candidate sits for the actual interview.

Finally, the number of platforms available for online interviews is growing, and it is essential the candidate practice and be familiar with the technology before the interview. Each has its own unique set of operational issues and problems are solved in different ways. Online interviews usually give the candidate just one chance to respond. Additional time for equipment failures, power outages, and technical malfunctions is rarely given. Therefore, knowledge of the platform and technology, as well as familiarity, comfort, and ease with its operation is essential.

So, how does one successfully participate in an online interview and get that job? Read on!

Nailing the Online Interview

Preparation and Practice

Without question, preparation and research is the key to success in almost any endeavor, and online job interviewing is no exception. Just as in a face-to-face interview, an applicant should spend a great deal of time researching the organization, its culture, management structure, financials, and industry. A close examination of the job description against the applicant's own qualifications is critical. Taking the time to honestly assess one's own strengths and weaknesses will allow the candidate to confidently respond to direct and focused questions by the employer about his/her qualifications and ability to succeed in the organization. Questions the applicant has about the employer should be written down and available to the applicant for reference, if the interview allows that type of communication. The candidate should anticipate what questions the employer is likely to ask and prepare and practice strong responses in advance. Even if the initial online interview does not give the applicant an opportunity to ask questions, those questions will be relevant in the next stage of the process.

Keep in mind that e-mail and texting removes "social cues such as gender, race, ethnicity, and age, as well as facial expressions and intonations routinely used in understanding face-to-face interactions" (James & Busher, 2009, p. 20). This can operate to an advantage or disadvantage. Therefore, review the responses to ensure they are appropriate: neither too aggressive nor difficult. Finally, keep in mind that the employer is only looking for relevance—fully answer the questions but do not expand or offer personal opinion, information, etc. unless asked to do so. Be sure the responses are clear and concise, enthusiastic yet professional, and do not ramble.

Technology and Setup

Each kind of technology has its own set of issues—and resolutions. Without question the candidate must be very familiar and comfortable with the operation of the technology and the parameters of the platform. If the candidate does not already own good equipment, he/she should buy, borrow, or rent the best equipment available. Wi-Fi can be unpredictable at different times of the day in different regions and geographic locations, and it is always preferable to eliminate any chance of disconnect or interference by using a solid wired connection. Batteries should always be fully charged and backup batteries available nearby. The interview should be conducted in a location where the candidate will not be disturbed. Clear, but not harsh, lighting is essential and so important that the candidate should consider seeking professional advice if there is any question on how to stage the background for the interview. The equipment should be set up so that the candidate can only be seen from the waist up. In general, the most flattering camera angle is slightly above eye level. This can easily be accomplished by elevating the webcam or computer. Framing is key: The camera should be at a proper distance that should show the candidate's face at a flattering angle—not too big and not too small. Remember how unattractive most "selfies" can be and make adjustments. Practice looking into the camera and avoid looking around, leaving the employer with the impression that the candidate doesn't make eye contact (Levin-Epstein, 2011). Maintain good posture. Avoid distractions such as hand gestures, touching hair, etc. Most importantly, the equipment should be solid and stable—wavering and movement of the webcam will create its own distraction to the viewer. Each of these areas should be practiced, critiqued, and adjusted as needed.

The Interview

Employers tend to evaluate employees on attendance, and promptness will indicate to the employer whether or not the candidate shares a work ethic that is important to the employer (Sessoms, n.d.). Arrival time (or login time) is critical if the employer has arranged for the interview to be conducted at a location or uses one of the many commercial technology companies or platforms to conduct the interview. A successful interview is one that communicates ease and confidence on the part of the applicant.

Practice is essential before the candidate actually sits for the interview. Practice the questions and answers and practice using the technology. Practice sessions are most effective when done as a full dress rehearsal. Even though the interview may be one way, and not real time, it is just as critical to remember how important nonverbal cues are in this instance as in a face-to-face interview. Looking directly into the camera, maintaining eye contact, physical appearance, facial expressions, and body movements and gestures all telegraph meaning to the viewer. Hair style, body piercing, tattoos, and choice of clothing all send a message to the viewer (Moore, Hixson, & Stacks, 2014). The candidate should always give serious thought as to what message he/she wants to convey to the employer and then choose clothing, hair style, etc. accordingly. A clear advantage of the online interview is that the candidate is in control of each of these areas. However, a mistake in any one of these areas will be repeated and negatively reinforced—each time the employer reviews the interview.

The background for the interview is of high importance. Distractions can completely negate an otherwise great interview and should always be removed. The viewer should see the candidate in a background setting that simulates a professional environment and a workspace that is clean and orderly. Distractions can include noise from other rooms (e.g., phone ringing, doorbells, television, wind chimes, dogs barking, lawn mowers, etc.) as well as inappropriate clothing, jewelry, or constant hand gestures (Hansen, 2014). Elimination of distractions to the greatest extent possible is critical.

Tone, modulation, and articulation of voice is significant. Research indicates that most people make judgments about an individual after hearing them speak—and usually that judgment is made immediately (Trudeau, 2014). Here again, honest evaluation of one's own strengths and weaknesses is important to one's success. If possible, work with a professional to soften or eliminate a heavy accent, articulate words, and regulate pace. Pay attention to grammar and syntax. At a minimum, consider recording the answers and playing them back for review so that necessary adjustments can be made in advance (Wells,1999).

Follow-Up

Manners are so important and convey to others thought and respect. All interviews should be followed up with a note thanking the employer for their time and effort in interviewing the candidate. If the interview was conducted live or via e-mail, a thank-you note sent via e-mail is appropriate. If the interview was conducted via text, a thank-you note sent via text is appropriate. In any case, a second note sent "snail mail" is also appropriate and serves as a positive reminder of the candidate to the employer.

Most candidates fail to follow up with a prospective employer when they do not get a job, and in most cases, this is a mistake. Consider approaching the employer for a candid and honest assessment of the applicant's performance in the interview and information as to why the applicant was not chosen for the job. This kind of information will better prepare the candidate for the next interview and avoid any pitfalls or shortcomings identified by the employer. Again, a follow-up note thanking the employer for taking the time to provide this kind of valuable information is appropriate and will leave a positive impression, which is always important in building a personal brand and career.

Summary

Without question, interviews in any format are stressful. Online interviews are particularly stressful in that the communication is generally one-way or asynchronous and offers little to no verbal or nonverbal cues, feedback, or signals or the opportunity to adjust or modify behavior during the interview itself. The added pressure of managing the technology can add to the stress and can take the focus away from the substance of the interview itself. Online interviews are widely used, highly popular, inexpensive to conduct, and offer the employer the ability to interview a much larger pool of candidates. Just like face-to-face interviews, practice and preparation are keys to success; taking the time to understand and master the process will project confidence and distinguish one applicant from another.

Discussion Questions

1. Given what you know about communication, what do you personally think is both gained and lost through online interviewing for the interviewer and the interviewee?
2. Would you be more or less impressed with a potential employer who relied upon online interviewing in his or her hiring process?
3. How would you advise someone entering the job market to both seek jobs and prepare for interviews given what you know about online interviewing?

Please see the companion website for additional resources at [www.routledge.com/cw/ amsbary].

References

Carniol, A. (2015). *Prepare for an online job interview in 24 hours*. Retrieved from http://mashable. com/2013/01/26/online-interview-prep/.

Doyle, A. (2015). *Online job interviews—Practice and preparation*. Retrieved April 23, 2015, from Jobsearch.about.com/od/videointerviews/a/online-job-interviews.htm

Hansen, R. (2014). *Online video job interview do's and don'ts for job-seekers*. Retrieved April 23, 2015, from www.quintcareers.com/online_video_interviewing_dos-donts.html

James, N., & Busher, H. (2009). *Online interviewing*. Thousand Oaks, CA: Sage.

Levin-Epstein, A. (2011). *Ace your Skype job interview: 14 Smart Tips*. Retrieved April 23, 2015, from www.cbsnews.com/news/ace-your-skype-job-interview-14-smart -tips/

Luckwaldt, J. (2013). *80 percent of job openings aren't advertised*. Retrieved from www.payscale. com/career-news/2013/03/80-percent-of-job-openings-arent-advertised

Mayhew, R. (n.d.). *Advantages and disadvantages of job hunting on the Internet*. Retrieved May 4, 2015, from http://work.chron.com/advantages-disadvantages-job-hunting-internet-9987.html

McGrory-Dixon, A. (2011). *Encourage innovation*. Retrieved May 4, 2015, from www.benefitspro. com/2011/07/18/study-employers-seek-diversity-to-encourage-innova

Moore, N., Hickson, M., & Stacks, D. (2014). *Nonverbal communication: Studies and applications* (6th ed.). New York: Oxford.

Sessoms, G. (n.d.). *Important of attendance in work ethics*. Retrieved May 7, 2015, from http:// work.chron.com/importance-attendance-work-ethics-5082.html

Trudeau, M. (2014). *You had me at hello: The science behind first impressions*. NPR Radio. Retrieved May 7, 2015, from www.npr.org/blogs/health/2014/05/05/308349318/you-had-me-at-hello-the-science-behind-first-impressions.

Wells, L. (1999). *The articulate voice: An introduction to voice and diction* (3rd ed.) Boston, MA: Allyn and Bacon.

5

PERFORMANCE APPRAISAL
AND EXIT INTERVIEWS

Carol had just completed her first year at a new job. By most standards, it had been a positive first year. Her productivity had been high, her colleagues liked her, and she had won a major industry award (an unusual achievement for a new employee). Then she received a notice that it was time for her annual performance review. She must meet with her supervisor and his assistant to discuss her performance for the year and her goals for the following year. She found the idea of having to defend her work in front of more experienced and higher-ranked employees to be somewhat intimidating. As the time for the interview approached, she expressed her fears to fellow employees, but that did little to relieve her anxiety. Eventually, she entered the room, sat down before the two reviewers, and the interview began. Thirty minutes later, she left smiling—happy to learn that both reviewers were elated with her work during the year. It was, she later noted, "Not as bad as I was expecting."

Maybe. But she didn't talk about it as a positive experience either. Furthermore, employees with a less admirable work record might leave a similar meeting with a list of criticisms that could be a major blow to their ego. Such possibilities reflect growing concerns among organizational employees with the role of performance appraisal interviews. Still, during a time when an increasing number of organizations are requiring individual assessments and documentation of employment decisions, such interviews are likely to remain a staple element in organizational procedures. Consequently, the typical person is likely to find themselves involved in numerous appraisal interviews—far more, in fact, than the number of employment interviews in which they are likely to engage. Once hired, they will have relatively few additional employment interviews. Performance appraisal interviews, however, may occur as frequently as once a year. Understanding the purpose and functions of such interviews is thus a necessary skill for progression within many organizations.

Purposes of Appraisal Interviews

Performance appraisals serve many purposes in modern organizations (Arvey & Murphy, 1998), with most of those functions serving as an attempt to integrate human resource activities into organizational policies (Fletcher, 2001). From that perspective, the performance appraisal is perhaps the single most important factor in helping an organization reach its goals. Goals that are formulated at the top of an organization are often lost in translation as they get filtered down to line personnel. Most employees of large organizations have seen more than one change in upper management that has had little or no effect on their day-to-day organizational lives despite broad statements of change made by upper management. If upper management truly wants to initiate change within an organization, it must clearly communicate those changes and, more importantly, evaluate its employees according to organizational goals.

At the heart of the superior/subordinate relationship is the performance appraisal. Almost every decision that a manager makes regarding employees ought to be grounded in a reliable and valid performance appraisal:

Promotions. Promotion decisions must be grounded in a complete performance appraisal. The manager in charge of promotions must not only understand who are his or her outstanding performers and worthy of promotion, but must also understand who is best suited for the new position. Just because someone is a good performer in one job does not necessarily mean they will do well in the next one. An effective manager understands who his or her employees are and what their strengths and weaknesses are, not merely their productivity.

Separations. Firings and layoffs are important issues in most organizations. Not only is turnover an economically and emotionally costly event, but it now carries costly legal and social ramifications for organizations. Lawsuits, and the threat of lawsuits, are a terrifying prospect for most organizations, and terminations must be handled delicately and correctly.

Pay. Most salary decisions must be based on some form of performance evaluation. Pay decisions include raises and bonuses. Some organizations use a merit model and make each decision on a case-by-case evaluation. In these organizations, careful records and clear communication is necessary for managers who must make these decisions. Other organizations use an equity model to make these decisions. In these organizations, individual performance is not so much an issue as unit productivity (Bain, 2001). Specific units are designated for a given raise or bonus, which is often expressed in terms of a percentage of salary.

Feedback. On a day-to-day basis, employees need to understand how they are viewed by their employers. Mistakes need to be pointed out and exemplary behavior needs to be recognized in a timely fashion. These assessments are often done by unit managers and supervisors and are usually informal in nature. How that feedback is handled can have a major impact on the organization and its employees. Positive feedback can motivate employees to accomplish more or make them too self-satisfied with past accomplishments. Negative feedback may motivate them to try harder or trigger a violent outburst that may do physical harm to other workers (Geddes & Baron, 1997). Such potential consequences of the feedback from appraisal interviews demonstrates how important it is to handle these encounters with thoughtful preparation.

Organizational Development. Training and development are critical issues in organizations. With rapidly changing technologies and business environments, it is critical for organizations to provide ongoing up-to-date training for employees. Assessments are a first critical step in providing this training so that organizations can identify where resources are best used.

Levels of Assessment

Performance is not always an easy thing to assess. The decisions that are made from these assessments are, therefore, also very difficult. Sometimes individual performance is a minor factor in making certain decisions. Organizations often divide evaluations into various levels (Szilagyi & Wallace, 1990):

Organizational outcomes are measured to determine the overall health of the organization. Layoff and bonus decisions are often made at this level.

Divisional outcomes are measure to determine efficiency of specific units. Beyond productivity, safety, moral, and turnover are also measured. Organizational development decisions are often made at this level.

Individual outcomes are important measures for managers to keep. Though individual productivity is not the only measure that organizations keep, it is still the primary unit of analysis when it comes to making decisions about a given employee.

Individual behaviors are often measured by organizations to help measure employees against a given ideal. Often called Human Engineering, these organizations keep track of a variety of behavioral measures (e.g., steps taken, hours per task, etc.) and evaluate employees, not so much on their output but on their day-to-day or task-to-task behaviors. The most popular method of behavioral assessment is the Behaviorally Anchored Ratings Scales (BARS), a topic that will be discussed later in this chapter.

Individual traits are often measured by managers in making assessments. Many organizations are shying away from such evaluations (at least on the formal level) because they are viewed as subjective on the part of the managers and not very instructive to the employees. A manager may feel that a given employee's attitude is substandard, but it is often difficult to know what to do when confronted with the phrase "You have a bad attitude." Most organizations would prefer a behavior assessment that shows how the bad attitude is manifest. For example, "You never stay late when we have a deadline to meet" (Dunnette, 1966; Dalton & Standholtz, 1990).

Legal Issues

As with hiring, the manager who engages in performance appraisals and assessments must be acutely aware of the day-to-day legal concerns that govern most workplaces. Some managers may feel that once an employee is hired that the legal restrictions may weaken, but this is not the case. It is arguable, in fact, that there are more legal concerns once someone is hired on. There are two issues that need to be firmly in the mind of a manager at all times: discrimination and harassment (Hickson & Stacks, 1997).

Discrimination is not just an issue of hiring. Anti-discrimination laws are aimed at a wide variety of employment issues. These include firing, promotion, compensation, working conditions, and all other terms of employment. Since most of these decisions are, to some extent, based upon performance appraisal and review, it is incumbent upon the manager to be systematic and thorough in engaging in these reviews. The manager must be able to demonstrate that an assessment is work related and not based on race, gender, national origin, physical handicap, or age.

Harassment, on the other hand, is a verbal or physical act that creates an uncomfortable environment for an employee based on sexual, racial, or other equal opportunity issues. On the face of it, this guideline may seem common sense and easy to follow. Few reasonable people would defend the use of racial epithets or sexually suggestive behavior in the modern American workplace. There are a number of concerns that an evaluating supervisor must be aware of, however, to make sure that he or she is in compliance with the law.

First, the issue of harassment is in the mind of the recipient. There does not need to be an intent to harass on anyone's part. Rather, all that is needed is for the recipient to feel harassed. A supervisor must refrain from actions that can be seen as harassing, especially during a performance interview. Any manager who would use diminutive terms like "sweetie," "missy," or "darling" while interviewing a female subordinate is certainly asking for trouble, even if the manager feels these terms demonstrate familiarity and friendliness.

Second, it is important to remember that managers have an affirmative responsibility to deal with harassment issues even when they are not the harasser. The court cases have been very clear on this issue: Even when the offending behavior came from other employees, an organization that allowed harassing behaviors to continue will be held accountable. If, during an interview, an African American employee says, "Everything is great with you, but Hal keeps making racial jokes in my presence and it bothers me," the interviewing manager is obligated to follow through on the employee's complaint. At the very least he or she must advise the employee about what procedural actions can be taken to stop the offending behavior. Advising the employee to "toughen up" or "roll with the punches," or telling him that "Hal bugs everyone!" is not enough. Most organizations have formal grievance procedures especially designed for such situations (Peterson, et al., 1994).

Common Problems with Performance Reviews

As with survey interviews, the two major problems managers face while conducting performance reviews are issues of reliability and validity. The reliability of a measure basically refers to its consistency, and its validity is its actual relation to what you are actually interested in knowing. A supervisor may give unreliable evaluations if outside noise or other distractions does not allow for a thoughtful review. If the supervisor is drawn to irrelevant issues, then the performance review would be invalid.

Any issue that affects a supervisor's inconsistency in obtaining results on performance appraisals would affect the supervisor's intrarater reliability. *Intrarater reliability* refers to the consistency with which a supervisor would assess similar situations in dissimilar ways. A big factor in this is the manager's state of mind. If the manager is in a good mood, then he or she might be more favorable than if he or she were in a bad mood. Time of day, whether the evaluation was before or after a meal, time of week, and time of year can all affect intrarater reliability.

Interrater reliability is how consistent different managers will be in assessing the same subject. Managers get reputations for being soft or hard, biased or fair, lax or strict. Ultimately, it shouldn't matter who is conducting an evaluation within an organization; the process should be similar no matter who is conducting it.

Szilagyi and Wallace (1990) have identified four common problems with the validity of performance reviews. One of the more pernicious problems with validity is stereotyping. Certainly, years of legislative and judicial effort have been directly focused on racial, ethnic, and sexual stereotyping. Although there has been widespread and continuing debate on how to overcome discrimination based on these stereotypes, there is a broad consensus that stereotyping is detrimental to the evaluation process. In short, everyone agrees that one should focus on the performance of the employee and avoid stereotyping him or her.

Researchers Nick Feltovich and Chris Papageogiou (2004) have shown in an experimental setting that the manager's preconceived ideas have a profound impact on their distributions of rewards. They found that the more strongly held a stereotype is, the harder it is to overcome it. They did suggest, however, that repeated exposure to people who broke the stereotypes did have some mitigating effect.

It is important to note, however, that not all stereotypes are racial, ethnic, or sexual. For instance, many professors prejudge their students who are athletes, assuming they are below average. Blonde women often face the same prejudices and stereotypes as other women with the added "dumb blonde" stereotypes (Foege, 2004). Whatever there source or target, stereotypes are a serious problem for managers wishing to conduct valid performance evaluations.

Similar to stereotyping, halo effects (Thorndike, 1920) also create a problem in validity. Unlike stereotypes, halo effects are opinions that we make about people early on, and like stereotypes we let these early opinions color our view of their future performance. We tend to create a mental halo around a person. We evaluate them as good or bad and then make future evaluations according to this halo. If our initial impression is good, we form a good halo; if the employee goes on to make mistakes, we are more likely to forgive those mistakes and claim, "Well, everyone messes up from time to time." If our initial impression was bad and we form a bad halo, then we are unlikely to forgive those same mistakes and claim, "I knew they were trouble, right from the start." By the same token, supervisors are likely to overrate the accomplishments of employees they personally like and underrate the accomplishments of those they don't like (Lefkowitz, 2000). Even if the individual is not liked, a halo effect can occur if the interviewer feels influenced by organizational politics, i.e., whether the individual is a political ally or supportive of an internal organizational opponent (Tziner, 1999).

The initial halo need not have anything to do with the issues at hand. Ross, Amabile, and Steinmetz (1977) found test subjects would make evaluations based on initial halos, even when the halos were based on inherently unfair, biased, situational factors. The subjects completely ignored the inherent biases and let the halos affect their ultimate evaluations. The researchers argued that this tendency was so basic to human thinking that they called it the Fundamental Attribution Error (Ross et al., 1977) and claimed it was at the heart of most of our evaluation errors.

A third set of errors that evaluators make are contrast errors (Becker & Miller, 2002). Unlike halo effects and stereotyping errors, contrast errors occur when a manager allows the evaluation of one employee to affect the evaluation of another. These contrasts can take a number of forms. For instance, a manager may find that a number of her employees have committed the same error. Early in the day, she may write the errors off, but after a time she gets frustrated that she sees the same thing over and over again. By the end of the day, she may give unduly harsh evaluations just because she's tired of seeing the same thing repeatedly.

On the other hand, most employees know it's a bad idea to be evaluated shortly after someone who gets an excellent evaluation. Employees in this situation often find themselves being unfairly contrasted with the company "shining star." Most would prefer to be evaluated after the company "mess-up artist." In each of these situations, previous evaluations create unfair and invalid evaluations of the current employee. Research has shown that any number of factors can contribute to a contrast effect, including the sequence of the interviews and any significant delay between the interview and the assignment of the ratings (Becker & Miller, 2002).

The fourth validity error is the similar-to-me error. In this case, the manager focuses on traits and behaviors that are similar (or dissimilar) to him- or herself to make the evaluation. This is a very natural and human characteristic. People often compare their subordinates to themselves. The comment "You remind me of myself when I was your age" is considered high praise. In fact, some similarities may be a good thing, but not always. It is important for managers to understand that there are often different ways of accomplishing the same task. Systems theorists call this concept *equifinality* (Katz & Kahn, 1966) and claim that it is important to respect people's difference as well as their similarities. It has been demonstrated that diversity, not similarity, leads to creativity and is ultimately more profitable (Hickson & Stacks, 1998).

McCroskey et al. (1975) have discussed the similar-to-me error in terms of the communication concept of homophily, and they argue that we are attracted to people who are similar to us in three distinct areas: *demographics, background,* and *attitudes.* Subsequent research has shown that such perceptions of similarity can have a direct impact on performance appraisals (Strauss, Barrick, & Connerley, 2001).

Demographic homophily is based on the basic categories that we use to initially assess people. Southerners tend to like other Southerners and dislike Northerners (Yankees). Often a source for racial and other stereotyping, we are generally more comfortable with those of our own race, religious background, region, ethnicity, age, and even some physical characteristics like eye color, body type, or height can be considered demographic homophily character tics.

Background homophily is based on similarity of experience. Sailors like other sailors and hate Marines. We like people who attended the same schools we did or belonged to the same fraternity. We like people when we find out that we share an activity like playing golf or bowling. Some have seen this as a root cause of sexual discrimination, because women managers and male managers often come from vastly different backgrounds and engage in different activities. Some consultants have begun teaching special classes to teach young women basic golf skills because golf is such a common game in the business world.

Attitudinal homophily is perhaps the deepest and most meaningful dimension of homophily (Strauss, Barrick, & Connerley, 2001). We are naturally drawn to those who share our seminal attitudes. A person's work ethic, feeling about honesty in business, or attitudes about religion are all things that may make up attitudinal homophily. It is important to note that our attitudes are deeply personal, and we tend not to reveal them until we know someone. Your mother or father may have warned you never to discuss religion or politics with people you don't know very well. For this reason, it is often difficult to learn someone's attitudes about something, and we make assumptions that are often wrong based on whatever clues we can learn about them. We may assume because someone is a Southern Baptist that they are politically conservative, or if they are a college professor that they are politically liberal. Both assumptions are often wrong.

Outcome Performance Review

One of the most popular forms of outcome assessment is Management by Objectives (MBO). This method encourages the manager and employee to work together to systematically establish a set of objectives that the employee should meet over the upcoming performance period. An early proponent of MBO, Peter Drucker (1954) claims that it addresses four critical factors in an employee's job: (1) that people work better when they have clear objectives and know how those objectives impact the larger organization; (2) people want to have input into their objectives; (3) people need clear feedback regarding their work; and (4) rewards need to be specifically linked to achievement of objectives.

The MBO process is divided into the following eight steps (Szilagyi, A., & Wallace, M., 1990):

1. *Diagnosis.* Overall, what are the current employment issues in the organization (i.e., employee shortages, technology improvements, etc.)?
2. *Planning.* What is the organizational commitment (resources) available to the training and development process?
3. *Defining the employee's job.* In this step, the manager and employee strive to learn what activities and contribution the employee makes to the organization as a whole.

This may be done in light of the employee's job description but may also evolve during the employee's tenure.

4. *Goal setting.* The employee develops and submits a list of goals to be accomplished during the next evaluation period.
5. *Superior review.* The supervisor reviews the goals submitted by the employee.
6. *Joint agreement.* Steps 4 and 5 are repeated until consensus is reached between the supervisor and employee.
7. *Interim review.* The superior and employee meet during the evaluation period to review progress towards the goals.
8. *Final review.* At the end of the review period, the supervisor and employee meet to formally review results. The process begins again.

The first distinguishing characteristic about MBO is that emphasis is placed on the outcomes, or goals, of the employee's work. The process does not focus on specific employee behaviors. Behaviors are only discussed in light of goals that were or were not met. Many organizations that use flextime favor this approach. They focus on what is accomplished, not when the employee was physically present.

The second distinguishing feature is that most of the MBO focus is on the future. Most of the process looks forward and does not dwell on past performance.

The third distinction is that it is an evolving process. With its focus on organization goals and job descriptions, MBO might almost seem bureaucratic in nature, but the final step acknowledges that the organization and its needs are constantly changing and that the employee is constantly evolving. The employee's role within the organization, therefore, also needs to be constantly renegotiated.

Stanley (2004) argues that because employees are intimately involved in negotiating their own goals and objectives, they will look more favorably upon organizational change. They will have more practical goals (often higher than management would have set on its own). They will feel greater loyalty to management and the organization because they have a say in its operation. Finally, MBO offers an important feedback tool to the organization to assess its own need to grow and change.

Behavioral Evaluations

In contrast to outcome evaluations, another school of thought is that managers should examine the specific behaviors exhibited by the employees and provide evaluation and feedback to them about their behaviors. Two early examples of behavioral style were the critical incident and forced choice methods. Both of these methods had the supervisor rate their employees on an objective behavioral grade sheet. Managers and organizations like these types of reviews because they feel that they are more easily defended if a legal challenge is launched against the organization (Jacobs et al., 1980).

Taking a page from the MBO employee/supervisor negotiated steps, William Kearney (1979) presented a step-by-step process that incorporates employee input into a behavioral evaluation now call Behaviorally Anchored Rating Scales (BARS). The process is broken down into a series of small steps and typically takes place over a short evaluation period:

1. *Orientation.* This is where the terminology and processes are discussed with the employee.
2. *Job review.* The supervisor meets with the employee and other job incumbents to identify relevant dimensions of performance.

3. *Develop anchors.* The supervisor develops a worksheet with the critical behaviors and the levels of expectations regarding those behaviors. These become the behavioral anchors.
4. *Reach consensus.* The supervisor must negotiate acceptance with the scale among all the job incumbents.
5. *Weight.* The users decide which of the scales (anchors) best represent critical job performance and weigh them accordingly.
6. *Publication.* The scales are distributed to all concerned parties.

It is important to note that the anchors are behavioral, not attitudinal. It is felt that by focusing on behavior, BARS has a much greater developmental value than it would if it focused on attitudinal questions. For example, managers are encouraged to avoid terms like "Employee shows enthusiasm" or "Employee has good attitude" and instead focus on behavioral concerns like "Employee greets customers with a smile." For this reason, BARS has been found to be an excellent training tool (Daley, 1992). However, as an appraisal tool, critics complain that it can lead to inflated evaluations and is less reliable than other methods (Solomon & Hoffman, 1991).

Forced Ranking

A method popularized by Jack Welch, former CEO of General Electric, to make upper management more lean and efficient is forced ranking. Simply put, forced ranking involves using a standardized measure and identifying the top 20 percent of your managers and putting them on the fast track, leaving the middle 70 percent alone, and then firing the bottom 10 percent. In Welch's (2000, p. 1) own words,

> Not removing that bottom 10% early in their careers is not only a management failure, but false kindness as well—a form of cruelty—because inevitably a new leader will come into a business and take out that bottom 10% right away, leaving them—sometimes midway through a career—stranded and having to start over somewhere else.

Forced ranking is seen as a way to make companies more competitive. Despite widespread criticism (Sears & McDermott, 2003), this method of performance appraisal is growing in popularity. It is now estimated that 20 percent of all Fortune 500 companies use some form of forced ranking (Johnson, 2004). It is stressed, however, that forced management needs to be clearly and fairly implemented, that it be limited to top managers, is best used with other performance review techniques, and will likely only work for about three years (Rodgers, 2002).

Improving Performance Appraisals

The problems associated with rating errors, reliability and validity problems, and the inherent problems associated with giving negative feedback are all problems that point to the potential weakness of performance appraisal interviews. These problems are big enough to cause some authorities to question the value of even using such interviews in the organizational setting (Juncaj, 2002), particularly for the stated purpose of making decisions about merit pay increases (Gray, 2002). Rasch (2004) notes that such interviews can be counterproductive, creating divisiveness within the organization, and recommends that organizations instead focus on professional growth that encourages employee success and leadership development training for supervisors.

That model, though, like each of the others discussed previously, has its own strengths and weaknesses. Many organizations consequently use a variety of methods, or blends of various techniques, to overcome those problems. Regardless of which method is used, or the gender of the raters (Shore & Tashchian, 2003), the individuals who participate in the process must believe in its validity for it to be effective (Tziner, Murphy, Cleveland, Beaudin, & Marchand, 1998; Tziner & Murphy, 1999). Furthermore, the effectiveness of the interview increases whenever the interviewer is more attentive, takes notes, and is more accountable for the evaluations (Mero, Motowidlo, & Alexandra, 2003). Success is also enhanced if the interviewer seeks objective information (Shore & Tashchian, 2002) from a variety of sources (Raymark, Balzer, & Delatorre, 1999) before making the final evaluation. The importance of seeking additional information and opinions becomes a bigger need if there are differences of opinions regarding the evaluation (Levy, Cawley, & Foti, 1998). The importance of complete information emphasizes the need for individual interviewers to improve their own interviewing and information-gathering skills rather than relying on any one specific technique. Earlier in this chapter, various problems surrounding performance appraisals were discussed. Although certain methods of appraisal may give the interviewer an edge in one dimension or another, there are things all appraisal interviewers should be aware of regardless of the technique employed. The perception of fairness on the part of the interviewee is as equally important as, if not more important than, the methods used.

An early motivational theorist, John S. Adams (1965), referred to this concept as **equity theory**. Equity theory (Adams, 1965; Walster, Walster, & Berscheid, 1978; Kabanoff, 1991) is based on the assumption that individuals evaluate their relationships by comparing the contributions they make to the benefits they receive and by comparing this ratio to the corresponding ratio of a comparison person or standard. Thus, equity theory posits that the perception of equity on the part of the employee will determine his or her level of motivation. Basically, he felt that inequity lead to dissatisfaction in the workplace.

It is important to note that equity does not mean everyone gets the same thing. It means that everyone wants to get what they feel is their fair share, depending on their own contribution. For this reason, employees of similar status and position often compare salaries, raises, and bonuses to see if anyone is getting what they feel is too little or too much. The problem for the manager is that the feeling of equity is just that, a feeling. Because people tend to overestimate their own importance in a workplace, it's very hard for a manager to actually achieve equity. But this theory can provide a nice conceptual framework for conducting better appraisal interviews. There are a number of steps each organization can take to ensure a fairer evaluation process:

1. *Standardize the process.* Whatever method of evaluation is employed, the process should be worked out independent of the manager who is conducting the evaluations of the employees who are being evaluated. This also requires a clear understanding of what characteristics are to be evaluated, which is an important component of both the behavioral and outcome methods of evaluation. Furthermore, the interviewers should have a clear understanding of that process, because knowledge of the process is directly associated with an effective appraisal system (Williams & Levy, 2000).
2. *Increase the number of items.* By increasing the number of items that are evaluated, the chance that one or two items will unreasonably skew the results of the

evaluation is reduced (Nunnally, 1967). Increasing the number of items effectively increases the reliability and validity of the appraisal (Lindell, 2001), even if multiple raters are involved in the evaluation (Saner, Klein, Bell, & Comfort, 1994).

3. *Use multiple evaluators.* By increasing the number of evaluators, you not only increase the interrater and intrarater reliability, but you also decrease the possible validity problems that you run into regarding homophily. Software programs are available to ease the process of computing the ratings and to evaluate the reliability of the process (Berry & Mielke, 1997). Still, employee satisfaction with the process will be highly dependent upon the credibility of the raters (Albright & Levy, 1995). While multiple raters can reach agreement on a single-item rating scale (Szalai, 1993), the effectiveness of the rating increases if multiple items are used (Saner, Klein, Bell, & Comfort, 1994).

4. *Increase the frequency.* A recent study of more than 2,000 workers found that less than one-third of them had been evaluated *at all* in the last year. To be effective, performance appraisals should be done in a timely manner. Whether they are done weekly, monthly, or quarterly will be dependent on many factors, but employees need feedback in order to improve their performance. Furthermore, even those who were evaluated once a year said they preferred more frequent evaluations (Manshor & Kamalanabhan, 2000).

5. *Focus on components of job performance.* As discussed earlier in this chapter, there are many growing legal concerns over the fairness of performance evaluations. For this reason alone, managers should be concerned with focusing solely on the components of job performance. This will also mitigate many of the stereotyping and halo effects discussed earlier. Furthermore, focusing on job performance reduces the use of words with strong emotional overtones (Timmreck, 1999).

6. *Deal with anxiety.* Carol's anxiety over her first performance appraisal interview was to be expected. She was facing a new communication encounter, with little experience to handle it. However, the supervisor could also have been facing similar anxiety, particularly if that person was new to the performance appraisal process. The problem with both situations is that the level of anxiety can interfere with the communication processes (Bartoo & Sias, 2004). It is to the advantage of both participants to address such anxiety early so that it will have minimal impact on the interview.

The hallmark of any effective performance evaluation will be equity and fairness. Regardless of the technique, the manager must approach the interview with an open mind and a desire to do an equitable job. Re (1987) argues the following maxims of equity that should be the hallmark of any evaluation:

He who seeks equity must do equity. It is important for management to communicate clearly and fairly with employees. This starts with the procedure itself, which must be viewed as a process that is fair to all participants. Furthermore, that perception of fairness must exist both within and outside of the interview setting. Employees will base their assessment of the appraisal on some elements within the appraisal system, such as its structure and evaluation policies, but will also be influenced by appraisal-related interactions that will occur at other times during the year (Giles, Findley, & Field, 1997).

Equity aids the vigilant, not those who slumber on their rights. Action should be taken to maintain an atmosphere of equity with an organization. This is an underlying principle of affirmative action.

Equity follows the law. To be equitable, managers must stay abreast of the obligations under the law.

Equity regards substance rather than form. It is not enough to say that you "meant well." You must establish a legal, reliable, and effective method of appraisal and stick to it.

Employee Responses

So far the bulk of this chapter has focused on the appraisal interviewer and not so much on the interviewee. The assumption in most cases is that if the manager does a good job, then the performance interview will be successful. This, unfortunately, is not the case. As stated in Chapter 1, interviewing is a two-party interaction. Therefore, the behavior of the interviewee, or in this case the employee, must be examined. Those conducting performance appraisals should be aware of how employees may respond, especially when they are faced with an unfavorable review. Monroe et al. (1989) offer the following taxonomy of equivocating subordinate responses:

Apparent compliance. Often the employee will seem overly polite or apologetic. He or she may make promises or be reluctant to offer his or her side of things. Often the words of such an employee are not followed up by actions. A manager should set a very clear set of goals and expectations when faced with such a response.

Relational leverage. On the other hand, the employee may offer too much in the way of defense. The employee may claim to know more about the subject, or invoke their tenure within the organization. This is often used with young or new managers. The manager must be confident in his or her evaluation. This is where training and preparation will pay off.

Alibis. The employee may offer excuses related to their health or overall workload. This is a delicate situation for the manager because the alibi may, in fact, be valid. The manager must be an effective listener. Also, using multiple evaluators can help in this situation.

Avoidance. Some employees will cancel meetings, or not answer e-mails or telephone calls to avoid an appraisal. By having regularly scheduled and frequent appraisals, you can reduce an employee's ability to avoid the situation.

The Exit Interview

A employee/employer interview that is conducted more for the benefit of the organization than the employee is the *exit interview*. Exit interviews are conducted when an employee leaves an organization. They may be conducted by organizations that are losing an employee (Giacalone & Duhon, 1991) or educational institutions who interview their departing graduates (Doll & Jacobs, 1988). They serve two major functions: (1) to provide closure for the departing employee and (2) to help the company understand why the person decided to leave (Roberts, 2003). Addressing the first component can reduce the chances of having a disgruntled former employee who speaks ill of the company (Sandberg, 2004). Addressing the second component can improve the efficiency and morale within the company for current employees.

Kinsman (2001) notes that effective exit interviews have two essential components. First, the departing employee must be candid and honest, with their comments expressed with the intent of making life better for other workers who remain. Sometimes that may be difficult, with employees reluctant to address and discuss some issues

(Knouse & Beard, 1996) and reluctant to give honest answers to others (Giacalone & Knouse, 1997). Often, though, it may be surprisingly easy to achieve. When a person is leaving a company, they have little to gain from expressing hostility. Still, if the interview degenerates into a venting session for the departing worker, the worker may feel better, but little is achieved. More frequently, the worker simply says they're leaving because they will be paid more, while not verbalizing the other factors that caused them to seek another job. Furthermore, the employee may have trouble verbalizing the source of their dissatisfaction. As Kinsman noted, "someone who thinks they're leaving for a bigger challenge or higher salary might simply be dissatisfied with the way they are treated" (p. 2G).

Second, the criticisms generated by exit interviews must be well received by the company. Candid comments from former workers accomplish little if the company is not receptive to improving the work environment. As Kinsman noted, "it is incumbent that the company be realistic in its assessment and courageous enough to improve its own business operations" (p. 1G). Smart companies hear and respond. In so doing, the organization can increase employee morale of those still on the job (Murphy, 2004) and reduce retention problems (Use exit interviews . . . , 1999).

Summary

Overall, the employer/employee interview provides an effective feedback tool not only for the employee but for the employer as well. Regardless of technique or method, managers and supervisors should approach such interviews well prepared and with an open mind.

Exit interviews are conducted when an employee leaves an organization. They serve two major functions: (1) to provide closure for the departing employee and (2) to help the company understand why the person decided to leave. When handled properly, exit interviews can make the employee feel better about the departure while providing the organization with information for improving its internal processes.

Discussion Questions

1. What type of appraisals (behavioral or outcome) are used in your college or university to assess your performance? Are they reliable? Are they valid?
2. What makes you especially defensive during a performance appraisal?
3. What stereotypes have you been a victim of and what have you done about it?

Please see the companion website for additional resources at [www.routledge.com/cw/ amsbary].

References

Adams, J. S. (1965). Inequity in social exchange. In L. Berkowitz (Ed.), *Advances in experimental social psychology* (Vol. 2, pp. 267–299). New York: Academic Press.

Albright, M. D., & Levy, P. E. (1995). The effects of source credibility and performance rating discrepancy on reactions to multiple raters. *Journal of Applied Social Psychology, 25,* 577–600.

Arvey, R. D., & Murphy, K. R. (1998). Performance evaluation in work settings. *Annual Review of Psychology, 49,* 141–168.

Bain, V. (2001). Individual performance isn't a solo activity. *Journal for Quality & Participation, 24*(3), 32–34.

Bartoo, H., & Sias, P. M. (2004). When enough is too much: Communication apprehension and employee information experiences. *Communication Quarterly, 52*, 15–26.

Becker, G. A., & Miller, C. E. (2002). Examining contrast effects in performance appraisals: Using appropriate controls and assessing accuracy. *Journal of Psychology, 136*, 667–683.

Berry, K. J., & Mielke Jr., P. W. (1997). Measuring the joint agreement between multiple raters. *Educational & Psychological Measurement, 57*, 527–530.

Daley, D. M. (1992). Pay for performance, performance appraisal, and total quality management. *Public Productivity and Management Review, 16*(3), 39–51.

Dalton, G., & Standholtz, K. (1990). How am I doing? *Executive Excellence, 7*(5), 6–8.

Doll, P. A., & Jacobs, K. W. (1988). The exit interview for graduating seniors. *Teaching of Psychology, 15*(4), 213–214.

Drucker, P. (1954). *The practice of management.* New York: Harper and Brothers.

Dunnette, D. (1966). *Personal selection and placement.* Belmont, CA: Wadsworth.

Feltovich, N., & Papageogiou, C. (2004). An experimental study of statistical discrimination by employers. *Southern Economic Journal, 70*(4), 837–849.

Fletcher, C. (2001). Performance appraisal and management: The developing research agenda. *Journal of Occupational & Organizational Psychology, 74*, 473–487.

Foege, A. (2004). The return of the dumb blonde. *Brandweek, 45*(9), 22.

Geddes, D., & Baron, R. A. (1997). Workplace aggression as a consequence of negative performance feedback. *Management Communication Quarterly, 10*, 433–454.

Giacalone, R. A., & Duhon, D. (1991). Assessing intended employee behavior in exit interviews. *Journal of Psychology, 125*(1), 83–90.

Giacalone, R. A., & Knouse, S. B. (1997). Motivation for and prevention of honest responding in exit interviews and surveys. *Journal of Psychology, 131*, 438–448.

Giles, W. F., Findley, H. M., & Field, H. S. (1997). Procedural fairness in performance appraisal: Beyond the review session. *Journal of Business & Psychology, 11*, 493–506.

Gray, G. (2002). Performance appraisals don't work. *IIE Solutions, 34*(5), 15–17.

Hickson, M., & Stacks, D. W. (1997). *Organizational communication in the personal context.* Needham Heights, MA: Allyn & Bacon.

Jacobs, R., Kafry, D., & Zedeck, S. (1980). Expectations of behaviorally anchored rating scales. *Personal Psychology, 33*(3), 595–640.

Johnson, G. (2004). Forced ranking: The good, the bad, and the alternative. *Training, 41*(5), 24–31.

Juncaj, T. (2002). Do performance appraisals work? *Quality Progress, 35*(11), 45–49.

Kabanoff, B. (1991). Equity, equality, power and conflict. *Academy of Management Review, 16*, 416–441.

Katz, D., & Kahn, R. L. (1966). *The social psychology of organizations.* New York: John Wiley and Sons.

Kearney, W. J. (1979). Behaviorally anchored rating scales: MBO's missing ingredient. *Personnel Journal, 58*(1), 75–83.

Kinsman, M. (2001, May 13). Exit interviews help both parties understand why employees leave. *Birmingham News,* 1G–2G.

Knouse, S. B., & Beard, J. W. (1996). Willingness to discuss exit interview topics: The impact of attitudes toward supervisor and authority. *Journal of Psychology, 130*, 249–261.

Lefkowitz, J. (2000). The role of interpersonal affective regard in supervisory performance ratings: A literature review and proposed causal model. *Journal of Occupational & Organizational Psychology, 73*, 67–85.

Levy, P. E., Cawley, B. D., & Foti, R. J. (1998). Reactions to appraisal discrepancies: Performance ratings and attributions. *Journal of Business & Psychology, 12*, 437–456.

Lindell, M. K. (2001). Assessing and testing interrater agreement on a single target using multi-item rating scales. *Applied Psychological Measurement, 25*(1), 89–99.

McCroskey, J.C., Richmond, V.P., & Daley, J.A. (1975). The development of a measure or perceived homophily in interpersonal communication. *Human Communication Research, 1,* 323–332.

Manshor, A. T., & Kamalanabhan, T. J. (2000). An examination of raters' and ratees' preferences in process and feedback in performance appraisal. *Psychological Reports, 86,* 203–314.

Mero, N. P., Motowidlo, S. J., & Alexandra, L. A. (2003). Effects of accountability on rating behavior and rater accuracy. *Journal of Applied Social Psychology, 33,* 3493–3514.

Monroe, C., Brarzi, M.G., & DiSalvo, V.S. (1989). Conflict behaviors of difficult employees. *Southern Communication Journal, 54,* 311–329.

Murray, J. (2004, June 11). Don't let them leave in silence. *Times Educational Supplement, 4587,* 32.

Nunnally, J. C. (1967). *Psychometric theory.* New York: McGraw Hill.

Peterson, T.R., Witte, K., Enkerlin-Hoefiich, E., Experocueta, L., Flora, J.T., Florey, N., Loughran, T., & Stuart. (1994). Using informant directed interviews to discover risk orientation: How formative evaluations based in interpretive analysis can improve persuasive safety campaigns. *Journal of Applied Communication Research, 22,* 199–213.

Rasch, L. (2004). Employee performance appraisal and the 95/5 rule. *Community College Journal of Research & Practice, 28,* 407–414.

Raymark, P. H., Balzer, W. K., & Delatorre, F. (1999). A preliminary investigation of the sources of information used by raters when appraising performance. *Journal of Business & Psychology, 14,* 319–339.

Re, E. D. (1987). *Cases and materials on remedies.* Mineola, NY: Foundation.

Roberts, C. (2003, November 6). Harvest the words of those who walk out. *BRW, 25*(43), 66.

Rodgers, K. (2002, April 2). Grade: Forced ranking strategies and techniques. *Personnel Today,* 21–22.

Ross, L., Amabile, T. M., & Steinmetz, J. L. (1977). Social roles, social control, and biases in social-perception processes. *Journal of Personality and Social Psychology, 35,* 485–494.

Sandberg, J. (2004, March 31). Departure tales: When farewells fare poorly, goodbyes aren't good. *Wall Street Journal* (Eastern Edition), *243*(63), B1.

Saner, H., Klein, S., Bell, R., & Comfort, K. B. (1994). The utility of multiple raters and tasks in science performance assessments. *Educational Assessment, 2,* 257–272.

Sears, D., & McDermott, D. (2003). The rise and fall of rank and yank. *Information Strategy: The Executive's Journal, 19*(3), 6–12.

Shore, T. H., & Tashchian, A. (2002). Accountability forces in performance appraisal: Effects on self-appraisal information, normative information, and task performance. *Journal of Business & Psychology, 17,* 261–274.

Shore, T. H., & Tashchian, A. (2003). Effects of sex on raters' accountability. *Psychological Reports, 92,* 693–702.

Solomon, R. J., & Hoffman, R. C. (1991). Evaluating the teaching of business administration: A comparison of two methods. *Journal of Education for Business, 66*(6), 360–365.

Stanley, T. L. (2004). The best management ideas are timeless. *Supervision, 65*(6), 9–12.

Strauss, J. P., Barrick, M. R., & Connerley, M. L. (2001). An investigation of personality similarity effects (relational and perceived) on peer and supervisor ratings and the role of familiarity and liking. *Journal of Occupational & Organizational Psychology, 74,* 637–657.

Szalai, J. P. (1993). The statistics of agreement on a single item or object by multiple raters. *Perceptual & Motor Skills, 77,* 377–378.

Szilagyi, A., & Wallace, M. (1990). *Organizational behavior and performance.* Glenview, IL: Scott, Foresman/Little and Brown.

Thorndike, E. L. (1920). A constant error on psychological rating. *Journal of Applied Psychology, 4,* 25–29.

Timmreck, T. C. (1999). Words for behavioral description in performance appraisals. *Psychological Reports, 84,* 201–295.

Tziner, A. (1999). The relationship between distal and proximal factors and the use of political considerations in performance appraisal. *Journal of Business & Psychology, 14,* 217–231.

Tziner, A., & Murphy, K. R. (1999). Additional evidence of attitudinal influences in performance appraisal. *Journal of Business & Psychology, 13,* 407–419.

Tziner, A., Murphy, K. R., Cleveland, J. N., Beaudin, G., & Marchand, S. (1998). Impact of rater beliefs regarding performance appraisal and its organizational context on appraisal quality. *Journal of Business & Psychology, 12,* 457–467.

Use exit interviews to improve teacher retention. (1999). *Curriculum Review, 39*(2), 6–7.

Walster, E., Walster, G., & Berscheid, E. (1978). *Equity theory and research.* Boston, MA: Allyn and Bacon.

Welch, J. F. (2000). Letter to shareholders. *GE 2000 Annual Report,* p. 1.

Williams, J. R., & Levy, P. E. (2000). Investigating some neglected criteria: The influence of organizational level and perceived system knowledge on appraisal reactions. *Journal of Business & Psychology, 14,* 501–514.

Section 3

INTERVIEWING IN THE MEDIA

6

NEWSPAPER INTERVIEWS

Read your daily newspaper, examine a typical story, and you'll notice that most are a combination of facts and quotes. The facts may be statistics or recounts of public records—something reporters get by examining public documents or other resource material—and they provide the factual basis for the story. But most of those facts would be dry and dull material without the accompanying quotes.

Most of those quotes come through journalistic interviews. Historians still debate when the first journalistic interviews were conducted, but the practice goes back at least to the 1860s (Schudson, 1994). Regardless, journalistic interviews share many of the common characteristics of other forms of interviews (Brady, 1976), but the results are used by the reporter to create a written story that conveys useful information to a reading public (Metzler, 1977; Raugust, 1994). The reporter must establish rapport with the interviewee, must proceed in a systematic manner to ask questions that elicit the desired information, and should conclude the interview in a manner that provides closure.

Depending on the situation, either open-ended or closed-ended questions may be used, but the open-ended format dominates the approach. Open-ended questions are more likely to elicit quotable responses.

There are some differences, though, with newspaper interviews, including basic use of terminology. The "interviewee," for example, is never referred to by that label. Instead, the proper professional term for journalists is "source."

The location of the interview is often chosen at the convenience of the interviewee. Furthermore, many interviews are conducted over the phone—a process that is less disruptive to the schedules of both participants. Telephone interviews are particularly popular for breaking news stories or those that face a daily deadline. Reporters may not have the time to travel to several different locations for short interviews with different people related to the same story. A few quick phone calls will suffice. In-person interviews are still used, though, particularly for feature stories and profiles. But one major difference is apparent—the priority that the reporter must place on accuracy. That priority dictates that reporters have an ethical responsibility to approach their interviews differently than most other professional interviewers. If that goal is attained, reporters can feel satisfaction in knowing that they are doing their job, getting their story, and holding people accountable for their actions (Rothstein, 2002).

The Priority of Accuracy

One of the authors is occasionally called by reporters to comment on the local and state political scene. The resulting stories usually quote the author and identify him as being with the communication studies department at UAB, the University of Alabama at Birmingham. The quotes are usually accurate, but the attribution is sometimes inaccurate.

The author is frequently identified as being either with the "political science" department or with the "University of Alabama." Minor mistakes, perhaps, but nonetheless unnecessary ones. Such mistakes result from poor interviewing techniques that disregard basic elements of journalistic interviews.

Journalists must remember what Fedler (1989) called "the importance of accuracy" and the corresponding "need to be fair" (pp. 186, 189). They should make every effort to ensure that their stories are both fair and accurate, on even small details. Spelling, for example, must be perfect, and the technique for doing that is simple. Before completing any interview, the reporter should verify the spelling of the interviewee's name and position. Furthermore, important facts elicited in one interview should be confirmed with at least one other source. That may be another person or some written record, but verification is essential. That emphasis on accuracy must be foremost in the reporter's mind before the interview proceeds.

Even then, there may be problems. Gordon and Kittross (1999) have argued that interviews are "an unreliable, often invalid, and even harmful way of obtaining information for the media" (p. 291). They point to three factors that can negate the usefulness of interviews. The first is the unreliability of eyewitness accounts—a problem that often plagues legal interviews—as a major problem. Even trained observers have been known to give inaccurate accounts of events. Second, they argue that many reporters use the interview as an easy alternative to sifting information from documents. Documents can often provide "smoking gun" evidence for the misdeeds of a public figure, for example, but reporters must sift through reams of documents to uncover such evidence. It is often easier to simply get a quote from someone. Good reporting, Gordon and Kittross argued, should involve both forms of research. For example, the Watergate scandal uncovered by Bernstein and Woodward (1994) is best known for its interviews with an unknown source referred to as "Deep Throat" (Garment, 2001). However, much of that story was based on information obtained from official and unofficial documents. Third, Gordon and Kittross note that quotes from interviews may be used as a substitute for a reporter's own opinion. When a reporter has a specific view of an event, they may be reluctant to express that individual view in print. If they can find a source who will provide a supportive quote, however, that is likely to become part of the story. Thus, the interview should be used to confirm, illustrate, or assist the readers with evaluating the story (Nylund, 2003).

The Interview Process

Homework

Before the interview starts, reporters should do the research on the topic and/or the person being interviewed. Research can begin with a simple search of the Internet (Prochnau, 2002), gathering information from official sources, and talking with others about the topic. The goal of this research is to (1) to maximize the information that will be obtained from the interview, and (2) prepare a list of questions or identify the information needed from the interview.

Pre-interview research is important. As Stephens and Lanson (1986) noted, "there is a direct relationship between how much the reporter knows *before* an interview and how much that reporter will find out *during* the interview" (p. 229). Goodman (2002) suggests that reporters ask themselves the questions they want answered before the interview as a means of starting pre-interview research. Pre-interview research also increases the reporter's ability to adapt questions as the interview progresses. As Rivers (1992), wrote, "If you have done your homework, you will know enough about the interviewee to modify your approach in the direction of more or less formality, respectful deference, or cheerful camaraderie, carefully framed speech or streetwise jargon" (p. 146).

Effective pre-interview research makes the interview more efficient. One of the authors was once asked to do a 2,000-word newspaper profile of a singer who would be performing a concert in the city. The deadline for the assignment was on a Thursday—three weeks away. That left plenty of time for preparation and the interview, which was scheduled for a week later.

A change in recording schedules disrupted that plan, though. When the interview was rescheduled, it was for the Wednesday before the Thursday deadline. That left the writer with less than 24 hours to write and polish the 2,000-word article.

The author handled that problem by intensifying research for the piece. Previous profiles of the artist were examined to identify relevant topics and to provide a better understanding of the subject of the story. Most of the article was essentially written in advance, with gaps left to put in the relevant quotes once they were obtained.

Portions of that article still had to be rewritten. A preliminary draft had included a reference to the singer's position on a social issue. The author planned to ask the singer a similar question and anticipated a similar response. When the question was posed, though, the singer responded with an unanticipated answer. A follow-up probe referred to the quote from the earlier interview. "Yeah, I know that's what he wrote," the singer said, "but I don't know where he got that from."

Research can also lead to questions that might otherwise be overlooked. While researching an article on singer Mark Chesnutt, the author came across an earlier article by *Billboard* that called him "Country Radio's Stealth Superstar" for Chesnutt's ability to rack up millions in radio play with little publicity. When the author referred to that article during the interview, Chesnutt replied, "They hit it right on the head. . . . *People* magazine and *Entertainment Weekly* did interviews with me, but neither ran a story. They said I wasn't interesting enough." That story and quote became the lead of the article (Powell, 1994).

These stories illustrate how research helps the reporter develop questions, identify needed information, and provide the background for probing during the interview. Exactly how that is done varies with individual reporters. Fedler (1989) recommends that reporters "write their questions in advance, then check off each question as they ask it so that they do not run out of questions or forget to ask an important question" (p. 511). Others work from a list of topics to be covered, listing the most important topics first. Either way works about the same. Even if written questions are used, the reporter generally uses the list only as a guideline. As Stephens and Lanson (1986) wrote, the written questions "rarely will be used exactly as they are written out or exactly in the same order—good interviewers always are open to new avenues of questioning should they present themselves" (p. 230).

Reporters should ask questions without arguing or debating issues with their sources. Reporters gather and report information. Debating the issues with their sources is not part of their job. In fact, it can hinder their effectiveness. The good reporter remains objective about all issues, and that objectivity makes their information useful. Any time that a reporter is viewed as taking sides, their ability to do their job is hampered. Furthermore, anything that indicates a lack of objectivity can inhibit the answers that the reporter will obtain. That's particularly true if the reporter indicates a bias toward the other side, or if the reporter disagrees with the source. As Felder (1989) noted, "Few sources will continue to speak freely after reporters disagree with them" (p. 512).

The best questions are short, simple, specific, and relevant to the story. As Fedler (1989) noted, "Vague questions elicit vague answers" (p. 512). **Specific questions** get more details and provide more useful information to the reporter. **Short questions** are also important, and long questions should also be avoided. This maxim is often ignored because many topics are complex and not easily summarized into simple questions. Still, the reporter has to seek simplification. Long answers are harder for the source to understand and thus increase the likelihood that they will not answer.

Unless the reporter is seeking a specific admission or denial of some guilt or specific behavior, **yes/no questions** should be avoided. Such questions limit the source's responses to answers that are rarely quotable. Instead, the reporter should use open-ended questions that start with such phrases as "describe," "why," "tell me how," and "explain." Rivers (1992) adds that "you should frame questions that are responsive to the natural flow of conversation but open-ended, implying that no right or wrong answer exists" (p. 147). Such an approach is more likely to elicit responses that will be useful in writing the story.

Another technique, one that's not frequently used in some other forms of interviews, is the use of **repetitive questions**. Reporters may ask the same question two, three, or four times. As Fedler (1989) noted, this technique is effective because "Each time a source retells a fact, he or she may add a few additional, and sometimes important, details" (p. 512).

Arranging the Interview

The interview process begins when the journalist sets up the interview. Most journalistic interviews are done over the phone. Topics often arise quickly, with deadlines approaching. The reporter must obtain some quotes on an issue quickly. There is often little time to prepare a list of questions, and the reporter also has little opportunity to plan a lengthy interrogation. Often, the quick telephone interview is oriented around one question that relates the source to the topic and asks for a response ("The mayor just announced that he's not running for re-election. What's your response to that?"). The advantage of such an approach is that it's quick and efficient. The interview is conducted at the same time as that of the initial contact.

Most sources eagerly participate in these quick, informal interviews because the process is mutually beneficial. While the reporter gains information for a story, the source gains exposure for themselves or a platform for their ideas. As Stephens and Lanson (1986) noted, "Most people who participate in public life, or who find themselves in the news, will be glad to talk with a reporter [because] they want a chance to state their case or to gain a little publicity" (p. 230). During the 2000 presidential election, for example, Republican senator John McCain gained the respect of the national press by his accessibility and willingness to bluntly answer questions (Mitchell, 1999).

Telephone interviews constitute the bulk of a reporter's interviewing channel, but some stories require one-on-one interactions. As Fedler noted, "Telephone calls . . . are not a very satisfactory means of obtaining in-depth interviews about controversial or complex issues and personalities" (p. 511). Stephens and Lanson (1986) add that while the phone is fast, it provides the reporter with less feedback for monitoring the source's responses (p. 230). That feedback can be critical on in-depth stories. That's why in-depth stories require in-person interviews. For such stories, the reporter must call in advance to make appointments. Proper etiquette during this call is for the reporter to identify themselves and the newspaper they work for and explain why they want to conduct an interview. The source also needs to know the deadline under which the reporter is working. That can provide a guideline for setting up an in-person interview.

A major question that can influence the slant of a story is the bias of the individual reporter or newspaper and the sources they select to tell a story. Source selection can influence local news (Berkowitz & TerKeurst, 1999; Gant & Dimmick, 2000), state (Wasserman, 1999), and national coverage (Viser, 2003). Source selection can be influenced by such factors as race (Domke, Garland, Billeaudeaux, & Hutcheson, 2003) and gender (Armstrong, 2004; Craft & Wanta, 2004; Zoch & Turk, 1998). Gender seems to be a particularly important variable, with male editors generally adopting a more negative focus than women (Craft & Wanta, 2004), and women reporters more likely to use women as sources for news stories (Armstrong, 2004).

Conducting the Interview

Once the interview actually begins, the reporter must adopt an open attitude that is receptive to new information. As Stephens and Lanson (1986) wrote, "Reporters should enter any interview ready to learn" (p. 229). That openness to new information is essential, for it may reveal a crucial story angle that the reporter had not anticipated.

The reporter must also make an early decision as to how they will keep a record of the interview. The two most common methods—note-taking and audio recording—both have their pluses and minuses. Alfino (2003) recommends doing both, but note-taking is the most common technique. As Fedler (1989) noted, most reporters (68%) prefer this method and never use tape recorders (p. 514). Instead, they take detailed notes, recording more information than they will ever use because they're never sure as to what will be useful. Statements that will make potential quotes are written out using the exact wording of the source. Once the interview is completed, they immediately review and transcribe those notes while the interview is still fresh on their minds. The problems with this approach are twofold, though. First, there is a question of accuracy. Sources who claim they were misquoted often point to faulty reporter notes as the reason. Second, the note-taking process can be intimidating to some sources. As Rivers (1992) noted, taking notes simply "scares some subjects" (p. 151). Still, the note-taking approach is the most commonly used technique, particularly for reporters facing daily deadlines.

The second technique—audio recording—is accurate but also more time consuming. The reporter, in effect, goes over the interview twice—once when it is conducted and a second time when the tape of the interview is transcribed. The result is that audiotaping can increase the accuracy of a reporter's quotes, but it is also more time consuming. Even if the reporter doesn't transcribe the entire interview, using it only to review the quotes they need, it can still be difficult to locate that quote on the tape. The result is more loss of time. For this reason, audio recording is often reserved for feature stories or magazine articles—stories that don't face immediate deadlines. Stephens and Lanson (1986) noted that audiotapes may also be useful for legal reasons because, "In investigations, tapes may provide evidence needed to protect the newspaper's and the reporter's credibility" (p. 231).

The first questions of the interview should be general, easy, and ones that make the source feel comfortable. Reporters generally don't start by asking for specific information, but instead begin with more general questions that are easy to answer. These might include such open-ended questions as "What happened?" and "What did you see?" If tough questions are anticipated as being part of the interview, they're not used here. As Stephens and Lanson (1986) noted, there are many different ways to open an interview, "[b]ut one that almost never works is to open with an accusatory question" (p. 231).

As the interview progresses, the reporter will move to more specific questions. As Biagi (1986) noted, "reporters are after specifics" (p. 232). The general questions get the sources talking, but the specific questions provide the most useful information. The specific questions should have been developed in advance based on the goal of the interview. As Stephens and Lanson wrote, "Reporters have a much better chance of getting what they want from an interview if they know what their goal is" (p. 231). Achieving that goal requires that the reporter (1) actively listens to the source's answers and (2) asks follow-ups that ensure that they understand the answer. Topics are not abandoned until the reporter feels comfortable with their understanding of the information.

During the entire process, the reporter attempts to talk with the source rather than simply asking questions of them. As Rivers (1992) noted, "The ideal interview strikes a balance between monologue and dialogue" (p. 152). If the source dominates the interview, they will control the topics that are discussed and the reporter may miss major issues. If the reporter does too much talking and asks too many questions, the source will become annoyed with the direction of the interview. Both extremes are to be avoided.

Closing the Interview

Some of the most effective quotes come in the closing stages of the interview, after the formal interview is actually completed. This is conducted by asking a simple overview question such as, "That's all my questions. Is there anything I've left out that you think needs to be covered?" or "Do you have anything else to add?" The source may then offer an idea that the reporter had overlooked, or more frequently, add a comment that is not rehearsed but summarizes the point more vividly than some of the "prepared" responses elicited during the earlier questions. Or, as Biagi (1989) noted, reporters sometimes get the "best material after the formal interview is over" (p. 235). Wilkerson (2002) said that this wealth of material from the final question occurs because "the source feels free to say almost anything" (p. 17).

One of the authors, for example, was interviewed by a newspaper regarding the 2000 presidential election between George W. Bush and Al Gore and was asked to predict the winner. His response was that it was too close to call. When the interview was completed, the reporter asked if he had anything else to add. "Not really," the author replied, "but anybody who says they know who will win is either a psychic or they're faking it." It was this last, spontaneous comment that was used by the reporter as a quote in the story.

The last question can also be reserved for the most sensitive question. Biagi (1986) advises reporters to "end tough," because "at the end of the interview you have less to lose by alienating subjects, and after a long interview they might be more inclined to let down their guard" (p. 235). Similarly, Rivers (1992) noted that the use of a final tough question may obtain information that may be difficult to get otherwise.

If the source is helpful and not antagonistic, the final question for the interview should be directed toward future interviews. Some questions may have gone unasked, or new developments may occur that cause the story to be rewritten before the day's deadline. Thus, the reporter should close every interview by asking the source how they can be contacted should another question come up. As Biagi (1986) states, this approach works with even reluctant sources because "Most sources will be impressed rather than annoyed by a diligent reporter who calls back to clarify points" (p. 235).

Interviews for feature stories, in particular, often require more than one interview—either with the source or with their friends and relatives. If another visit with the source will be required, that interview can be scheduled then. If friends and relatives are needed to provide more insight, then their names and phone numbers should be obtained.

Types of Journalistic Interviews

News/Feature Interviews

Most of the information provided in this chapter so far focuses on the standard journalist interview (i.e., those that are conducted for the purpose of writing a typical news story or feature article). Such interviews will consume the bulk of those conducted by reporters during a typical workday. However, some types of news stories may require a change in technique. Those that often use a different approach are round-up stories and interviews with reluctant sources. As Stephens and Lanson (1986) noted, "not every journalistic interview is an attempt to make a person sweat, twitch, tremble, and bread down and admit guilt. In fact, the majority of interviews are just friendly attempts to get some helpful information and some usable quotes" (p. 331).

Press Conferences

The second most common form of the journalistic interview is the press conference. The press conference is a semi-formal arrangement in which the source speaks with several reporters at the same time. Politicians often hold press conferences to make major political announcements. Coaches and players hold press conferences after games, so that sports reporters can get their comments on winning and losing. The approach is highly efficient if somewhat impersonal. As Fedler (1989) noted, "Most press conferences . . . are more convenient for sources than for reporters" (p. 518).

Still, the press conference offers reporters a chance to ask questions, just not as many as they would for an individual interview. At a large press conference, any individual reporter may have the opportunity to ask only one or two questions. However, the source's responses to any question—whether asked by the reporter or not—are considered fair game for quoting. The principal interviewing strategy is to focus on topic priority. Given that you may be able to ask only one question, make sure it's the right question—the one needed to flesh out the angle for the story.

One problem with press conferences is that they are sometimes conducive to an adversarial relationship between the press and the interviewee. Clayman and Heritage (2002) examined presidential press conferences from Dwight Eisenhower to Ronald Reagan and detected an increasingly adversarial relationship over those 40 years of press conferences. The interviewee has considerable power in that the person holding the press conference gets to select whose questions they will accept. Not surprisingly, President George W. Bush was known to prefer recognizing foreign journalists, who were usually deferential with their questions (Stevenson, 2004).

Roundup Interviews

Most interviews are a number of questions asked to one individual. Roundup interviews take the opposite approach—asking a single question to a number of different people. The purpose of a roundup interview is to study a single question or issue from different perspectives. Diane Osen (2002), for example, was interested in identifying which books had influenced the lives of successful authors. The result was a book, *The Book that Changed My Life*, which answered that question from the perspective of writers who successfully competed for national book awards.

Reluctant Sources

Investigative interviews pose complex and potentially frustrating problems for reporters (Lieberman, 2004), while placing them in situations that require careful ethical consideration (Berkowitz & Limor, 2003). The interviews are essential, because the reporter needs information from an inside source to reveal a heretofore unknown problem. However, the people who can provide the necessary information are often reluctant to do so—for fear of retribution—or outright hostile because they are the subjects of the investigation. Reluctant sources are not necessarily dishonest people. President Harry Truman, for example, who gets high marks from historians for the integrity of his presidential tenure, often had a contentious relationship with the newspaper reporters of the day (Mitchell, 1998). Interviews with reluctant sources must be preceded by extensive research, and the questions must then be limited to a highly specific area. Only then should the reporter approach the reluctant witness, confront them with the research information, and ask for a comment. In that situation, even the "no comment" reply becomes a useful quote. A variation of this approach is used when the reporter catches up with the source without advance notice and confronts the source with the information. This approach, called the **ambush interview**, is useful if no other means has been successful at getting a response. However, it can create ethical dilemmas for the reporter who confronts a source with new information without giving them a chance to review it. The source, caught off guard, may respond angrily even if the information is to their advantage.

Sometimes the hostility of the witness is based on a distrust of the media (Arpan & Raney, 2003). As Fedler (1989) noted, some people are merely nervous around reporters and some "may distrust reporters and fear that a topic is too complex for reporters to understand or that reporters will be inaccurate or sensational. Hostile sources frequently complain—sometimes justifiably—that reporters have misquoted them and made embarrassing errors in previous stories" (p. 513). In those instances, reporters can increase source receptivity by understanding why the source is reluctant. Another approach is to convince them that there is an advantage to speaking with you. After all, a "no comment" line in a news story looks bad on the source. It could be less damaging to them if they have a chance to explain their side of the story.

Proximity may be important to the success of the interview with a reluctant source. Stephens and Lanson (1986) noted that, "The closer a reporter can get to a potential source, the harder it is for that person to turn down an interview" (p. 230). During the Iraq war, this principle was taken to an extreme degree, with some reporters embedded with the military units they were covering (Pfau et al., 2004). In other instances, getting close to the source sometimes means interviewing associates of the primary target. If so, it's essential that the reporter treat those associates in a highly professional manner. If the target feels that the associates have been subjected to a fair interview, they become more likely to agree to talk to the reporter themselves.

A fourth approach to investigative interviews is the use of deception, or what Stephen and Lanson (1986) call "the trap." It may seem ironic that journalism, a profession that ideally seeks the truth, frequently uses deception as a technique for obtaining it. Deceptive techniques used by reporters include impersonations, non-identification, and fabrication of their purpose, but is justified on the basis of a pragmatic harm-benefit framework (Lee, 2004). In interviews, deception is sometimes used by a reporter who approaches the source and requests an interview on an unrelated issue. Once the interview begins, most of the questions will focus on that issue. Later though, the reporter can bring up the investigative issue and ask the source to explain some details about it. Fedler (1989) notes that this approach can be effective in eliciting both new information and confirming the accuracy of one's research information.

Biagi (1986) suggested three different techniques for "trapping" reluctant sources: the funnel interview, the covertly sequenced interview, and the machine gun interview. The *funnel interview* uses the standard funnel technique of moving from general to specific questions. For reluctant sources, though, the technique is revised slightly in the latter stages. As the questions become more specific, the reporter hones in more directly on those controversial elements that are alleged to have happened. In this instance, then, the goal of the funnel technique is to force the source into a corner by getting them to respond to a general question first. Once they have answered the general questions, it becomes harder to evade the specific questions that follow.

The *covertly sequenced interview* takes a different approach. Rather than saving the tough questions for last, this approach spreads the tough questions throughout the interview. After asking a few general questions, a tough specific question is tossed in. Assuming that the source responds, the reporter then follows with more general, easy questions. Then abruptly, another tough one is sprinkled in. The goal behind this interviewing strategy is to surprise the source and/or possibly catch them in contradictions. Its potential weakness, though, is that the source may try to evade each question and feel they have been successful at doing so when the reporter returns to safer topics.

The *machine gun interview* is a third alternative. Again, the reporter starts with general questions. But, at some point during the interview, the reporter tosses in a series of tough questions—one followed quickly by another. The goal here is to put the reluctant source on the defensive, asking specific questions that leave little room for evasion. It has the advantage of reducing evasiveness, but it can also increase the defensive responses of the source. And, it is generally not effective if done in the early stages of the interview.

Another situation in which a reporter may encounter a reluctant source is an interview with a victim of tragedy. In this instance, the source is not defensive about the topic or accused of doing anything wrong. Still, the very nature of the tragedy that they have suffered may make them unwilling to talk with the press. Any attempts to impose on their mourning, in fact, will cause the reporter to be viewed as insensitive and crude. Still, information may be necessary to provide other people with a sense of the suffering. In those instances, the reporter must approach the victims "gently, without hassling" (Stephens & Lanson, 1986, p. 230). Bucqueroux and Carter (1999) recommend explaining to the victim the goal of providing breaking news to the public. Still, sensitivity to their feelings must be a top priority.

Levels of Confidentiality

Most journalistic interviews are straight-forward, question-and-answer exchanges in which the source provides the reporter with information that can be used in the story. Sometimes, though, special rules can apply in terms of the level of confidentiality for the interview. The source may feel comfortable providing the reporter with the information but feel uncomfortable at being quoted on the topic. In those instances, one of four levels of confidentiality may be applied to the interview through mutual consent of both the source and the reporter. These levels of confidentiality are critical to the journalistic process. Without a sense of confidentiality, many sources would not provide the information needed for a story, particularly for investigative pieces. Depending on the situation, four different levels of confidentiality are possible—indirect quotation, off the record, not for attribution, and background.

- **Indirect Quotation**. The reporter uses an indirect quotation when they summarize the substance of a source's information without providing a verbatim quote. This is the lowest level of confidentiality. In many cases, in fact, the source of the information is identified. However, the indirect summation allows the journalist to simplify complex ideas without using the technical language of the source.
- **Not for attribution**. "Not for attribution" refers to information that the reporter can use in the story, but that information should not be attributed to a named source. Such information often appears in stories attributed to "a reliable source," "a long-time friend," "a source close to the president," etc. Usually, the source is not named for fear of embarrassment or professional retaliation. In other instances, though, this approach is used by government officials who may want to leak information that—officially—they are supposed to keep confidential.
- **Background**. Background information refers to information that may be used by a writer entirely on his or her own responsibility. The source who provides the information cannot be identified as the source. Typically, the writer presents the information as though it had been developed from original research. It is frequently used in those situations in which even a general reference to an unidentified source might lead to revealing the name of the source.
- **Off the Record**. "Off the record" is the highest level of confidentiality in the interview. At this level, the source expects the reporter to hold the information in complete confidence. It is withheld totally from publication. So why even bother to reveal it? Sometimes such information is useful in providing writers with information that will orient them to future events that will require special handling.

The reporter should make sure that the source knows the rules at the beginning of the interview. The source can ask to go off the record at any point in the interview, but the request has to be made before the source answers the relevant question—not afterward. Changes in the level of confidentiality cannot be made on a post-hoc basis. As Fedler (1989) wrote, "If a source grants an interview and—at the end of the interview—says it was off the record, reporters are not obliged to cooperate" (p. 517).

Summary

Journalism interviews must place a priority on (1) accuracy and (2) fairness when interviewing a news "source." That begins with small details such as an accurate spelling of the source's name and title. It continues with the use of quotes from the interview that fairly represent the person's views. Reporters must be careful when gathering information through interviews, because the process is subject to the same problems that plague any information gathered from witnesses of an event—i.e., the potential for inaccurate perceptions.

Like other forms of interviews, good journalistic interviews start with good pre-interview research. Pre-interview research increases the reporter's ability to ask useful questions and to probe for additional information on short responses.

The purpose of the questions for the reporter is to gather information. Thus, the questions should be asked without arguing or debating the issue with the source. A range of question types will be used, including broad, open-ended questions to elicit unprompted responses ("Tell me what you saw") to specific questions designed to get more details ("Did you say you saw two men or three men?").

Some journalistic interviews are done in person, but telephone interviews comprise the major channel for news-gathering interviews. That approach, unfortunately, allows the reporter to get less feedback from the interviewee, but it is often necessary when writing to meet daily deadlines.

The structure of a journalistic interview is similar to that of many other formats. The reporter typically opens with easy, general questions that make the source feel comfortable. As the interview progresses, the reporter will ask more specific questions, until the interview approaches an apparent closing in which the reporter asks, "Do you have anything else to add?" That final question often gets the most spontaneous and useful quotes, because the source feels more at ease by then.

Journalistic interviews can occur in numerous formats. News/features interviews are standard and soft interviews designed to obtain quotes and information for use in a typical news story. Press conferences are a semi-formal group interview in which the source speaks to several reporters at one time. Roundup interviews are those in which a single question or topic is addressed to a number of different people.

Journalists take different approaches when dealing with reluctant sources, sometimes using ambush interviews as a means of getting a response, or using some form of deception to elicit the information from the source. Interview techniques used for reluctant sources include the funnel interview, the covertly sequenced interview, and the machine gun interview.

Journalists must be particularly careful when interviewing victims. The very nature of a tragedy may make victims unwilling to talk with the press. Attempts to interview them in such a situation may be viewed as insensitive. The reporter must approach such situations with tact and sympathy for the victim.

Finally, not all discussions with news sources can be used by the reporter. How much and how it can be used depends on the level of confidentiality agreed on by the source and the reporter. Only those interviews that are "on the record" can be used with full quotations and attribution. "Indirect quotation" is used when the reporter merely summarizes what is said by the source. "Not for attribution" refers to information that the reporter can use in the story, but that information cannot be attributed to the source. "Background" is information provided by the source so the reporter can better understand the situation, but again, that information cannot be attributed to the source. "Off the record" is the highest level of confidentiality, with the source expecting the reporter to hold the information in complete confidence.

Such variations in confidentiality, combined with the variable nature of the source's participation, adds to the complexity of journalistic interviews.

Discussion Questions

1. Review a newspaper article and identify the quotes. What questions and interviewing techniques do you think were used to elicit those quotes? Now review other portions of the story. Can you identify any other paragraphs or sentences that were probably based on the interview, even though those sections are not quotes?
2. Assume that you've been assigned to write a newspaper article on a meeting of the city council. You would start by reviewing what actions the council has taken in its past few meetings. Then you would make sure that you attended the meeting so that you could cover it properly. Finally, you would plan to interview some of those

at the meetings. Who would that be? The council members? Those in the audience? What questions would you ask? Why?

 Please see the companion website for additional resources at [www.routledge.com/cw/amsbary].

References

Alfino, L. (2003, May). 10 tips for top-notch interviews. *Writer*, *115*(5), 39–41.

Armstrong, C. (2004). The influence of reporter gender on source selection in newspaper stories. *Journalism & Mass Communication Quarterly, 81*, 139–154.

Arpan, L. M., & Raney, A. A. (2003). An experimental investigation of news sources and the hostile media effect. *Journalism & Mass Communication Quarterly, 80*, 265–281.

Berkowitz, D., & Limor, Y. (2003). Professional confidence and situational ethics: Assessing the social-professional dialectic in journalistic ethics decisions. *Journalism & Mass Communication Quarterly, 80*, 783–801.

Berkowitz, D., & TerKeurst, J. V. (1999). Community as interpretive community: Rethinking the journalist-source relationship. *Journal of Communication, 49*(3), 125–136.

Bernstein, C., & Woodward, B. (1994). *All the president's men.* New York: Touchstone.

Brady, J. (1976). *The craft of interviewing.* New York: Random House.

Biagi, S. (1989). *Interviews that work: A practice guide for journalists.* Belmont, CA: Wadsworth.

Bucqueroux, B., & Carter, S. (1999, December). Interviewing victims. *Quill, 87*(9), 19–21.

Clayman, S. E., & Heritage, J. (2002). Questioning presidents: Journalistic deference and adversarialness in the press conferences of U.S. Presidents Eisenhower and Reagan. *Journal of Communication, 52*, 749–775.

Craft, S., & Wanta, W. (2004). Women in the newsroom: Influences of female editors and reporters on the news agenda. *Journalism & Mass Communication Quarterly, 81*, 124–138.

Domke, D., Garland, P., Billeaudeaux, A., & Hutcheson, J. (2003). Insights into U.S. racial hierarchy: Racial profiling, news sources, and September II. *Journal of Communication, 53*, 606–623.

Fedler, F. (1989). *Reporting for the print media* (4th ed.). San Diego, CA: Harcourt Brace.

Gant, C., & Dimmick, J. (2000). Making local news: A holistic analysis of sources, selection criteria, and topics. *Journalism & Mass Communication Quarterly, 77*, 628–638.

Garment, L. (2001). *In search of deep throat: The greatest political mystery of our time.* New York: Basic Books.

Goodman, E. (2002). Important questions happen before reporting beings. *Nieman Reports, 56*(2), 86–91.

Gordon, A. D., & Kittross, J. M. (1999). *Controversies in media ethics.* New York: Longman.

Lee, S. L. (2004). Lying to tell the truth: Journalists and the social context of deception. *Mass Communication & Society, 7*, 97–120.

Lieberman, T. (2004). Answer the &%$#* question! *Columbia Journalism Review, 42*(5), 40–44.

Metzler, K. (1977). *Creative interviewing.* New York: Prentice-Hall.

Mitchell, A. (1999, December 12). Underdog McCain develops anti-campaign style. *New York Times*, p. 26Y.

Mitchell, F. D. (1998). *Harry S. Truman and the news media: Contentious relations, belated respect.* Columbia: University of Missouri Press.

Nylund, M. (2003). Quoting in front-page journalism: Illustrating, evaluating and confirming the news. *Media, Culture & Society, 25*, 844–851.

Osen, D. (Ed.). (2002). *The book that changed my life: Interviews with National Book Award winners and finalists.* New York: Modern Library.

Pfau, M., Haigh, M., Gettle, M., Donnelly, M., Scott, G., Warr, D., & Wittenberg, E. (2004). Embedding journalists in military combat units: Impact on newspaper story frames and tone. *Journalism & Mass Communication Quarterly, 81*, 74–88.

Powell, L. (1994). Country's quiet phenomenon. *Orlando Sentinel: Calendar*, p. 6, 8.

Prochnau, W. (2002). How did I do this before Google? *American Journalism Review, 24*(9), 24–29.

Raugust, K. (1994, December). Using quotes in nonfiction. *Writer, 107*(12), 23–24.

Rivers, W. L. (1992). *Freelancer and staff writer.* Belmont, CA: Wadsworth.

Rothstein, D. (2002). Questions help to hold people in power accountable. *Nieman Reports, 56*(2), 93.

Schudson, M. (1994, October). Inventing the interview. *American Heritage, 45*(6), 46–48.

Stephens, M., & Lanson, G. (1986). *Writing and reporting the news.* New York: Holt, Rinehard & Wilson.

Stevenson, R. W. (2004, July 4). Presidential interviews follow a script (but not always). *New York Times, 153*(52900), 3.

Viser, M. (2003). Attempted objectivity: An analysis of the New York Times and Ha'aretz and their portrayals of the Palestinian-Israeli Conflict. *Harvard International Journal of Press/Politics, 8*(4), 114–120.

Wasserman, D. P. (1999). The local contours of campaign coverage. *Communication Research, 26*, 701–725.

Wilkerson, I. (2002). Interviewing sources. *Nieman Reports, 56*(1), 16–17.

Zoch, L. M., & Turk, J. V. (1998). Women making news: Gender as a variable in source selection and use. *Journalism & Mass Communication Quarterly, 75*, 762–775.

7

INTERVIEWS ON RADIO
AND TELEVISION

One of the authors, while being interviewed for a local news segment, found himself answering each of the four questions with a series of clichés and generalities. After the fourth question, the reporter acknowledged his thanks and starting putting up his equipment.

"I should apologize," the author said. "I only gave you broad generalities and few specifics."

"That's all right," the reporter responded. "This is television. All we need are broad generalities."

While the reporter was speaking with a little self-directed sarcasm, he had a point. Reporters for both newspapers and televisions conduct journalistic interviews, but they do so with different techniques. The newspaper reporter is looking for quotes and information that can flesh out the details of a story. The television reporter is looking for a soundbite that can illustrate a point. These two different goals result in two different interviewing situations.

The Soundbite

A television reporter may interview a source for 10 minutes, but little of that interview will actually be broadcast. Most stories will run one minute or less, and the reporter rarely has time to include much of the interview. Instead, the reporter will typically summarize the story with a limited number of quotes (usually just one), typically using only about 10 seconds of what the speaker says (Jones, 1988, p. 53). Dramatic statements may run as long as 12 seconds, but that's rare. Ten seconds is typically the top range, a guideline that is consistent with written quotes for a newspaper story that are usually limited to "a sentence or two—about ten seconds if they were to be spoken out loud" (Redmond, Shook, & Lattimore, 2001, p. 176). These short quotes are called "soundbites" or "actualities," and they must be short statements that illustrate the story. As Redmond, Shook, and Lattimore (2001, p. 176) noted: "When electronic media stories average between 20 to 70 seconds, bites longer than ten seconds begin to dominate the editorial content."

Reporters use soundbites for four purposes: (1) to provide credibility to the story, (2) to provide factual information, (3) to add visual realism to a story, and (4) to reveal something about the speaker. Jones (1988) called these four factors the FACE formula for describing what the reporter is seeking. The FACE acronym stands for these four elements:

Feelings. To let the audience know what the source is feeling
Analysis. To provide an assessment of the situation in one phrase or sentence.
Compelling C's—catastrophe, crisis, conflict, change, crime, corruption, or color
Energy. A dynamic delivery that conveys emotions.

Redmond, Shook, and Lattimore (2001, p. 172) argue that credibility should be the primary goal by adding "an air of authority, first-person experience, and expert support for the points made." Similarly, Shook (1982, p. 67) noted that "The soundbite . . . is the point of emphasis that proves the story and what's been said about it both visually and in the reporter's narrative." As such, most of the four purposes for doing the story are interrelated, with each effective soundbite adding credibility, factual information, visual realism, and information about the source.

Soundbites have become such an integral part of television news that they may sometimes be overused. As Redmond, Shook, and Lattimore (2001, p. 172) noted,

> Sometimes reporters think of soundbites as an essential part of the story, but the best soundbites are not self-contained reports. They help illustrate a story in somewhat the same way a newspaper picture might, and typically they add a dimension that the script could not.

Getting the soundbite is a two-step process of (1) eliciting the statement from the source and (2) selecting that portion of the interview that provides the most impact. That means that the selection priority is on impact—not summation effectiveness. "Sound-bites are not there to tell the story but, instead, to enhance the report and help provide a sense of 'being there'" (Redmond, Shook, & Lattimore, 2001, p. 172). To increase the chance of getting a soundbite that conveys that feeling, they also suggest that a reporter should be willing to ask a source to explain a point again, particularly if the first response is rambling or too long. "What you are after is a short, concise, clear answer that just about anyone could understand," they note (Redmond, Shook, & Lattimore, 2001, p. 175). Interestingly, the source is more likely to provide such a statement when they are asked the same question a second time. Their answer to the question when it is first posed is often a planned summary. When the question is asked a second time, they'll often relax and "give you a more conversational answer" (p. 175).

Types of Broadcast Interviews

Redmond, Shook, and Lattimore (2001) identified four distinct types of broadcast interviews: (1) live interviews, (2) spot interviews, (3) public official interviews, and (4) celebrity interviews.

Live Interviews

Television reporters use live interviews to provide interest and capture a mood. As Redmond, Shook, and Lattimore noted (2001, p. 243), "It is one thing to hear the reporter's account of an air disaster and quite another to hear an observer's still strong impressions of a mid-air collision." Such interviews are staples of cable news networks such as CNN (Robinson, 2002) and are a frequent element in network coverage. They "provide the credibility, mood, vivid details and unexpected insights that help give news reports authenticity and vitality" (Redmond, Shook, & Lattimore, 2001, p. 243). To be most effective, though, the interviewee should be adept at summarizing points quickly. As Jones (1987) noted, "If you're interviewed during a live shot, the pressure to condense what you say is greater than in any other interview form. . . . There's no chance to edit" (p. 52).

Live interviews face their own set of problems. First, both the interviewer and interviewee may be uncomfortable in front of the camera, and the reporter has little time to make them feel at ease. The reporter must be able to meet people easily and help them feel comfortable despite the pressures of the moment. At the same time, though, many television reporters are uncomfortable with the live format (Tuggle & Huffman, 1999). Second, there is no way for the reporter to guarantee that the story gets a concise and effective answer. If the interviewee doesn't want to answer the question, they can simply be evasive and ambiguous. The best that the reporter can do is to identify the evasiveness and move on. Third, the live interview sometimes deteriorates into a substitute for true reporting. Following the terrorists attacks of September 11, 2001, all of the networks went to extensive live coverage of the subsequent attacks (Reynolds & Barnett, 2003). Still, with so much time to fill, and information sometimes slow to develop, some of the reporters engaged in some speculation at times to explain events on which they were not prepared to report. As Redmond, Shook, and Lattimore (2001) observed, "Reporters who arrive on the scene and must go on the air immediately frequently fall back on a few seconds for an on-camera introduction, a live interview, and a brief 'that's it from here' conclusion" (p. 243). Even when that approach works, it usually results in an incomplete story. Fourth, the use of the live interview can be turned into a plea for action, particularly when it is associated with saturation coverage of a real-time event (Robinson, 2002). Finally, the live interview is highly susceptible to the "reporter as story" syndrome. As Redmond, Shook, and Lattimore (2001, p. 245) noted:

> Television reporters often become local celebrities by virtue of their frequent appearances on the airways. If they appear too much, though, their story can be hindered. On live interviews, this syndrome often manifests itself with a reporter asking questions that are longer than the answers. An effective interview must be the opposite—a short question that elicits a slightly longer answer that directly addresses the issue needed to explain the story to the audience.

Shook (1982, p. 82) suggests that the reporter make plans to control the interview prior to going on the air. This involves establishing a predetermined cue—usually a hand signal, touch, or pre-determined final question—that tells the interviewee that the interview must end within 15 seconds. Furthermore, the reporter must be prepared to interrupt a source who spends too much time on a single question. To avoid that, the reporter must have another question ready to ask whenever the person pauses. In some instances, the reporter might have to interrupt the source in mid-sentence; if so, do it politely, saying, "Forgive me, but . . ." Finally, the reporter must have a final exit line planned in advance. The exit line serves to put a conclusion on the live interview while also providing a cue for the director to zoom off from a tight shot and be ready to cut back to the studio.

Spot Interviews

These interviews often occur around breaking news. They are used so that eyewitnesses can describe what they saw and felt as witnesses to a dramatic event such as a home fire or automobile accident. This approach allows the audience to get a firsthand sense of the emotions and the drama faced by the participants at that event. This approach is not without its critics. The most obvious problem is that the reporter can be insensitive and intrude on the private grief of an individual who has just faced a tragic loss.

Reporters who do spot interviews with victims or their families are always subject to crossing ethical and legal lines that differentiate the public's right to know and the victims' rights to privacy. The ethical questions regarding invasion of privacy are ongoing issues with which editors and reporters constantly grapple (Hanson, 2002). Sometimes, however, such questions may go beyond the ethical dimension and also include legal questions. Release of improper information by the reporter could subject the reporter to possible legal action (TV Newsman can be sued . . ., 1995) and/or potentially alienate the television audience (Seamans, 2001).

Public Official Interviews

There is some debate regarding the extent to which television effectively covers local public officials, but the city hall beat is a staple of local television news (Coulson & Lacy, 2003). Redmond, Shook, and Lattimore (2001) argued that the goal of public official interviews should be to expose the sincerity or hypocrisy of an official who speaks on public issues. "Expose" may be too harsh of a term to describe all public official inter-views, though. "Reveal" might be more accurate. Ideally, the public official interview should be one in which the reporter asks questions that the public would have asked, if they had the opportunity. The reporter becomes a surrogate interviewer for the public, seeking information that the public will find useful. In other words, according to Red-mond, Shook, & Lattimore (2001, p. 17), broadcast reporters

> are responsible for asking questions your audience would ask if given the oppor-tunity, seeking clarification if the interviewee wanders, keeping the interview an exchange of information instead of a conveyor belt of information from special interests, and pacing the interview so it builds to a satisfying conclusion.

Some of the most intensive public official interviews occur on Sunday mornings on shows such as NBC's *Meet the Press*, CBS's *Face the Nation*, and ABC's *This Week* (Simon, 1987). These interviews are discussed in more detail in Chapter 9, but some review is appropriate here. The format of the shows are similar. Each has a reporter or reporters directing questions at public officials or other newsworthy individuals. In most cases, those guests are either high-ranking administration officials or people who are in leadership positions in Congress who are asked to answer tough questions related to issues of the day. Public officials agree to participate, thus gaining exposure for themselves and their ideas. An effective interview on any of the shows can dramati-cally increase recognition of an issue, pushing it to the forefront of the media's agenda. Furthermore, most of the guests are experienced at answering such questions. Their interview-response skills are often just as well developed as the interview-questioning skills of the reporters.

Veteran reporter Molly Ivins (1991) has criticized these shows, though, particularly those who interview representatives of opposing sides of an issue. Her criticism is that in an effort to present both sides, these shows can potentially misrepresent the relative value of the side with the strongest argument. Ivins was particularly critical of shows such as *MacNeil/Lehrer* and *Nightline*, writing that such shows "frequently give us a face-off between those who see reality and those who have missed it entirely" (p. 232).

An *ambush interview* is a controversial form of the public official interview in which "reporters who are unable to schedule an interview with an individual often stake out the person's home or office until they are able to ambush the person as he or she comes into or goes out of the building" (White, 2002, p. 371). Ambush interviews are remark-ably easy to do, given the recent advances in camera and microphone technology. A television crew has the same access to public places and freedom of movement as anyone else, causing Jones (1988) to note that "In a public place, you have almost no right of personal privacy" (p. 168). Still, because of their invasiveness, such interviews are ethically questionable, and yet sometimes necessary. Lesley Stahl (1999), of CBS, calls it "an opportunity for reporters to relinquish their dignity." While the technique has always been available to broadcast reporters, Stahl argues that its popularity exploded during the Watergate era, when that was the only effective way to get comments from some participants. Since then, the technique has become more commonplace. The reporter's ethical dilemma is deciding when the technique should be used. ABC News correspondent Barry Serafin has argued that an ambush interview is justified only when there's "a genuine public accountability involved" that relates to the public interest.

Jones (1988), writing from the interviewee's perspective, describes the ambush interview as a "heads they win, tails you lose" situation (p. 123). He recommends that public figures should politely refuse to do them by making an appointment for a full interview at a later time ("I don't have time now, but can you come back at three this afternoon?"). Another option is to first request an off-camera interview to set the rules regarding what will be off and on the record before the ambush interview is completed. Both approaches give interviewees time to prepare for the interview.

Celebrity Interviews

The celebrity interview is a growing phenomenon for broadcast stations. Celebrities like the publicity that comes from broadcast appearances, while the broadcast outlets like the entertainment and star value that comes with interviewing the celebrity. As a result, a number of national network and syndicated shows (*Jay Leno, David Letterman, Regis and Kelly*) feature such interviews as major segments of their programming. At the local level, celebrities who are passing through town to promote a new movie or book often find themselves doing interviews for local stations. Such interviews rarely generate major news stories, but that's not their purpose. From the station's point of view, the goal is primarily that of entertainment. If the interview is above average, it will also provide the audience with an intimate look at the celebrity. The reporter's guideline here is that "The reporter is not the story" (Shook, 1982, p. 66). The focus of the interview should remain on the celebrity—not the reporter.

Tricks of the Trade

The goal of most broadcast interviews, as ABC's Ted Koppel (2000) noted, is "extracting information from a guest" (p. viii). Most of the standard techniques of interviewing apply to broadcast interviews. However, there are some significant variations that could be called "tricks of the trade" for broadcast reporters.

Spontaneity

Redmond, Shook, and Lattimore (2001) noted that "The best (broadcast) interviews are spontaneous, not stilted, rehearsed or contrived" (p. 172). To encourage this approach, most reporters avoid pre-written questions and instead work from a **key word question list**, which identifies topics to be covered in the interview. "Questions cannot be prepared in detail or totality because interviews often develop spontaneously," Redmond, Shook, and Lattimore (p. 173) added. "The attentive interviewer capitalizes on the situation at hand by listening carefully to responses and guiding the interview so it develops naturally" (p. 173). To increase that spontaneity, White (2002) suggests that the reporter's question list should not be obvious to the interviewee but should be put to one side and referred to "only when necessary" (p. 258).

Nonverbal Behavior

Providing positive nonverbal feedback is a positive characteristic in most forms of interviewing. In television interviews, however, the reporter's control over their nonverbal behavior is twice as important. The reporter must remember at all times that both the interviewee and the television audience are observing the behavior. Thus, White (2002) noted, "Television reporters must be concerned about their facial expressions and head movements during an interview, particularly in a studio situation when two or more cameras are being used. . . . [A] reporter cannot be shown expressing agreement or disagreement" (p. 265). Furthermore, effective use of movement and nonverbal behavior increases audience attention and knowledge acquisition (Ravaja, 2004).

Nonverbal behavior is also used to induce responses from the interviewee. As such, expert interviewers use their nonverbal behavior to enhance the responses from the interviewee rather than as expressions of their own position, attitudes, or values. As ABC's Ted Koppel wrote, "my tone or apparent mood or facial expression has little or nothing to do with what I really think" (p. viii). Instead, a raised eyebrow or shift in tone of voice is used to induce the interviewee to continue speaking. The most common technique for doing this is silence, i.e., when an interviewee completes an answer, the reporter keeps looking at them and pointing the microphone at them. The nonverbal behavior tells the interviewee to continue talking. The advantage of this technique is that the individuals will likely continue talking, believing that they need to provide more information. As Redmond, Shook, and Lattimore (2001, p. 175) noted, "The first answer to a question can be rather dull. The ensuing additional detail can be the stuff of exclusive revelations."

The nonverbal behavior of the interviewee is also critical. As White (2002) noted, "Many people interviewed by reporters are shy by nature or intimidated by microphones and cameras" (p. 257). Someone who is tense on camera can make the audience feel uncomfortable and ruin an otherwise good interview. The reporter must use their own nonverbal behavior to prepare the source for the interview and make the interviewee more comfortable, a process that White (2002) calls "warming up the head" (p. 258). That includes maintaining an open and relaxed position while maintaining constant eye contact with the interviewee. White notes that eye contact will also enhance the listening skills of the reporter because "It's easier for reporters to concentrate on what people are saying if they look them right in the eye" (p. 258). The crew can help in that endeavor by not shining lights in the interviewee's eyes and putting the microphone in an inconspicuous place.

Ice-breakers

Putting the interviewee at ease continues with the first few questions of the interview. The first question is a formal one: "Could you say and spell your name for the camera?" This makes it easier for the editor to put titles on screen with a character generator for airing of the interview. That question is followed by a series of other simple questions that the reporter has no intention of using. Their sole purpose is to make the interviewee more comfortable and allow them to acclimate to the broadcast environment. As Redmond, Shook, and Lattimore (2001) noted, "Once people start talking, they settle down a bit" (p. 175).

Listening

Redmond, Shook, and Lattimore (2001) once noted, "Many people, even so-called professional interviewers, are so intent upon formulating their next question that they fail to hear what the interviewee is saying" (p. 172). The problem, they added, is that "You can kill the life of an interview quickly by concentrating so intently on your next question that you fail to hear" (p. 173). When reporters don't listen, the interviewee picks up on their lack of interest and their responses become monotone. Even worse, reporters who don't listen miss the opportunity to ask important follow-up probes. "The questions you think are important are only an interview guide," Redmond, Shook, and Lattimore warn. "Often the richest material is found when those questions are used as a framework for exploring a subject and you ask follow-ups freely along the way" (p. 176). Without listening, they add, the reporter may "miss the follow-up opportunity that could lead to an Emmy-winning disclosure" (p. 176).

White (2002) notes that failure to listen can often create embarrassing situations for a reporter. "Many inexperienced reporters are so intent on asking their prepared questions that they fail to listen to the answers," he wrote. "They often do not realize that their previous question was not answered fully, or at all. Sometimes, to the embarrassment of all, the reporter asks a question that already has been answered" (pp. 257–258).

Repeating Questions

Unlike some other interviews, it's perfectly acceptable for a broadcast reporter to repeat a question and give the interviewee a second chance at answering it. This approach is often used whenever the first answer provides the information needed for the story but is too long to use as a soundbite. White (2002) recommends eliciting a second response by saying, "That was great, but could you cover that same ground again in about half the time?" (p. 261). As Redmond, Shook, and Lattimore noted, "Often when you ask to have something explained again, the interviewee will smile, relax a little and give you a more conversational answer. Then you'll have a great soundbite" (p. 175).

Testing Equipment

A broadcast interview is worthless if the reporter doesn't have sound or an image of broadcast quality. That means both audio and video equipment must be tested before the interview begins. The camera should have a fresh battery, and the room should be lit so that a good visual image is obtained. Microphones must be pretested, since different types will pick up different sounds. The most common forms of microphones used for broadcast interviews are the lavalier, the shotgun, and the wireless. Each has its own advantages and disadvantages. The lavalier is attached to the interviewee's clothing to pick up their responses and little else. The shotgun mike can be used at farther distances (up to 30 feet) but will also pick up outside noise that may detract from the quality of the recording. The wireless microphone is a small, inconspicuous lavalier-type mic that broadcasts to a receiver a few yards away; it allows the interviewee more freedom of movement and is thus used with "walking" interviews. The problem, though, is that each different microphone will likely have different levels of audio sensitivity. One may record the interviewee's voice while blocking out other noises, whereas another may pick up the hum of an air conditioner in the background. The crew must test the mike in advance of each interview to see how it will perform in that setting.

Establishing Rapport

White (2002) notes that different reporters have different views on building rapport with the news source. Some like to ask a few questions before the interview starts, while giving the source an overview of the questions that will be asked. As White noted, "The advantage of *warming up* the head is that it gives the person time to collect his or her thoughts, usually ensuring a smoother interview. . . . Warming up an interviewee also tends to put the person more at ease" (p. 258). However, there are some instances in which the reporter will not want the interviewee to realize all of the questions that will be asked. If any tough questions or surprise questions are anticipated by the source, that anticipation can alter their responses. Still, in those instances in which the reporter is not seeking controversial information, the warming-up procedure is fairly common.

Opening the Interview

The first questions are intended to get basic information. Ask the person to say their name, spell it, and identify their title. That can be followed by basic information regarding their employment, education, and/or marital status. These questions provide the information for placing a subtitle with the person's name on the screen during the broadcast of the interview and also allow them to get used to the camera and the question-and-answer process.

Asking Questions

Question techniques used by broadcast reporters are similar to those of newspaper reporters. Most use carefully phrased **open-ended questions** that will not encourage a "yes/no" response. The reporter wants a one-sentence summary of the person's belief, not a one-word response to an idea. Furthermore, the reporter should avoid the temptation to use leading questions. This can be difficult to do, particularly since the reporter is often looking for emotional reactions. Still, it's not considered proper to try to trigger such reactions. Thus, the reporter should ask, "What did you think when you first returned home?" rather than "Were you upset when you first saw how badly your home had been damaged?" The goal is to restrict the questions to those that gather information about what the person knows or thinks about the topic.

Tough questions are those that the interviewee will resent. As with newspaper interviews, these are often held until the end of the interview. Some reporters, in fact, will avoid asking them at all rather than risk their relationship with the interviewee or offend the audience if they are asked without sufficient cause. Still, they have to be asked in some situations. White (2002) suggests that it helps "to blame the tough questions on other people" (p. 259), such as your boss or the source's critics ("Some of your critics say . . ."). Redmond, Shook, and Lattimore (2001) suggest that "Tough questions should be saved for interviewees who intentionally try to change the subject or who talk nonstop to avoid the subject" (p. 173). Even when tough questions are asked, the interviewee may avoid the answer. If so, the reporter should point out that the question was not answered. White (2002) suggests that this be done politely by saying, "I'm sorry, but you still haven't answered my question" (p. 261). If the interviewee still avoids the question, that response itself can be newsworthy. As White (2002) added, "When the response is, 'That's all I'm going to say on the subject,' that in itself makes a statement" (p. 261). If the response is to say nothing, the resulting silence can be particularly devastating when replayed on television.

The **surprise question** is a specific variation of the tough question that is designed to "catch the interviewee off guard" (White, 2002, p. 259). It requires advance preparation and research on the part of the reporter. Furthermore, the general advice follows the protocol of courtroom examination: Don't ask a question unless you already know the answer. If the source tries to avoid the question, or gives an inaccurate response, the reporter must know the question and probable answer well enough to ask a quick follow-up for clarification ("But that's not what you said last week. Have you changed your mind?"). Jones (1988) warns his readers about responding to surprise questions, particularly those that the interviewee considers unfair. "Controlled anger is the key here," he wrote. "A seething resentment that the reporter would stoop so low. And a clear, positive statement, delivered with deep feeling" (p. 131).

The **closing question** for the interview is usually the same: "Did I forget something?" or "Is there anything else you'd like to add?" The pressures to conduct the interview and to get it completed in time to edit and air will often cause the reporter to overlook something important. A simple final question to address that possibility easily solves that problem. And, that final question often provides the best soundbite. The open-ended nature of the question allows the interviewee essentially to interview themselves. They often respond with a statement that honestly and accurately reflects their feelings and beliefs. The result can be an effective soundbite.

Another crucial skill for the interview is knowing when to stop. White (2002) noted that "Reporters just entering the field tend to ask too many questions, usually because they are understandably insecure" (p. 262). But the television journalist has a limited amount of time available for the soundbite. Asking too many questions leads to too much material and too much time being spent on a single project. Another quote from another source will be more valuable than extending the time interviewing a single source.

The Other Side of the Microphone

Conducting interviews is part of the job for television reporters. Most are adept and skillful, the byproduct of years of training and experience. The participant who is likely to have less experience and less training is usually on the other side of the microphone—the interviewee. Many people who appear on camera may do so during the only television interview in which they will ever participate. They have little chance to build up experience and are often at a disadvantage in the interview situation. Others, however, may find that part of their job includes participating in media interviews. In the entertainment industry, interviews are a normal part of the job (Murphy, 2002). Professionals from such diverse fields as politics (Powell & Cowart, 2003) and medicine (Jud, 1999) often have to face the camera and answer a reporter's questions, while a consulting industry has developed to help businesspeople in dealing with and scheduling of TV interviews (Novotny, 2000). Similarly, many new authors find that broadcast interviews are a key element in promoting their latest work (Jud, 2003). Still, as Jud has noted, "What makes a good guest for a show doesn't always make a good show for the guest." Experienced interviewers work to ensure that a broadcast interview tells their story, not just the story that the journalist wants told.

Different writers have made a variety of suggestions for being effective on camera. Hyde (1999) places a priority on remaining calm. Jud (1999) suggested that the person who participates in a television interview should use what she calls "the seven C's" as their goals for the interview; i.e., try to come across as Creative, Credible, Current, Convincing, Complete, Clear, and Concise. Jud (2003) has also emphasized the need to identify key points to mention during the interview. Myers (2000) noted the importance of sincerity in influencing public perceptions to the interview. Jones (1988) suggested that, for live interviews or press conferences, the interviewee should get the tough questions out of the way first, so that "Then you have the rest of the show to counter with a brighter side" (p. 50). If any of the anticipated questions are expected to be tough or controversial, it's also wise to make a copy of the interview yourself. Reporters have been known to take quotes out of context and thus convey something that was not representative of the interview. Reporters have also been known to do reverse shooting of questions, i.e., getting a response from an interviewee subsequently taping a different question and editing it into the presentation as if it were the original question. Keeping a complete tape of the interview provides evidence if such techniques are used.

Chris Matthews, host of CNN's *Hardball*, believes that passion is a key factor for a political reporter. "If someone has no passions, he or she has no business either running for office, standing on a downtown corner holding a bullhorn, or hosting a political talk show," Matthews (2001, p. 214) wrote. Bill O'Reilly, former host of the Fox News Channel's *The O'Reilly Factor*, has a similar view. O'Reilly notes that one reason conservative talk show hosts are more successful than liberal hosts is because liberals "are usually nonjudgmental," and that limits their ability to take a strong position when interviewing others (O'Reilly, 2000, p. 51). Matthews hopes that his guests bring their own passion to his show. Specifically, he identifies five things that he hopes that they will bring to his show: facts, spontaneity, honesty, feistiness, and laughter (p. 215). The goal, he adds, is to provide information, viewpoints, and entertainment. "This isn't the inquisition," he writes. "No one really gets hurt. In fact, guests usually want to come back for more" (p. 215).

Jones (1988) noted that the importance of the soundbite means that people who are interviewed for broadcast news must develop "a stopwatch in your head" (p. 67). Statements that they want included in the broadcast should be limited to 10 seconds. White (2002) gives a similar time estimate, saying the interviewee should "usually try to express their views in about 12 seconds to make sure their answers are not edited" (p. 261). Conversely, a source can limit the chances of the station airing an answer to an adverse question by simply spending 20 seconds or more answering it. As Shook (1982) noted, "the people who are the most important newsmakers often have become television performers over the years. They know the clock is in their favor and they can talk for three minutes and still not give meaningful answers to the reporter's questions" (p. 68).

Jones (1988) also suggests that the interviewee should use the reporter's name when answering questions. This acknowledges the reporter's role while building rapport during the interview, and that can make both participants feel more comfortable during the interview. That comfort level is important. As Jones noted, "The camera detects phonies" (p. 28). Any indication of tenseness can be interpreted as insincerity, thus damaging the interviewee's cause. To ensure that sincerity is present, Jones also advises against memorizing answers. "The first thought that comes to your mind is usually the best, the brightest, and the most sincere," he wrote (Jones,1988 p. 31).

Sincerity must be supported by honesty. Some interviewees are so tempted to paint themselves in a positive light that they stretch the truth in some of their replies. Such actions almost inevitably create problems. As Jones (1988) noted, "If you're caught in an on-camera lie, television will never forget. It will be played over and over. You can't say you were misquoted" (p. 127).

Another approach is to view the interview as an interpersonal conversation rather than giving in to the temptation to treat it like a public speech. Jones (1988) calls this the "living room" mentality, recommending that the interviewee "Talk as if only one or two people are listening . . . [because] . . . There may be half a million people out there listening—but they're not all together in one place" (p. 27).

Perhaps the major tool available to the interviewee, though, is the topic shift. A topic shift occurs when the interviewee takes a question and then rephrases it into one on a different topic. Brian Jud (2003), host of the television show *The Book Authority*, offers two suggestions for handling topic shifts. First, if the interviewee believes the question slants material in the wrong direction, they can say, "That's a good question, but if you look at it from a different perspective . . ." Another option, particularly if the question is actually a statement about the interviewer's belief, the guest can reply, "Most people think that's true, but look at it in the context of . . ."

Telephone Interviews

Television interviews are usually conducted face-to-face, but radio reporters—like newspaper reporters—can often conduct their interviews on the phone. Still, the radio reporter faces some hurdles in telephone interviews that the newspaper reporter doesn't worry about. The biggest problem is that the lack of visual feedback can make it difficult for the reporter "to know when the newsmaker has finished giving an answer" (White, 2002, p. 265). As a result, radio reporters sometimes find themselves interrupting the interviewee before they are finished answering the question. In a live, "talk-radio-style" interview, such interruptions are irritating to the audience. In a recorded interview, of which only a portion will be used, it can make it harder to edit the interview for a good soundbite. Because of this, White suggests that even radio reporters should use telephone interviews only as a last resort when it is impossible to interview the individual in person. If the phone is used, the reporter must monitor the conversation for such disruption, apologize to the source, and ask them to repeat the answer.

On occasion, television reporters will also use telephone interviews. For television reporters, telephone interviews are usually informational in nature. The reporter uses the phone to gather breaking information to see if a story warrants additional coverage. In fast-breaking news, the interview may be re-broadcast, sometimes using a photo of the interviewee. However, if the interview goes beyond the informational stage and is recorded for possible broadcast use, the interviewee must be informed. In many states, it is illegal to record someone on the phone without their permission.

Checkbook Journalism

A growing ethical issue for broadcast journalists is the concept of "checkbook journalism," i.e., paying interviewees for their interviews. As Day (1997, p. 188) noted,

> These large payments for interviews with such high-profile public figures attract a lot of attention and a predictable round of criticism, even from within the media establishment itself. Checkbook journalism raises the ethical hackles of some reporters and editors because it encourages the marketing of information that may not be accurate.

Day (1997) first noted that trend became a major problem during coverage of the O.J. Simpson trials, resulting in "a thriving cottage industry in checkbook journalism among the tabloid media as they unashamedly offered financial inducements to potential witnesses to tell their stories to a national audience" (p. 109). Since then, the trend has grown into a form of packaged entertainment that sometimes has reached extreme levels.

Checkbook journalism typically takes three different forms. The most overt is the direct exchange of money for the interview. As Day (1997) noted, "Some news organizations . . . have been known to pay accident victims for exclusive interviews" (p. 188).

A more subtle form is indirect payments. The news organization pays for the transportation, lodging, and meals of the person in exchange for the interview. While no money directly changes hands, the inducement of a free vacation is sometimes sufficient enticement to secure the interview.

A third version of checkbook journalism is the consultant's ploy, i.e., hiring an individual who is a participant in the story as a consultant for the story. This approach is more frequently used on long-term stories. It obtains the services of the interview for an extended period of time and makes it harder for the opposition to get an interview with them.

Generally, the entire concept of checkbook journalism raises ethical questions for broadcasters. As Day (1997) noted, "Although paying sources for news or exclusive interviews is common in other parts of the world, it is still publicly disparaged among most mainstream American news organizations" (p. 189). There are, however, those who consider it an acceptable means of obtaining interviews in modern society (Checkbook journalism bounces back, 1991). Many interviewees lack the financial resources to make themselves available to the media at no cost. If they take time off from their jobs, they might need financial compensation for their loss. And, those who sign on as consultants for stories are often truly professional consultants—lawyers or professional services consultants who have expertise in the topic being covered. They generally do not provide their services for free—even to media outlets. As such, their views can bring insights to a story that might not otherwise be available.

Summary

The essence of an effective television interview is the priority that broadcast reporters place on the soundbite. The reporter should always remember that the purpose of the interview is not to gather information but to elicit a powerful concise statement (emotional or factual) from a credible source, to enclose within your package. Broadcast interviews differ from newspaper interviews in several aspects. Live television interviews enhance coverage of ongoing events, while pre-recorded soundbites are used to flesh out the details of a story. Meanwhile, those who are the subject of such interviews must remember that the audience is both listening to and looking at them.

Discussion Questions

1. Do you think most interviewers are fair to their interviewees on most television networks?
2. What recourse do you feel a public official or celebrity should have if they have been treated unfairly by the press?
3. If you were an on-air interviewer, how would you deal with an interviewee who refused to answer your questions and just stuck to their talking points?

Please see the companion website for additional resources at [www.routledge.com/cw/amsbary].

References

Checkbook journalism bounces back. (1991, December 9). *Broadcasting*, 5.

Coulson, D. C., & Lacy, S. (2003). Television reporters' perceptions of how television and newspaper competition affects city hall coverage. *Mass Communication & Society, 6,* 161–174.

Day, L. A. (1997). *Ethics in media communications: Cases and controversies.* Belmont, CA: Wadsworth.

Hanson, G. (2002). Learning journalism ethics: The classroom versus the real world. *Journal of Mass Media Ethics, 17,* 235–246.

Hyde, P. (1999). Whatever you do, don't be nervous! (And other tricks of the pundit trade). *Masthead, 51*(4), 26–27.

Ivins, M. (1991). *Molly Ivins can't say that, can she?* New York: Random House.

Jones, C. (1988). *How to speak TV.* Tallahassee, FL: Video Consultants.

Jud, B. (1999). The seven C's of effective media interviews. *Creative Nursing, 5*(4), 11–12.

Jud, B. (2003, March 5). How to do radio and TV interviews that actually sell your book. *1st News from 1st Books,* p. 2.

Koppel, T. (2000). *Off camera: Private thoughts made public.* New York: Alfred A. Knopf.

Matthews, C. (2001). *Now, let me tell you what I really think.* New York: Simon & Schuster.

Murphy, G. (2002). *Interview tactics.* Retrieved from www.interview-tactics.com

Myers, G. (2000). Entitlement and sincerity in broadcast interviews about Princess Diana. *Media, Culture & Society, 22*(2), 167–185.

Novotny, P. (2000). From polis to agora: The marketing of political consultants. *Harvard International Journal of Press/Politics, 5*(3), 12–26.

O'Reilly, B. (2000). *The O'Reilly factor.* New York: Broadway.

Powell, L., & Cowart, J. (2003). *Political campaigns communication: Inside and out.* Boston: Allyn & Bacon.

Ravaja, N. (2004). Effects of image motion on a small screen on emotion, attention, and memory: Moving-face versus static-face newscaster. *Journal of Broadcasting & Electronic Media, 48,* 108–133.

Redmond, J., Shook, F., & Lattimore, D. (2001). *The broadcast news process* (6th ed.). Englewood, CO: Morton.

Reynolds, A., & Barnett, B. (2003). This just in . . . How national TV news handled the breaking "live" coverage of September 11. *Journalism & Mass Communication Quarterly, 80,* 689–703.

Robinson, P. (2002). *The CNN effect: The myth of news, foreign policy and intervention.* New York: Routledge.

Seamans, I. (2001). Viewer dissatisfaction understates the anger at local TV news. *Nieman Reports, 55*(3), 97–98.

Shook, F. (1982). *The process of electronic news gathering.* Englewood, CA: Morton.

Simon, R. (1987, March 14). Those Sunday interview shows: They're tougher now, but are they better?" *TV Guide, 35*(11), 4–7.

Stahl, L. (1999). *Reporting live.* Boston, MA: Simon & Schuster.

Tuggle, C. A., & Huffman, S. (1999). Live news reporting: Professional judgment or technological pressure? *Journal of Broadcasting & Electronic Media, 43,* 492–505.

TV newsman can be sued for telling youngsters about a murder. (1995, March 25). *Editor & Publisher, 128*(12), 34–35.

White, T. (2002). *Broadcast news: Writing, reporting, and producing.* Boston, MA: Focal Press.

8

INTERVIEWS IN THE POLITICAL ARENA

It started out as a routine news conference. John, a candidate for governor, was leading in the polls and seemed headed to victory in the statewide contest. He had called the conference to discuss his new plan for lowering the crime rate in the state, something that would likely be another boost to his campaign.

After presenting the plan to reporters, though, he opened the floor for questions. After a few follow-up questions on the crime topic, one reporter brought up a different issue—rumors that he was having an affair with a subordinate and using state automobiles to ferry her to their liaisons. The reporter closed by noting another rumor—that a local newspaper had photos that documented the issue. John replied quickly and angrily, saying there was no truth to the rumors and condemning the use of a rumor campaign against him. He also denied the possibility that the paper had any photos that would prove anything and dared the news organization to print them if they had them. The next day, John's answers to that question dominated the press coverage of the campaign. Two days later, the newspaper ran their photos. John eventually lost the campaign by a narrow margin.

That incident reflects the importance of interviews in today's political arena. Interviews with the press or with representatives of governmental bodies are a daily activity for many such officials, and nearly all eventually find themselves in interview situations. Reporters obtain information for political coverage from two major sources: (1) public statements by the public official and (2) interviews with the official and those around them. Often the name of the individual who provided the information is not provided in the news story. That situation requires that both the political reporter and their source have a clear understanding of the level of confidentiality in which the interview is conducted. As noted in the chapter on journalistic interviews, political reporters adhere to the same levels of confidentiality as other reporters. And, they employ those levels more frequently than do other reporters.

Those interview situations are often critical—both to the careers of the public officials involved and to the public that they represent. Quotes from those interviews become fodder for news coverage that can make or break a political career. Knowing that, most career politicians are well trained at handling the political interview. Their training, however, sometimes emphasizes equivocation and topic shifting, i.e., techniques aimed at avoiding any direct response to a question.

This chapter will outline some of the interviewing situations that apply to the political arena, particularly in terms of media interviews, debates, and interviews before legislative committees. The discussion will include the role of each type of interview and a delineation of some of the techniques used by the participants—those doing the interviews and those being interviewed. Hopefully, those who plan on entering the political arena will benefit from the information presented here. However, a larger purpose for this chapter is directed toward the average citizen in today's environment of media and democracy. By understanding the process of political interviews, we believe that citizens (particularly voters) will be better able to make more sense of the communication that occurs in that context.

The Press Secretary

A key figure in political interviews is the press secretary. The press secretary serves as the major conduit of news and information between the public official and the news media. As Perloff (1998, p. 69) noted, "It is a dicey job," one in which verbal missteps can have serious consequences. Not surprisingly, then, the press secretary not only plans and works on interviews for the public figure but also engages in day-to-day interviews with reporters on behalf of the public figure.

The role is such an integral part of today's political communication process that it is easy to forget that it is a relatively new role. For decades, most statewide campaigns did not bother to use one. Even at the presidential level, the position did not formally exist until the administration of Herbert Hoover (Nelson, 1998). Stephen Early's performance during 12 years as Franklin Roosevelt's press secretary generally defined how the job should be handled, at least in the eyes of the press (Mitchell, 1998).

Gradually, the role of the press secretary filtered down to other political offices and into campaigns. Grover Smith served in the function of press secretary for Sen. John Sparkman (D-Ala.) during the 1950s. At the time, however, senators had no official press secretaries, and Smith's official title was "research assistant." Smith eventually organized the first press secretary association for the Senate and got recognition for the group when newsman David Brinkley agreed to speak to them. Smith subsequently arranged for the official contact lists for each senator to include a person in each office who was identified as the press secretary (Powell & Cowart, 2003).

In political campaigns, the role is distinctly separated from other campaign functions, with the press secretary acting as both manager of the message and "messenger boy" (Grossman & Kumar, 1981, p. 130). The press secretary serves as a conduit for information to the press, keeping reporters alerted to the candidate's schedule, scheduling press conferences, and writing press releases for standard announcements. As a conduit, the press secretary serves as a gatekeeper between the candidate and the press, i.e., managing which reporters get interviews with the candidate or public official. Using that "gate" to control access to the candidate requires a careful balance. Too much can be detrimental, offering too many opportunities for negative press; too little can be even worse, creating an antagonistic relationship that also leads to negative coverage.

The extent to which the press secretary interacts with the press often depends on the extent to which the press seeks interviews. One factor that can influence interview requests, particularly for political candidates, is the financial strength of the campaign. Journalists cover candidates in rough proportion to their spending (Powell & Cowart, 1988). The more money a candidate spends, the more the press wants to cover the campaign and the more likely that reporters will seek interviews with the candidate or other campaign representatives. Thus, campaigns often work to enhance their campaign reporting status, knowing that the release of such information will trigger interview requests.

Although approaches to the role can vary, depending on the personality of the individual, most press secretaries aim for a positive working relationship with the press with the intent of maintaining that relationship through the ups and downs of the campaign. As a result, some campaigns use both the campaign manager and the press secretary in "good-cop/bad-cop" roles. When the campaign feels it is necessary to criticize the press, the criticism is more likely to come from the campaign manager; that way, the criticisms do not hinder the press secretary's working relationship with reporters.

As a conduit of information, the press secretary has several options for passing information on to the press. These options are essentially the same as the levels of confidentiality mentioned in Chapter 6 on newspaper interviews. Interviews can be "on the record" (comments may be quoted and the name of the source identified), "not for attribution" (information can be used, but not attributed to a named source), "on background" (the quote can be used but the source can be identified only by status or position, not by name), or "off the record" (the information can't be used at all; it is provided merely to help them understand the larger context of an issue or situation). Some information may also be "embargoed", in that the information is provided to a reporter in advance of a planned event, but the information cannot be used until the event occurs.

Some information may bypass the press secretary entirely through the process of news "leaks." Leaks are used on premature information that the source wants the press to have but that they are unable to disclose through normal channels ("This reporter has learned . . .").

Media Interviews

Newspaper Interviews

News coverage is an integral part of both political campaigns and political office holding that has a long history. Press coverage of politics goes back to the beginning of active campaigning. It became a major factor in the twentieth century, though, as the mass media expanded to include newspapers, radio, and television. The nature of the relationship between the press and public officials has varied significantly. President Franklin Roosevelt, for example, had a close relationship with many reporters in the national press and would often give them impromptu interviews, whereas Richard Nixon was openly hostile and skeptical of the press (Crouse, 1974).

The most frequent form of coverage available to politicians, candidates, and campaigns is that of straight news. The story is reported, hypothetically in an unbiased manner, and presented as information that will keep the readers and listeners informed. Public officials make conscious efforts to seek such coverage (Ansolabehere, Behr, & Iyengar, 1994). Typically, success in achieving news coverage is referred to as "free media," or "earned media."

Politicians may avoid such interviews, though, when coverage turns to scandals, controversy, or the personal lives of the public officials. The news media, however, often seem to be most active when covering such topics. During 1999, when controversy broke out over Republican George W. Bush's possible use of drugs, one reporter noted that "the frenzy that is gripping the Washington press comes from the merest whiff of scandal" (Fillipelli, 1999). Sabato (1991) described the trend as a "feeding frenzy" in which journalists destroy a candidate. Similarly, Patterson (1994) has argued that the focus on scandals has made the political system ineffective by destroying trust in political institutions. In many cases, neither the politician nor the media look good during scandal coverage, since nobody appears interested in a serious discussion of the campaign. The candidates focus on spin control, sometimes ducking in-depth interviews while trying to put the scandal in the best possible light for themselves and the worst possible for their opponents. The press focuses on sensation, often offering serious issues only as justification for sensational images and controversy. As Yardley (1999) noted, "It is a shootout in which there are no good guys" (p. 6C).

During the 1884 presidential campaign, Grover Cleveland was beset by accusations that he had fathered an illegitimate child. Cleveland's only response to reporters who approached him about the issue was "Tell the truth," and most reporters did not pursue the matter. Not so today. Modern campaigns often represent a "politics of intimacy" (Parry-Giles & Parry-Giles, 1996) in which a candidate's personal life is considered fair game. During the 2000 presidential campaign, candidates were asked a multitude of questions that had little to do with the issues of the office, but a lot to do with what they did in private. During Hillary Clinton's campaign for U.S. Senator from New York, a radio talk show host in Buffalo asked the first lady if she had been "sexually unfaithful" to her husband (Hu, 2000, January 20); Clinton called the questions "out of bounds" but answered them anyway (she denied the charges). Topics considered appropriate by reporters ranged from the sometimes controversial to the mundane, including questions about their sex lives, religious views, physical and mental health, income, advisors, friends, favorite books, movies, and political philosophers.

Two issues seem to be raised by this type of political reporting. At what point do reporters cross the line, delving into matters that are none of their nor the public's business? To what extent does such intrusion keep quality candidates from even running for public office. The latter is difficult to answer; during the Clinton-Lewinsky controversy, Republican Gov. George W. Bush speculated that he might not seek the Republican nomination for president if he and his family would have to be subjected to such scrutiny, but he ultimately decided to run anyway. Right or wrong, though, the press seems intent on examining candidates' private lives, and the pressure to do so increases with the increased visibility of the office being sought. Candidates who run for public office today have to expect some news coverage of their private lives.

Sometimes public officials will try to use an interview as a means of diffusing a potential scandal. During a 1987 congressional primary in Tennessee, front-runner Bob Clement was sued for alienation of affection by a man who claimed Clement had an affair with the man's wife. Clement denied the allegations, but reporters had more questions. Rather than holding a news conference to address the allegations, Clement and his wife together met with reporters in individual interviews, in their home, and answered their questions on the charges. Despite the stress associated with responding to such charges, Clement was perceived as at ease and honest during the individual interviews, and the press shifted their attention to whether his opponents might be behind the allegations. Their investigations subsequently revealed that one of the opponents had indeed been behind the charges, and Clement went on to an easy win in the campaign (Powell & Cowart, 2003).

On other occasions, the strategy may backfire. In 1972, Senator Edward "Ted" Kennedy was considered a major Democrat candidate for president, but he was dogged by questions concerning a major scandal—the Chappaquiddick incident (Tedrow, Tedrow, & Tedrow, 1980; Lange & DeWitt, 1993). To have a realistic chance to win the Democratic nomination, Kennedy needed to address that situation. In an attempt to do so, Kennedy agreed to an in-depth interview with the CBS program *60 Minutes*, knowing that questions about the incident would be raised during the interview. When those questions arose, however, he responded in a highly defensive and agitated manner. The subsequent broadcast of the interview doomed his chances for the presidency (Lester, 1972; Lippman, 1976).

Public officials make frequent use of the press conference in which they speak with several reporters at the same time. As noted in an earlier chapter, "Most press conferences . . . are more convenient for sources than for reporters"(Fedler, 1989, p. 518)—a factor that makes them highly desirable for public officials. In major political offices, such as the White House, press briefings will be held on a daily basis. During times of major crises, they will occur even more frequently than that. The speaker at such briefings is usually the press secretary or another administration official—not the president. The public official only appears at major press briefings.

The press conference is also a means that public officials will use to diffuse a controversial situation. They typically do this by making a prepared statement on the controversy before opening the floor to questions. The prepared statement will be designed to pre-empt the toughest questions, allowing the individual to define the issue in their own terms before the questions begin. Even when this tactic doesn't fully succeed, it will answer some of the reporters' questions in advance and reduce the likelihood of an extensive debate on the topic with the reporters (Rowley, 2003).

An increasingly popular form of news coverage of politicians is the personality profile, i.e., a story that attempts to allow media consumers to get a better understanding of the public official as an individual. Some public figures take advantage of this effect by using their public exposure to increase coverage for issues that are of interest to them. The most obvious situation in which this occurs is with the presidential first ladies, some of whom fought to protect their privacy, whereas others used their public recognition as a forum for favorite issues. Some, such as Barbara Bush, become celebrities in their own right (Wertheimer, 2000). Eleanor Roosevelt became a famous public figure whose public persona was quite distinct from that of husband Franklin Roosevelt (Lash, 1971); by using the public exposure that came with her position, she was able to advance the case for a number of issues that concerned her. Conversely, Betty Ford's personal bouts with alcohol started out as a private problem that emerged as a public crusade for others to seek rehabilitation (Gutgold, 2000). Other first ladies—such as Edith (Mrs. Teddy) Roosevelt (Hastings, 2000)—sometimes fought against public intrusion into their lives, preferring instead to focus on a sense of home life for themselves and their families. Either way, such coverage requires interviews to complete the story.

Sometimes such interviews can lead to major news stories. During his 1976 campaign for president, Jimmy Carter made national headlines when he did an interview with *Playboy* magazine and said he had sinned at times by having "lust in my heart" (Schram, 1976).

Editorials and op-ed (opinion) pieces in newspapers often have little direct impact on election outcomes (Powell & Cowart, 2003). Few people read the editorials, and those who do tend to be politicos who have already decided how they will vote. Still, endorsements can have an impact on down-ballot campaigns. Furthermore, newspaper editorials can have a major, indirect impact if the campaign chooses to use editorial content in its campaign advertisements. Being able to cite a newspaper brings instant credibility to a television ad, and candidates love to use headlines as a visual association for a verbal message. That's why most public officials willingly go through a process known as the editorial interview.

Prior to making endorsements in any electoral campaign, most major newspapers conduct a series of panel interviews with the candidates. All candidates for the offices under consideration are typically invited to meet with the editorial panel on an individual basis. The panel is composed of the paper's editors and political reporters, and each member of the panel can ask the candidate questions about his/her policies. Most candidates readily agree to subject themselves to this grilling, even those who don't expect to get the paper's endorsement. Obtaining the endorsement becomes a plum that can be touted in other campaign venues. And, even if the endorsement is not obtained, the interview provides the candidate with the opportunity to explain their positions to the gatekeepers of the newspaper—hopefully enabling those editors and reporters to provide more accurate coverage of the campaign.

Broadcast Interviews

Broadcast news coverage of politicians falls into two distinct categories—recorded interviews for broadcast news and live interviews.

Recorded interviews that are used for broadcast news are similar—in many ways—to interviews for newspaper coverage. From the reporters' view, the purpose is the same, i.e., to use quotes from the interview as part of a news story on the public official. There are some slight differences, however, particularly in terms of techniques that produce a good story and enhance positive coverage for the official. Interviews with newspaper reporters are usually more casual than are those with broadcast reporters. The newspaper reporter may have a recorder, but there are no cameras, lapel microphones, or other equipment that will be distracting to the interviewee. Furthermore, the interviewee is allowed more leeway in their responses.

Take, for example, this question: "What will be the impact of this piece of legislation on the public?" In a newspaper interview, the public official can use "hedges" (statements that delay or qualify the response) before giving the essence of an answer. Thus the interviewee might respond to such a question by saying, "Well, in my opinion, when you look at all the factors, I think you'll see that most of the public will be better off under this new law." That statement, in that form, is boring and would not come across well on television. However, it works well for a newspaper interview. The reporter can simply edit out the boring aspects of the statement and report it as a quote like this: "I think . . . most of the public will be better off under this new law."

Similar attempts to edit such a quote for broadcast purposes nearly always produce a choppy and unnatural look. The broadcast reporter is looking for a similar statement—but one made in a definitive way that stands alone by itself as a soundbite. For television interviews, then, the public official must think in terms of the soundbite that will be used to illustrate the news story.

In that situation, it is important to remember that only a small portion of the interview will actually be aired. The interview itself will take several minutes. When it is aired, however, only about 12 seconds of his comments will actually be used. The reporter will choose the bite that makes the story look good and allows for presentation of the story in a narrative format (Grabe & Zhou, 1999, 2003). From the campaign's perspective, it's important that it be the right 12 seconds. From the perspective of the interviewee, the goal is message consistency, i.e., that the soundbite used by the reporter carries the message preferred by the official. This can be remarkably easy to handle, but it takes a little advance preparation.

1. **Decide, in advance, what you want that soundbite to be.** In the brief amount of time before the interview starts, the public official usually decides what they want that soundbite to be. They formulate a single statement that can be stated in 12 seconds or less and that reflects the desired message for that time and place. Often interviewees are coached to pivot their response into a prepared soundbite, even if it does not strictly answer the question. Often interviewees are coached with a number of predetermined collection of soundbites to work into their interviews. These collections are referred to as talking points.
2. **It's okay to mumble and be monotonic, as long as it's not during the soundbite.** Most novices to television interviews forget that making a mistake is no big

deal. When they mumble or stumble over words, they become embarrassed and make more mistakes. Actually, recorded broadcast interviews are highly forgiving of such mistakes. Remember, most of the interview will never be aired, and such mistakes are routinely edited out of the story.

3. **It's okay to start over**. If the interviewee gets into a sentence and finds that they're stumbling over words or phrases, it's acceptable to simply stop in mid-sentence. That kills that section as a potential soundbite. The politician can then tell the reporter, "Let me say that again," and then repeat the answer more emphatically.

4. **Emphasize the soundbite.** Many public officials have learned to use the technique of pausing before they say the soundbite. Then, when they say it, they say it with passion. That's what the reporter is looking for—a distinct statement that effectively and dramatically summarizes the story.

Political consultant John Rowley (2003) has argued that preparation is the key to good media interviews for public officials. He wrote (p. 210):

> The first rule of candidate media relations is to not make any mistakes. Elections are not won or lost as a result of candidate generating a great positive news story or delivering a pithy positive quote. But a number of elections every year turn upon one mistake a candidate made in an interview. That is why the best candidates not only have ideas and are good communicators, but they practice their responses to the toughest questions before the red light of a TV camera is on and tape is rolling.

Some candidates feel more comfortable during live broadcast interviews than during news interviews. During the early stages of his 2000 presidential campaign, for example, George W. Bush seemed highly uncomfortable when responding to reporter's questions, but he was more adept at one-on-one interviews. Some reporters noted that in his early TV appearances, questions from reporters "caused him to send a panicky look into the camera" that contrasted sharply with the "easy charm" exhibited during his first appearance on CNN's *Larry King Live* (James, 1999). Much of the difference was due to the location of the camera; instead of speaking at a press conference, where Bush often felt like an open target, the Larry King interview was conducted in "the warm, woody setting of a Nashville saloon." Democrat Bill Bradley made a similar use of location to soften his image. During some early campaign events, Bradley often sounded aloof and abstract. Those negative tones disappeared, however, when the ex-professional basketball player shot baskets at Madison Square Garden with Ed Bradley for a *60 Minutes* interview and when he sat on the court for an interview with Wolf Blitzer on CNN's *Late Edition*.

Spin Doctors

Some candidates and public officials use "spin doctors" as surrogate interviewees on major stories. The role of the spin doctor is to interpret news events in a manner that is beneficial to their client. The goal of the "spin doctor" is "spin control," a term popularized during the Reagan administration. Maltese (1994, p. 215) defines *spin control* as "twisting (a story) to one's advantage, using surrogates, press releases, radio actualities, and other friendly sources to deliver the line from an angle that puts the story in the best possible light." Spin doctors are most effective at spin control in the area of breaking news. Coverage of breaking news is considerably more difficult for reporters (particularly TV reporters), because they often lack the time to verify how other media outlets are covering the same story. That uncertainty offers spin doctors a chance to be interviewed and to define the story positively for their client, hoping that other news outlets will pick up on the same "spin." Political consultant John Rowley (2003) disputes the negative connotations associated with the term "spinning" (p. 208):

> They call it spinning. We call it aggressive follow up. If a hard-nosed reporter appears to be inclined to do a damaging story, there is more work to do. The campaign communications director should continue following up to make the campaign's points, to provide additional documentation, and in some cases to provide more access to the candidate to answer unanswered questions.

Priming

The goal of the "spin" is message priming, i.e., establishing expectations for judging political messages. This process goes back to an academic concept known as *news priming*. Iyengar and Kinder (1987) argued that news priming is part of the news process in that the media establishes standards used by voters to evaluate the government, the president, and political candidates. These standards are developed as a set of expectations that are used as the basis of judgments of the political activity that the voters see and hear in the media. This theory was subsequently supported by research regarding extensive 1986 media coverage on the Reagan Administration's covert diversion of funds to the Nicaraguan Contras. Voters' evaluations of Reagan were strongly linked to the amount of coverage that issue received (Krosnick & Kinder, 1990).

The news priming function is the primary reason that elected officials and candidates want to dominate the media agenda (Perloff, 1998, p. 218). Spinning is one technique that they used in attempt to influence priming. The spin process is particularly active just prior to and after major public performances such as televised debates. Spin doctors typically participate in this process by trying to deflate expectations prior to an event and making positive comparisons with the expectations on a post-hoc basis. During their press interviews, spin doctors might try to lower expectations of upcoming performances ("Our candidate doesn't have as much debate experience as our opponent, but we expect he will do well") or try to encourage reporters to look at particular points of a candidate's performance ("The important thing is what he had to say on the economy").

Framing

Message framing is news priming on a holistic level. If the media accepts the way a politician frames an issue, then subsequent coverage of that issue tends to be beneficial for that politician. Most research on framing has focused on news coverage, with the results indicating that the way the media frames an issue can have a major impact on public opinion and voter behavior (Devitt, 1997; Gamson, 1996, Graber, 1987; Iroio & Huxman, 1996; McCombs & Shaw, 1993; McLeod & Detenber, 1999). More specifically, framing can have an impact on candidate credibility by framing voter attributions of blame or praise (Iyengar, 1996). Framing works because political attitudes are expressions of underlying arguments recalled from memory (Kelly, 1983; Zaller, 1992; Chong, 1993, 1999).

On a campaign level, framing is achieved with the campaign theme. Miller (1999) noted that campaign themes attempt to construct a reality by framing the interpretation of external events and providing a suggestion as to how the electorate should decide the election. The theme expresses an attitude, defines the rhetorical situation, and provides a mechanism for responding to reporters' questions. A campaign theme, then, acts as a controlling concept, naming and revealing attitudes toward events, providing a "strategic answer" to questions posed by situations (Burke, 1973, p. 1). The frame simplifies external events, defining them with cues for decision making. Clinton's 1996 campaign theme, Bridge to the 21st Century, framed the election context as a decision about the future. Simultaneously it expressed confidence in his earlier programs, optimism, and excitement about the ambiguous future of the next millennium (Miller, 1999). Ronald Reagan's "common culture" evoked benevolent capitalism and civic virtue as elements of the cornerstones of the American myth (Patterson, 1999). When he needed a political scapegoat, Reagan often framed the federal bureaucracy as a "benign political scapegoat" that could be the target of his verbal assaults (Braden, 2001).

Word Choice

Framing is influenced by word choice. Prior to being interviewed, public officials pay careful attention to choosing the right word or words to use during the interview. Words can simultaneously create labels, convey a speaker's feelings on a topic, and signal emotional distance between the speaker and the issue (Fraser & Gordon, 1994). The goal is to select the "right" word, i.e., "the word that does exactly what you want it to do, and nothing else" (Perlman, 1998, p. 129). The spokesperson usually tries to avoid long words that may be hard to pronounce and hard for the audience to understand. As Noonan (1998) noted, "big things are best said, are almost always said, in small words" (p. 54). Once a word or phrase is identified, it may be used repetitively—part of a process known as staying "on message" (Norris, Curtice, Sanders, Scammell, & Semetko, 1999). The authors worked on one campaign in which the guidelines for a candidate's radio interview included working in the phrase "fiscal conservative" three times. During the 2000 presidential election, George W. Bush never talked about spending "cuts" to reduce government expenditures, but always used the word "savings" as his euphemism (Bruni, 2000). During the 1980 New Hampshire primary, Ronald Reagan's consultants countered concerns that Reagan was too old (then 69) by using the phrase "oldest and wisest" in speeches and in their conversations with reporters, thus putting a positive connotation on the age issue. Deborah Tannen (2000) noted that George W. Bush's campaign rhetoric was filled with words that would appeal to women voters, including references to "children," "dreams," "hope," "love," and "hearts."

Sunday News Shows

In national politics, some of the most influential news television occurs on Sunday mornings (when few people are watching television) on interview shows such as NBC's *Meet the Press*, CBS's *Face the Nation*, and ABC's *This Week*. As TV commentator Roger Simon (1987, p. 4) once noted, those shows are all based on the assumption "that important political and government figures, faced with vigorous questioning, just might slip and commit news."

The format of the shows are similar. Each has a reporter or reporters directing questions at public officials or other newsworthy individuals. In most cases, those guests are either high-ranking administration officials or people who are in leadership positions in Congress. The oldest of the shows, *Meet the Press*, made its debut in 1951. For the remainder of that decade, the questions were gentle, with reporters typically showing respect toward their guests. Simon (1987, p. 5) noted that, in the beginning, "persistent follow-up questions were somehow considered bad manners." Today, tough questions are the rule, not the exception. Furthermore, appearances on the shows may offer little opportunity to reach undecided voters; the audience tends to be made up of active voters (Hofstetter et al., 1994), most of whom have already made their voting decision.

So why do politicians agree to participate? First, they want to get exposure for themselves and their ideas. Despite the small audience, all of the Sunday interview shows generate a great deal of spinoff coverage. Comments made on the show are reported on the evening television news and distributed in print to all of the major newspapers. An effective interview on any of the shows can dramatically increase recognition of an issue, pushing it to the forefront of the media's agenda. Second, most of the guests are not afraid of the tough questioning. Most, if not all, have been interviewed thousands of times before they make their first Sunday-morning appearance. Their interview-response skills are often just as well developed as the interview-questioning skills of the reporters. As Simon (1987, p. 6) wrote, "if they don't want to say something, it is hard to make them say it."

Campaign Debates

Perhaps one of the most critical interview situations in political campaigns is the televised debates. Debates have been major components of every presidential campaign since the Ford-Carter debates of 1976 (Hess, 1988), and they are regular components of most gubernatorial campaigns. They are now such an institutionalized and ritualistic part of campaigns that voters expect them to occur (Kraus, 2000), even though they are not legally required as part of the campaign. Furthermore, despite concerns over political malaise and lack of interest among voters, televised debates typically have a large viewing audience—larger than any other presidential campaign event (Buchanan, 1991).

Presidential debates are truly critical events. They offer candidates a chance to enhance their credibility while addressing issues that the media might have overlooked (Hellweg, Pfau, & Brydon, 1992). Furthermore, although such elements are merely one of several sources of voter information, debates typically have some type of impact on the voting public (Chaffee, 1978). For candidates, debates can orient voters about the personalities of the candidates, highlight differences in political philosophy, and focus attention on the candidates (Glenn, 2001). For voters, debates can increase interest and participation in a campaign (Delli Carpini et al., 1997; Buchanan, 1991), increase voters' information about the campaign (Becker et al., 1978), enhance their ability to discuss the campaign with others (Miller & MacKuen, 1979), and trigger increased interpersonal communication about the campaign (Jamieson & Birdsell, 1988). For the media, debate allows some reporters access to the candidates in a situation that allows for cross-examination questioning, thus allowing the voters to see how the candidates respond to pressure situations (Glenn, 2001). One immediate effect is a short-term impact on the salience of issues (Swanson & Swanson, 1978; Atkin et al., 1979). In the immediate aftermath of the debate, the issues addressed by the candidates are likely to receive increased coverage from the news media and an enhanced perception of salience by the voting public. Debates can also influence the image and perceptions of the candidates, although the impact does not typically alter any voting intentions (Abramowitz, 1978).

Still, debates are not perfect forums for candidate-voter communication (Jamieson & Birdsell, 1988). Media questions can be superficial, and even persistent questioning may reveal little information. Candidates often resort to repeating segments from their stump speeches or use the debate as a forum for attacking their opponent (Glenn, 2001). Voter response to these factors is often affected by three factors: (1) the expectations of the candidates, (2) the performances of the candidates, and (3) the political ideologies of the voters. The expectations of the candidates often come from other elements of the campaign, depending on the image that the candidates project and the issues they discuss (Hellweg, Pfau, & Brydon, 1992). In the 2000 election, George W. Bush entered the debates following a series of campaign misstatements that had raised doubts about his ability to perform well during the debates. While his resulting performance was not particularly stellar, it wasn't bad either. He subsequently came out of the debates with an improved image with the voters.

The performance of the candidates is also a factor. Debates present the candidates to the voters for a longer and more intense view of the candidates than either news or through advertising, giving the public a chance to familiarize themselves with the candidates (Jamieson & Birdsell, 1988, p. 28). Vancil and Pendell (1984) noted that the candidates can use that opportunity to demonstrate a presidential image; if they succeed at doing that, they will typically be perceived as the winner of the debate. Candidate performance can also lose debates with poor performances. As is discussed later in "mistake-based critical events," a candidate who blunders during a debate can suffer serious damage. As Lawrence (2000) noted, "Mistakes are replayed endlessly on news and TV." During the Bush-Gore debates, for example, Al Gore drew negative attention from the press with a series of inaccurate statements, including the claim that he had visited Texas following a natural disaster in the state. The resulting news coverage about the misrepresentations occupied the news agenda for several days and necessitated a subsequent apology from Gore. Similarly, in 1988, Michael Dukakis lost ground when he was asked if he would favor capital punishment for the killer if his wife were raped and murdered. Instead of expressing emotion, he listed the policy reasons behind his opposition to the policy (Lawrence, 2000). Mistakes are not always verbal in nature. In 1992, President Bush was criticized for glancing at his watch during a debate, as if he were anxious for it to be over.

While the press will focus increased attention on factual errors, voters often react negatively to personal mistakes. Personal behavior during the campaigns are often evaluated in terms of voter expectations. Hinck and Hinck (1998) argue for evaluating such responses in terms of *politeness theory*. Their work is an expansion on Brown and Levinson's (1987) theory that politeness is a universal value that operates across cultures. According to politeness theory, one standard used by voters to evaluate candidates is the expectation that the candidates maintain a relationship of respect and regard for the opposing candidate. Any deviation from this standard makes the voters uncomfortable and can cause a negative reaction toward the candidate who violates the norm. The candidates used politeness strategies in both the 1992 and 1996 debates (Hinck & Hinck, 2000). The factor emerged again, in a negative manner, for Al Gore during the 2000 debates. At times, Gore made the voters uncomfortable with his overly aggressive debate style, his audible sighs, and his tendency to move closer to Bush when the latter was answering a question. Such moments become pivotal points in the debate because (1) the viewers are attuned to potential violations of politeness and (2) they view behaviors at that moment as indicative of broader values and competence. They recognize key moments when a candidate's public face is threatened, and how the candidate handles those moments affects the voters' perception of their competence in handling dramatic conflict within the debate.

Finally, voters' impressions of the debates are based heavily on their political ideology, position on issues, and prior support of a candidate (Martel, 1983). Despite the secondary impact that debates can have on voters' information, they typically have little impact on voter decisions (Abramowitz, 1978). Decided voters typically score their candidate as the winner. For them, the debates act more like a pep rally. Rather than changing their vote, it merely reinforces their support, particularly if the candidate meets their expectations. Even the positive impact of increased knowledge and information is tempered by the voters' predispositions. Although they generally increase their knowledge of the campaign, the voters may still misunderstand much of the information in the debate (Jacoby, Troutman, & Whittler, 1986). Ultimately, debates play a pivotal role in campaigns, but their impact can be muted by other campaign factors.

Campaigns frequently prepare for debates through "role playing." Campaign staff members play the roles of reporters, asking the candidate tough questions and follow-ups. At least one person may play the role of the opponent, seeking to throw the candidate off balance with an unanticipated question or challenge.

Lawrence (2000) noted that debate contenders also typically rehearse a few "gotchas." Noonan (1998) traces the trend to 1984 when Walter Mondale criticized the substance behind Gary Hart's positions by asking "Where's the beef?" "After the success of Mondale's line," Noonan noted, "the word went forth: candidates needed to be supplied by their staff with zippy sound bites before they went into a debate or an interview" (p. 98). In 1984, Ronald Reagan faced concerns about his age with a response that he had planned in advance: "I want you to know that I will not make age an issue of this campaign. I am not going to exploit for political purposes my opponent's youth and inexperience." Everybody laughed, including opponent Walter Mondale, and the issue never arose again. Jamieson (1988) noted that the line also functioned as a cover for weak performances by Reagan in other parts of the debate, particularly a somewhat rambling closing statement. "What saves him . . . is the brevity of the light-hearted joke contrasted with the four-minute length of the final speech," Jamieson wrote. "The former lends itself to the news clip, the latter does not" (p. 113).

A different type of "gotcha" was used by Lloyd Bentsen in the 1988 presidential debate with Dan Quayle. After Quayle said he had as much experience as John F. Kennedy when he sought the presidency, Bentsen responded, "Senator, I served with Jack Kennedy. I knew Jack Kennedy. Jack Kennedy was a friend of mine. Senator, you are no Jack Kennedy." The line is still remembered as the classic example of a put-down in campaign politics. Still, such one-liners are rare in presidential debates, since it is typically difficult for any candidate to accomplish their goals with a single answer or line. Noonan (1998) credits that rarity to the media literacy of the voters: "the American public has become very sophisticated about such lines," she wrote, "so sophisticated that they now discount them" (p. 97).

Preparations for the candidate may include both verbal and nonverbal training. Goodman and Gring (1999), in an analysis of the 1992 and 1996 presidential town hall debates, noted that Clinton often re-positioned himself so that each television image of him either included the American flag in the background (in 1992) or pictured him with the audience (in 1996). They concluded that Clinton "made a conscious effort to maximize his visual impact during the town hall debates," a factor that implied that he had planned and practiced the positioning in advance of the actual debate.

Outside of this, a few other rules are often used in debate preparation. These include:

1. **Don't start sentences with "I think" or "I believe."** There is often a tendency for a public official to preface their answers with hedge statements such as "I think" or "I believe." The problem with those two phrases are twofold, i.e., they are (1) too egocentric and (2) too weak. Notice the difference, for example, between saying

"I think we can lead the nation to a great future" and "We can lead the nature to a great future." The second version is stronger, whereas the first version is a tacit admission that the speaker might be wrong.

2. **Don't worry about time**. Many forums are framed around rules that specify that the candidate has a specific length of time to answer a question—usually about two minutes. Some candidates feel obligated to speak for the entire two minutes—a perception that can adversely affect their responses as they try to "stretch" their answer to the appropriate length. In reality, it doesn't matter how long or how short their answer might be, as long as the answer is a good one. The audience is looking for an answer, not a two-minute-long answer. If the answer is a good one, it doesn't matter if it's 15 seconds, 30 seconds, 60 seconds, or 90 seconds. The audience doesn't keep track of how long a candidate speaks, but only of what they say.

3. **Answer the question in the first sentence**. Sometimes candidates will answer a question, but only after they explain why. In essence, their answer comes at the end of the answer. By then, many of the audience members would have quit listening. The audience listens to the first sentence, using it to judge whether the speaker is truly answering the question or merely trying to avoid the question. If they don't hear it in that first sentence, they evaluate the candidate as indecisive—even if the candidate eventually answers the question later in the response. Therefore, the first sentence in a response should leave the audience with the impression that the candidate is decisive and knowledgeable on the topic.

4. **Offer support for the answer immediately after giving it, preferably in a bullet point format, and end with a "bookend" that reinforces the main idea**. Combined with the previous recommendation, the ideal format for answering a debate interview question is (1) answer the question in the first sentence, (2) explain why, including at least one fact to demonstrate knowledge of the topic, and (3) end by referring back to the first sentence. Thus, if the question is, "What will be your top priority as governor?" the answer should be something along the lines of the following:

We must turn around the economy so we can raise the standard of living for everyone in the state (ANSWER TO QUESTION). Our economy is so bad right now that we're losing thousands of people every year who move out of state in search of jobs. Further, the current administration is doing nothing to actively recruit new industry (EXPLAINS WHY). I'll be the leader who'll change that (BOOKEND).

This approach to candidate preparation is not universal. Different political consultants have different ideas that they stress. Still, the goal is essentially the same regardless of which style of preparation is used, i.e., to have the candidate perceived as a knowledgeable and intelligent person who understands the needs of the public.

Legislative Hearings

As a sitting member of the U.S. Supreme Court, Justice Clarence Thomas is in a position to rule on the constitutionality of numerous cases that come before the court. Before he could take his position, though, he—like all of the other justices on the Supreme Court—had to go through a rigorous interview process in which he was questioned about his qualifications by a legislative committee.

That legislative review is a process that is required for a number of executive appointments—both at the federal and state levels. The purpose of the interview is decision-making. The nominee appears before the committee that oversees the office to which the person has been appointed. The committee will be composed of both Democrats and Republicans, and each committee member is allowed to ask the nominee questions. Such questions are usually limited to a specific time (usually about ten minutes), but additional questions can be submitted in writing.

Sometimes these hearings are perfunctory in nature, with the U.S. Senate committee convening merely to meet the candidate and to confirm the president's judgment. In fact, the Senate has confirmed 89 percent of the judicial nominees sent to it by the president (Yalof, 2001). Other times, they can be brutal. In those instances, the committee members often break into two groups—usually along party lines—in terms of support and opposition for the nominee. Supporters usually use their time for two purposes: (1) to ask "softball" questions that allow the nominees to talk about their strengths, and (2) to ask questions that will refute points raised by the opposition. Opponents usually approach these interviews as if they're cross-examining a witness in the court case. They're usually well trained for this approach, too, since many politicians start out as lawyers.

Opponents usually try to impeach the character of a nominee. Robert Bork, a Ronald Reagan nominee, was turned down by the committee after Democrats on the judicial committee raised questions about his legal ideology (Simon, 1992). Similarly, Clarence Thomas, a George Bush nominee, was subjected to intense questioning about his professional behavior in an office setting (including charges of sexual harassment) before he was nominated (Simon, 1992; Thomas, 2001). In Thomas's case, his professional behavior became a bigger issue than his legal philosophy (Gerber, 2002). The most common technique is to question the nominee about inconsistencies from the past record. Any person nominated for a high government post will have a lengthy public record that can be examined—and it will be. The opposing legislators will have their staff sift through and research the nominee's background. That material will be supplemented by research done by special interest groups who oppose the nominee.

The questioning process is similar to that of a cross-examination in the courtroom. The legislator reads something that the nominee has written in the past and gets him/her to confirm that the statement or fact ("Did you write a friend-of-the-court brief in which you supported the defendant in that case?"). The legislator then identifies an inconsistency about the fact ("Weren't you the only person out of 35 who filed such briefs to support the defendant?"). The nominee, to have any chance to pass, must respond positively and aggressively to such questions ("Yes, I was, but I was also the only one who was right. The court agreed with me").

Meanwhile, supporters of the nominee are listening to each question and answer, particularly those who have yet to ask any questions. They have also had their staff conduct research on the nominee—also supported with material from special interest groups. As opponents ask questions that hurt the candidate, the supporters plan questions that will refute the allegation implied by the opponents' questions. Furthermore, these questions will be part of an organized campaign aimed at gaining support for the nominee. Some critics have charged, in fact, that Clarence Thomas won his nomination despite strong opposition from the Democrats on the Judiciary Committee because the Republicans were better organized than their Democrat opponents (Mayer & Abramson, 1994).

A second type of interview done by legislative committee is the witness hearing. In most instances, particularly for non-controversial topics, the goal of a witness hearing is information gathering. The legislative committee meets to discuss a topic being considered for legislative action. Experts in the field are asked to meet with the committee so that the committee can learn more about the topic before presenting its recommendation to the full legislative body. The process typically starts with the witness making a formal presentation of their basic ideas. When that is completed, each member of the committee can then ask questions of the witness. The presentation is usually intended to be persuasive, i.e., the expert argues for a change in the law that supports their position ("Smoking is dangerous to one's health, and we must do more to curtail smoking by teenagers"). The questions are usually probes intended to gather more information ("Is there any evidence that tobacco companies are targeting teenagers?").

Sometimes witnesses will also be interviewed for nomination hearings. During the Clarence Thomas hearing, for example, opponents brought in a former Thomas co-worker—Anita Hill—to testify against him (Hill, 1997). Her testimony (i.e., that Thomas had subjected her to sexual harassment) triggered a public counter-strategy from the Republicans that included an attempt to impeach her character as a witness (Brock, 1994).

Sometimes, witness hearings are held to promote the agenda of a group or an individual politician. The most infamous legislative hearing to fall in this category would be the congressional hearings of the House Committee on Un-American Activities headed by Senator Joseph McCarthy in the mid-1950s (Reeves, 1997). McCarthy used the congressional hearing as a stage for interviewing those suspected of being Communist spies (Fried, 1997). The concern over spying in the U.S. was real; the Soviet Union had established an extensive spy network using Communist sympathizers (Buckley & Bozell, 1977; Herman, 2000). McCarthy's ability to tie into that issue and the fears that surrounded it made him a national political figure (Herman, 2000). As the hearings progressed, though, the questions presented during the hearings shifted from interviews to interrogation. The questions used in the interrogation were designed to elicit guilt by association or by reluctance to answer, particularly for those witnesses who were associated with the Hollywood film industry. Those who refused to testify soon found themselves blacklisted from future film work (Schrecker, 1998).

Summary

Interviewing skills are a major element in the careers of public officials. Interviews with the press or with representatives of governmental bodies are daily activities for many such officials. Furthermore, those interview situations are often critical—both to the careers of the public officials involved and to the public that they represent. This chapter has outlined some of the interviewing situations that apply to the political arena, particularly in terms of media interviews, debates, and interviews before legislative committees.

Media interviews faced by public officials include news interviews, press conferences, and live broadcast interviews. Such interviews become particularly intense if a controversy about the official's career emerges. Interviews also become important during political campaigns, particularly in debate formats in which journalists ask each candidate questions about the policy positions. Finally, interviews are also important inside the political arena, particularly when public officials have to appear as witnesses or nominees before legislative committees.

Discussion Questions

1. Observe a televised presidential news conference. What process is used to decide which reporters get to ask questions? Is each reporter allowed a follow-up question? How does one question relate to the one that follows it, or are the two questions unrelated?

2. Watch one of the Sunday morning political interview shows. Who asks the questions? What techniques are used to encourage the interviewee to be open with their responses? Would you describe this as an easy or a tough interview for the interviewee? Why?

3. Analyze a televised political debate. Who asks the questions—reporters, candidates, or both? What's the format for the questions and the answers? Are some of the questions too long? Are some of the answers too short?

 Please see the companion website for additional resources at [www.routledge.com/cw/9781138080959].

References

Abramowitz, A. I. (1978). The impact of a presidential debate on voter rationality. *American Journal of Political Science, 22,* 680–690.

Ansolabehere, S., Behr, R., & Iyengar, S. (1994). Riding the wave and claiming ownership over issues: The joint effects of advertising and news coverage in campaigns. *Public Opinion Quarterly, 58,* 335–337.

Atkin, C., Hocking, J., & McDermott, S. (1979). Home state voter response and secondary media coverage: In S. Kraus (Ed.), *The great debates: Carter vs. Ford, 1976* (pp. 429–436). Bloomington, IN: Indiana University Press.

Braden, S. W. (2001). *The rhetorical use of the benign political scapegoat: Ronald Reagan attacks the federal government.* Paper presented at the annual meeting of the Southern States Communication Association, Lexington, KY.

Becker, L.B., Sobowale, I.A., Cobbey, R.E., & Eyal, C.H. (1978). Debate effect on voters' understanding of candidates and issues. In G.G. Bishop, R.G. Meadow, and M. Jackson (Eds.). *The presidential debates: Media, electoral, and policy perspectives* (pp. 126–139). New York: Praeger.

Brock, D. (1994). *The real Anita Hill.* New York: Free Press.

Brown, P., & Levinson, S. C. (1987). *Politeness: Some universals in language usage.* New York: Cambridge University Press.

Bruni, F. (2000, May 8). Bush runs, with a lexicon of his own. *New York Times,* p. A11.

Buchanan, B. (1991). *Electing a president: The Markle Commission research on campaign '88.* Austin, TX: University of Texas Press.

Buckley, W. F., & Bozell, L. B. (1977). *McCarthy and his enemies: The record and its meaning.* New York: Crown.

Burke, K. (1973). *The philosophy of literary form* (3rd ed.). Berkeley, CA: University of California Press.

Chaffee, S. H. (1978). Presidential debates: Are they helpful to voters? *Communication Monographs, 45,* 330–346.

Chong, D. (1993). How people think, reason, and feel about rights and liberties. *American Journal of Political Science, 37,* 867–899.

Chong, D. (1999). Creating common frames of reference on political issues. In D. C. Mutz, P. M. Sniderman, & R. A. Brody (Eds.), *Political persuasion and attitude change* (pp. 195–224). Ann Arbor, MI: University of Michigan Press.

Crouse, T. (1974). *The boys on the bus.* New York: Ballantine Books.

Delli Caprpini, M., Ketter, S., & Webb, S. (1997). The impact of presidential debates. In P. Norris (Ed.), *Politics and the press: The news media and their influence gaps* (pp. 145–164). Boulder, CO: Lynne Rienner Publishing.

Devitt, E. G., Jr. (1997). Framing politicians: The transformation of candidate arguments in presidential campaign news coverage, 1980, 1988, 1992, and 1996. *American Behavioral Scientist, 40,* 1139–1160.

Felder, F. (1989). *Reporting for the print media* (4th ed.). San Diego: Harcourt Brace.

Fillipelli, S. (1999, August 29). A buzz about Bush. *Birmingham News*, p. 1C, 6C.

Fraser, N., & Gordon, L. (1994). A genealogy of dependency. *Signs, 19*, 309–336.

Fried, A. (1997). *McCarthyism: The great American red scare.* New York: Oxford University Press.

Gamson, W. A. (1996). Media discourse as a framing resource. In A. N. Crigler (Ed.), *The psychology of political communication* (pp. 111–131). Ann Arbor, MI: University of Michigan Press.

Gerber, S. D. (2002). *First principles: The jurisprudence of Clarence Thomas.* New York: New York University Press.

Glenn, R. (2001). *Debating the debates: Assessing the value of televised presidential debates in producing an informed electorate.* Paper presented at the annual meeting of the Southern States Communication Association, Lexington, KY.

Goodman, M., & Gring, M. (1999). *The visual byte: Bill Clinton and the polysemic town hall meeting.* Southern Speech Communication Association, St. Louis, MO.

Grabe, M. E., & Zhou, S. (1999). Sourcing and reporting in news magazine programs: 60 Minutes versus Hard Copy. *Journalism & Mass Communication Quarterly, 76*, 293–311.

Grabe, M. E., & Zhou, S. (2003). News as Aristotelian drama: The case of 60 Minutes. *Mass Communication & Society, 6*, 313–336.

Graber, D. A. (1987). Framing election news broadcasts: News context and its impact on the 1984 election. *Social Science Quarterly, 68*, 552–568.

Grossman, M. B., & Kumar, M. J. (1981). *Portraying the president: The white house and the news media.* Baltimore, MD: Johns Hopkins Press.

Gutgold, N. D. (2000). *Living out loud: How Betty Ford expanded the boundaries of the role of the First Lady.* Paper presented at the annual meeting of the Eastern Communication Association, Pittsburgh, PA.

Hastings, C. M. (2000). *A home of her own: Edith Roosevelt's construction of Private White.* Paper presented at the annual meeting of the Eastern Communication Association, Pittsburgh, PA.

Hellweg, S. A., Pfau, M., & Brydon, S. R. (1992). *Televised presidential debates: Advocacy in America.* New York: Praeger.

Herman, A. (2000). *Joseph McCarthy: Re-examining the life and legacy of America's most hated senator.* New York: Free Press.

Hess, S. (1988). *The presidential campaign.* Washington, DC: The Brookings Institution.

Hill, A. (1997). *Speaking truth to power.* New York: Doubleday.

Hinck, E. A., & Hinck, S. S. (1998). *Audience reactions to Clinton and Dole: Some evidence for explaining audience assessments in terms of political strategies.* Paper for the National Communication Association convention, New York.

Hinck, E. A., & Hinck, S. S. (2000). Politeness theory and political debates. In D. Bystrom, D. B. Carlin, L. L. Kaid, M. Kern, & M. S. McKinney (Eds.), *Communication politics: Engaging the public in campaign 2000 and beyond* (pp. 124–130). Washington, DC: Proceedings of the National Communication Association Summer Conference.

Hofstetter, C. R., Donovan, M. C., Klauber, M. R., Cole, A., Huie, A. J., & Yuasa, T. (1994). Political talk radio: A Stereotype reconsidered. *Political Research Quarterly, 47*, 467–479.

Hu, W. (2000, January 20). Interviewer gets personal with First Lady. *New York Times*, p. C37.

Iroio, S. H., & Huxman, S. S. (1996). Media coverage of political issues and the framing of personal concerns. *Journal of Communication, 46*, 97–115.

Iyengar, S. (1996). Framing responsibility for political issues. *Annals of the American Academy of Political and Social Science, 456*, 59–70.

Iyengar, S., & Kinder, D. R. (1987). *News that matters.* Chicago: University of Chicago Press.

Jacoby, J., Troutman, T. R., & Whittler, T. E. (1986). Viewer miscomprehension of the 1980 presidential debate: A research note. *Political Psychology, 7*, 297–308.

James, C. (1999, December 19). We're ready for our close-ups now. *New York Times*, p. Y30.

Jamieson, K. H. (1988). *Eloquence in an electronic age: The transformation of political speechmaking.* New York: Oxford University Press.

Jamieson, K. H., & Birdsell, D. S. (1988). *Presidential debates: The challenge of creating an informed electorate.* New York: Oxford University Press.

Kelly, S., Jr. (1983). *Interpreting elections.* Princeton, NJ: Princeton University Press.

Kraus, S. (2000). *Televised presidential debates and public policy* (2nd ed.). Hillsdale, NJ: Lawrence Erlbaum.

Krosnick, J. A., & Kinder, D. R. (1990). Altering the foundations of support for the president through priming. *American Political Science Review, 84,* 497–512.

Lange, J. E. T., & DeWitt, K. (1993). *Chappaquiddick: The real story.* New York: St. Martin's Press.

Lash, J. P. (1971). *Eleanor and Franklin.* New York: Signet.

Lawrence, J. (2000, October 3). Candidates look to previous debates to sharpen strategies. *USA Today,* p. 14A.

Lester, D. (1972). *Ted Kennedy triumphs and tragedies.* New York: Putnam.

Lippman, T. (1976). *Senator Ted Kennedy.* New York: W. W. Norton.

Maltese, J. A. (1994). *Spin control: The White House office of communications and the management of presidential news.* Chapel Hill, NC: University of North Carolina Press.

Martel, M. (1983). *Political campaign debates: Images, strategies, and tactics.* New York: Longman.

Mayer, J., & Abramson, J. (1994). *Strange justice: The selling of Clarence Thomas.* Boston, MA: Houghton Mifflin.

McCombs, M. E., & Shaw, D. L. (1993). The evolution of agenda-setting research: Twenty-five years in the marketplace of ideas. *Public Opinion Quarterly, 36,* 176–185.

McLeod, J. M., & Detenber, B. H. (1999). Framing effects of television news coverage of social protest. *Journal of Communication, 49,* 3–23.

Miller, A. H., & MacKuen, M. (1979). Informing the electorate: A national study. In S. Kraus (Ed.), *The great debates: Carter vs. Ford, 1976.* Bloomington, IN: Indiana University Press.

Miller, J. J. (1999). *The campaign theme and an election's controlling frame.* Paper for the Southern Communication Association convention, St. Louis, MO.

Mitchell, F. D. (1998). *Harry S. Truman and the news media: Contentious relations, belated respect.* Columbia: University of Missouri Press.

Nelson, W. D. (1998). *Who speaks for the President? The White House press secretary from Cleveland to Clinton.* Syracuse: Syracuse University Press.

Noonan, P. (1998). *On speaking well.* New York: Regan Books.

Norris, P., Curtice, J., Sanders, D., Scammell, M., & Semetko, H. A. (1999). *On message: Communicating the campaign.* London: Sage.

Parry-Giles, T., & Parry-Giles, S. J. (1996). Political socophilia, presidential campaigning and the intimacy of American Politics. *Communication Studies, 47,* 191–205.

Patterson, R. (1999). *Bill Bennett and 'common culture' politics: Moral and economic fusion in the Reagan presidency.* Paper for the Eastern Communication Association, Charleston, W.V.

Patterson, T. E. (1994). *Out of order.* New York: Knopf.

Perlman, A. M. (1998). *Writing great speeches.* Boston, MA: Allyn & Bacon.

Perloff, R. M. (1998). *Political communication: Politics, press, and the public in America.* Mahwah, NJ: Lawrence Erlbaum.

Powell, L., & Cowart, J. (2003). *Political campaign communication: Inside and out.* Boston, MA: Allyn & Bacon.

Reeves, T. C. (1997). *The life and times of Joe McCarthy: A biography.* New York: Madison Books.

Rowley, J. (2003). Free media relations: The state of the fourth estate. In L. Powell & J. Cowart (Eds.), *Political campaign communication: Inside and out* (pp. Xx–xx). Boston, MA: Allyn & Bacon.

Sabato, L. J. (1991). *Feeding frenzy: How attack journalism has transformed American politics.* New York: Free Press.

Schram, M. (1976). *Running for president: A journal of the Carter campaign.* New York: Pocket Books.

Schrecker, E. (1998). *Many are the times: McCarthyism in America.* New York: Little, Brown.

Simon, P. (1992). *Advice and consent: Clarence Thomas, Robert Bork, and the intriguing history of the Supreme Court nomination battles*. Washington, DC: National Press Books.

Simon, R. (1987, March 14). Those Sunday interview shows: They're tougher now, but are they better? *TV Guide, 35*(11), 4–7.

Swanson, L. L., & Swanson, D. L. (1978). The agenda-setting function of the first Ford-Carter debate. *Communication Monographs, 45*, 347–353.

Tannen, D. (200, Jan. 20). Bush's sweet talk. *New York Times*, 149(512730), p. A19.

Tedrow, T. L., Tedrow, R. L., & Tedrow, T. (1980). *Death at Chappaquiddick*. Gretna, LA: Pelican Publishing.

Thomas, A. P. (2001). *Clarence Thomas: A biography*. San Francisco, CA: Encounter Books.

Vancil, D. L., & Pendell, S. D. (1984). Winning presidential debates. *Western Journal of Speech Communication, 48*, 62–74.

Wertheimer, M. M. (2000). *Barbara Bush's refashioning of the White House*. Paper presented at the annual meeting of the Eastern Communication Association, Pittsburgh, PA.

Yalof, D. A. (2001). *Pursuit of justices*. Chicago: University of Chicago Press.

Yardley, J. (1999, August 29). Candidates focus on spin, media focus on sensation. *Birmingham News*, p. 1C, 6C.

Zaller, J. R. (1992). *The nature and origin of mass opinion*. Cambridge: Cambridge University Press.

Section 4

RESEARCH INTERVIEWS

9

QUALITATIVE RESEARCH INTERVIEWS

An ethnologist spends six months in the foothills of Appalachia interviewing the local residents regarding their lifestyles and religious beliefs before writing a book on the religious rituals of rural Appalachia.

A sociologist visits maximum security penitentiaries across the nation to interview criminals on death row to understand why some people become mass murderers.

A historian interviews the widow of a war hero. Her answers provide insights into the historical figure's private life while providing a guideline for seeking out written sources on the man's life.

Each of these examples represents an instance in which interviews are used as a research methodology. Researchers working with interview techniques have used the process to investigate such wide-ranging topics as local politics (Mullen, 2003), national politics (Olsen, 2003), family relationships (Boose & Flowers, 1989), and non-profit organizations (Gutgold, 2003). By asking questions, researchers seek to gather information that becomes research data. As the interviews continue, that data is compared to other data on the same topic as the research seeks to draw some conclusion about an event or group of people.

Researchers have also found that qualitative research interviews can be used to explain and supplement data obtained from quantitative research studies. Such an integration of interview techniques has contributed to our understanding of aggression (Bushman & Anderson, 1998) and intercultural communication (McKinley & Jensen, 2003). The potential for integrating qualitative interviews with other forms of research offers a dramatic opportunity to expand our collective understanding of the human condition. So far, three major interview approaches have been used for this purpose: (1) in-depth interviews, (2) focus groups, and (3) informal interviews done as part of participant-observation research.

In-Depth Interviews

In-depth, or extended, interviews are one-on-one sessions in which an interviewer explores a topic in detail with one interviewee. Such interviews are frequently used in communication research through face-to-face interviews. Some pollsters and market researchers also use the technique for telephone interviews. The goal of such interviews is to gain an intimate familiarity with the points of view of the person being interviewed. Stacks and Hocking (1999) note that the approach is particularly useful in studying research questions that are either value- or policy-oriented. Historians also used the approach as an introductory method for learning about a person's life from the perspective of people who knew him. Researchers have used the technique to examine such topics as social problems (Bandy, 2004), social activism (Moore, 2003), depression

(Loewenthal, MacLeod, Lee, Cook, & Goldblatt, 2002), and psychiatric recovery (Smith, 2000).

One example of in-depth interviews in the academic setting is the *Retrospective Interview Technique (RIT)*, an approach that aims to help individuals reconstruct events and circumstances in a chronological order (Huston, Surra, Fitzgerald, & Cate, 1981). The technique asks participants to graph and discuss the changes that occurred over time in some aspect of their relationship. As a research methodology, it has been used to study romantic relationships (Baxter & Bullis, 1986; Baxter, 2001), post-divorce changes (Graham, 1997), parent-child relationships (Golish, 2000), behavioral patterns of children (McVeigh, Norris, & de Wet, 2004), blended families (Baxter, Braithwaite, & Nicholson, 1999), occupational therapy (Eklund, Rottpeter, & Vikstrom, 2003), career paths (Allen & Pickett, 1987), teacher-student interaction (Norby, 2002), marital conflict (Erbert, 2000), child abuse (Bifulco, Brown, & Harris, 1994), and intercultural communication (Adams & Stalder, 2002).

Another version of the in-depth interview is the *known associate interview*. In the known associate interview, the researcher interviews individuals who are known to be friends, family, and/or business associates of a particular person. The goal of this approach is to gain some insight of that person as part of a larger research project about them. Such information can be invaluable in doing a thorough investigation into the individual or topic. Scott Berg (1999), for example, won a Pulitzer Prize for his 1999 biography of Charles Lindbergh—a work that would have been less successful without the cooperation of Lindbergh's widow, Anne Morrow Lindbergh. By talking with her, he was able to obtain an understanding of Lindbergh's private life, his private thoughts, and the public aspects of the man that warranted additional investigation.

Another form of in-depth interviewing is *field interviewing* (McCracken, 1988). Field interviewing is a semi-directed conversation in which the researcher seeks to elicit the participants' point of view on a topic. The interviews are typically conducted in the participants' environment or "field." The participants will be more comfortable in that context, and the context also helps to provide cues for directing the conversation. The interviewer starts out with a general idea of the topic to be covered but draws upon comments and issues raised by the participants to direct the discussion.

In many instances, field interviews end up being extended conversations rather than true interviews. Once a topic is raised, a few probes keep the conversation flowing. Sometimes those conversations can be rather lengthy, resulting in some researchers referring to them as "long interviews" (McCracken, 1988). Lindsley (1999), for example, spent four hours on some of the interviews she used to study cultural themes in American-owned businesses in Mexico. Similarly, Chen and Chen (2002) used in-depth interviews with 16 Hong Kong businesspeople who did business with the People's Republic of China to identify eight cultural factors that affect business negotiations. Still, because the participant controls so much of the conversation, the researcher can potentially elicit details that could not be obtained with any other methodology. That's one reason Berger (1998) noted that the approach is a highly effective tool for understanding how people view the world.

Keyton (2001) notes that field interviews are particularly useful for learning "about events and interactions that cannot be directly observed" (p. 295). Government agencies use field interviews to evaluate their programs and to make policy decisions (Murphy, 1980). While the entire event or topic may be difficult to understand, the interview allows the researcher to at least understand it from the perspective of the participant. Furthermore, such interviews may point the researcher toward other people who can provide important information (Peterson et al., 1994).

Sometimes the approach is used as a tool for ethnology research. Markowitz (2000), for example, investigated the impact of the fall of Communism on young people in Soviet Russia using in-depth interviews with more than 100 Russian teenagers between 1995 and 1996. She concluded that the end of the Soviet system had an adverse effect on these young people. The lack of cultural stability and social predictability left them with few guidelines for future behavior, she concluded, and created disillusionment and high-risk behaviors among those Russian youths. Kotter and Cohen (2002) interviewed 400 people in 100 organizations to study the way employees can actively influence change within the companies.

Field interviews can also be used as a first-stage research tool prior to conducting a more formal research project. They can be particularly useful for this purpose when working with cultural or ethnographic research. Huer and Saenz (2003) conducted a series of field interviews and informal conversations with Mexican Americans and Vietnamese Americans before completing their research project. The informal field interviews provided them with a better understanding of the cultures, thus enabling them to ask better questions of the survey and focus group aspects of the project.

Market researchers sometimes use extended telephone interviews as an alternative to focus groups. Because of their length, the sample size for extended interviews is usually smaller than that for a full survey or poll. The goal, though, is usually the same—to gather qualitative data that can provide a more complete answer to a research question. Because each interview is conducted on an individual basis, the extended interview eliminates any group influence on an individual's opinions and statements. Those individual opinions are then put into a single database for the purpose of drawing research conclusions. The disadvantage of the technique, particularly in comparison to focus groups, is that it is time-consuming and can be expensive. Furthermore, because it is time consuming, the total sample for such interviews may be small and thus limit the generalizability of the results.

To counter this problem, in-depth interviewers often go to great lengths to ensure that the people they interview are representative of the types of individuals that they wish to study. Some will use demographic screening questions, much like those used for focus group recruitment. Others have used the "snowball" technique in which one interview participant is asked to help identify others who fit the desired profile. If the study is investigating the communication behaviors of diabetics, the interviewers may first talk to friends who are diabetic. They then ask those participants to suggest other diabetics who would like to participate in the project. Still others use convenience sampling by going directly to groups whose membership reflect the target audience. A study into coping behaviors among women who suffered breast cancer, for example, might look to cancer support groups for potential participants.

The format of a field interview starts with a traditional approach. The early questions are intended to orient the participant to the purpose of the interview and to put them at ease. Asking some biographical questions at this stage can get the participant talking about a familiar topic while providing the interviewer with an understanding of the context (McCracken, 1988). As the interview progresses, the questions should be designed to allow the participant to tell their own story. Open-ended questions, combined with a liberal use of probes, is the primary technique. Closed-ended questions are used as follow-ups to clarify information.

The advantage of an in-depth interview is that it allows the researcher to get heavily involved with a single aspect of a research project. The interview may actually be a series of interviews conducted over days, weeks, or months. The researcher often has time to explore different angles, different topics, and different directions related to the topic. That level of involvement allows for a more complete understanding of the other person than could ever be achieved through survey research or through focus groups. However, such advantages come with major weaknesses. First, it is highly time consuming—so much so that in-depth interviews with all of those knowledgeable on any one topic is probably impractical. Second, only one perspective can be obtained at a time; while the researcher may know one individual's perspective in detail, it can be difficult to verify if that perspective is accurate and objective. Third, that limited perspective necessarily leads to questions about reliability and validity. Reliability rises out of concerns that the opinions of the interviewee may not be representative of others' views. Validity questions arise out of the possibility that the researcher may impose some of their own opinions on the data. Even the most objective researchers will examine the data in light of their own experiences; since only one view is being analyzed, there are no counter-balancing sources of information to help maintain the researcher's objectivity.

Focus Groups

A focus group is a group of people who are gathered together at a common location to discuss some topic under the direction of a moderator (Wellner, 2003). In most cases, the size of the group is relatively small (usually 10 to 15 participants). As a result, data from focus groups lack the generalizability of similar responses obtained from a poll or survey. That weakness aside, in-depth information can be obtained. Johnson (1996) argues that focus groups offer a radically different approach to research social relations. In essence, polls and surveys provide a "quantitative" assessment of a public opinion issue. Focus groups can go "beyond surveys" (Bullock & Jones, 1999, p. 38) and provide "qualitative" data about the same issue (Morgan, 1997). Nayyar (2003) describes focus groups as "a window" into how the participants "think and feel" (p. 6). Or, as Joseph Glick (1999, p. 121) noted, "The strength of the focus group is that it allows people to be people." Surveys can tell a researcher what is happening, but focus groups can tell them why. As Hansen, Cottle, Negrine, and Newbold (1998) noted, the semi-structured nature of the focus groups allows the researcher "a potentially much richer and more sensitive type of data" (p. 258).

Three factors are critical to the success of a focus group: a good research question, a good facilitator, and the recruitment of a good sample. The research question is essential, because it is unlikely that researchers will elicit useful information when they do not know what they are seeking. Developing those questions requires advance planning and thoughtful consideration (Betts & Baranowski, 1996; MacDougall, 2001; Tiberius, 2001). The research question guides both the development of the group discussion guide and the selection of the participants, who are usually chosen on the basis of some demographic or psycho-graphic criteria. Thus, inadequate planning on the research question can doom the success of the project (Morgan, 1995).

Similarly, the facilitator is a key person in the process (Glick, 1999). The role is so critical that some authorities recommend using a professional moderator for the role (Shoaf, 2003). The moderator's job is to encourage discussion by all participants, guide the discussion along the topic of interest, but not to influence the discussion in any manner. They often have an outline guide or a questionnaire to remind them of the information being sought, yet they must use their personal research skill to guide the discussion without letting the questionnaire become an artificial part of the process (Keyton, 2001). Opening questions are generally broad and designed to encourage participation. As the interview progresses, a funnel technique is used to narrow the discussion to the specific research question that is being studied. Doing that requires a skillful moderator but can produce useful information that may not be easily obtained by other techniques. The group format generates discussion (Carey & Smith, 1994) and conflict, which allows new ideas to emerge (Morgan & Krueger, 1993). As Glick (1999) noted, "When non-consensus and disagreements are encouraged, two things generally emerge in group discussion: opinion becomes nuanced in ways that begin to reveal underlying thought frameworks, and people often invoke powerful images" (p. 117). If the group moves too much toward consensus, the moderator has to play the role of the "devil's advocate" and generate discussion from a counter viewpoint (MacDougall & Baum, 1997).

Researchers often have materials with them that can be used to stimulate discussion. The most popular of these are copies of television ads, with group participants serving as critics and explaining their responses to the ads. The researchers typically monitor the entire process. Frequently, the monitoring occurs at the same time as the discussion, with the researchers observing the discussion behind a one-way mirror. In addition, the entire process is videotaped, providing for frequent viewings at a later date to verify conclusions.

Usually, though, the researcher is not looking for generalizable answers. Instead, the goal of focus group research is to obtain new insights into the target audience and their views, which works to supplement the work of other forms of research and for preparing a media campaign. For instance, focus groups have led to the development of advertising campaign slogans, using terminology provided by the focus group participants. Or, ads may be re-edited based on comments of the participants. Other times, it can lead to the development of new ideas or messages that are subsequently tested with survey research (Wimmer & Dominick, 1994, p. 148).

Ideally, the facilitator is just one member of at least a two-person team (Robinson, 1999). One person leads the discussion, while the other observes and take notes on the discussion. If multiple groups are used, the two individuals may rotate roles, particularly if it is appropriate based on the nature of the groups. A male-female team would probably swap roles in those groups in which participants were selected by gender. The woman would facilitate the women's group, while the man would handle that role for the men's group.

Focus groups have also seen increased use recently as a tool for academic study. Janesick (1998) recommends it for those situations in which the research is a new area of study or if the target group is well defined. Keyton (2001) notes that it is particularly useful in gathering comparative data, i.e., "information about the same topic from different types of people" (p. 307). The range of topics for which it is appropriate is a wide one. Press and Cole (1995) examined attitudes toward abortion with focus group methodology. Reilly, Muldoon, and Byrne (2004) used the approach to study violence in Northern Ireland. Stjerna, Lauritzen, and Tillgren (2004) used it to study tobacco use among teenagers. Morrison (2002) used focus groups to examine intercultural communication, while others have argued that focus groups are particularly effective because of the researcher's ability to use them for culturally sensitive topics (Calderon, Baker, & Wolf, 2000; Murdaugh, Russell, & Sowell, 2000). The technique has also been used in health communication to study public health topics such as attitudes toward medical research (Asai et al., 2004), mental health (Schilder et al., 2004), cardiovascular disease (Powell & Amsbary, 2001a), and health concerns of women and children (Powell & Amsbary, 2001b). Other public agencies have found it useful in studying such topics as prison incarceration and family violence (Wolf, Uyen, Hobart, & Kernic, 2003). In fact, Hyde and Yi (2000) argue that it should be considered an important research tool for broad topics in public management.

Focus groups have a wide range of other applications. Swenson and Griswold (1992) recommended their use in journalism and in program intervention work. Political campaigns use focus groups to pre-test television ads, monitor audience responses to presentations, and identify audience language habits that can be used in campaign messages (Williams, 2004). One Republican pollster who frequently used focus groups is Richard Wirthlin, who provided data for former President Ronald Reagan. Every time Reagan gave a televised speech, Wirthlin had focus groups watching and using hand-held devices to record their responses to the speech, second by second. Wirthlin used the resulting data to identify what worked and what did not work for each speech. The information was then used in preparing the next speech (Taylor, 1990, p. 218).

As mentioned before, because of the small sample size, the representativeness of focus group results is questionable. As a result, recruitment of a proper sample is essential (MacDougall, 2001). Some researchers have argued that keeping control of the groups' participants is the most important part of the process, noting that specific criteria as to why individuals are included should be developed in advance (Mansell, Bennett, Northway, Mead, & Moseley, 2004). A general rule of thumb is that you need at least two groups, for comparison purposes, with 10 to 15 participants in each group. Sometimes focus group participants are recruited though newspaper advertisements or announcements at group meetings (Press & Cole, 1995). More frequently, though, they are recruited from the target population via pre-interview telephone calls. Part of the telephone conversation will include a short demographic survey to make sure that the person qualifies for the study ("Are you at least 18 years old? Has anybody in your family seen a doctor about health problems such as high blood pressure in the past year?"). Typically, the recruitment process will recruit 15 to 18 possible participants, with a second round of calls made to these participants on the day of the focus group meeting. Not all will show up, but the researcher is usually satisfied if the final group numbers 10 to 15 participants.

Each participant is usually paid an honorarium for their participation, with the fees varying depending on the anticipated length of the discussion. If the group has a high turnout (i.e., more than 15 recruited participants show up), some of those participants will be paid their fee and told they don't have to stay any longer. Groups that become too large can become too unwieldy to interview properly.

Focus groups have some major limitations (Morgan, 1995). Wimmer and Dominick (1994, p. 149) argue that, considering the small sample size and qualitative methodology, gathering quantitative data is inappropriate for a focus group. Several observers have noted that focus groups lack the statistical validity and reliability of quantitative research methods (e.g., Hunter, 2000; Carey, 1995). That problem may be particularly acute if the group has one or two dominant members who quickly lead the other participants to a false consensus (Morgan, 1997). For this reason, most academicians argue that focus group data should be viewed as only preliminary data that should be verified with more in-depth research.

Another problem with focus groups is their representativeness. The sample for focus groups essentially consists of volunteers who are often provided monetary incentives to participate. Such groups may not be representative of the overall population from which they were selected. That is particularly true if those participants are "professional subjects" who are constantly used by research organizations for a number of projects. Once someone volunteers to participate in a focus group, the research organization often keeps their name (complete with phone number and demographic data) on file. When they need another participant with those demographic criteria, the research organization may first call people who have participated before, creating a sample of people who are frequently used for similar research. Constant repetition of this process leads to focus groups composed of unrepresentative samples.

An additional problem has to do with the role of the researcher, i.e., the ability of the researcher to conduct an impartial analysis (Weinberger et al., 1998). It is remarkably easy for the researcher to let personal biases into the resulting report. Analysis of any focus group discussion requires that the researcher view the data from three different perspectives—that of the individual, the group, and the group interaction (Duggleby, 2004). Regardless of impartiality, Sim (1998) noted that the process limits the ability of any researcher to obtain some information. Attempts to infer attitudinal consensus can't be done, since any view expressed by the group may be a result of the interaction instead of individually held attitudes. Reed and Roskell (1997), for example, noted the importance of following the sequence of the discussion and the social context of the discussion. Similarly, Kitzinger (1994) noted that the interaction of the group is a key attribute of focus groups, and yet researchers rarely include the impact of that inter-action in their reports. Traulsen, Almarsdottir, and Bjornsdottir (2004) suggest that an added level of analysis—an interview with the moderator—is needed to address this problem. Still, even that may not totally eliminate researcher bias. For the same rea-son, researchers will have trouble assessing the strength of those opinions, which, in turn, makes it harder for the researcher to make comparisons among groups. Stockdale (2002) suggests that some of the potential researcher bias can be eliminated if the researcher relies more on quantitative analysis of the resulting group discussion, using spreadsheets to analyze and compare the resulting data. Others have suggested using online focus groups, noting the advantage of that approach in providing a written record of the discussion (Schneider, Kerwin, Frechtling, & Vivari, 2002; Murray, 1997).

Finally, the use of focus groups raises some ethical questions that researchers must address. The biggest concern has to do with the impact of the group on the participants, particularly those with personal vulnerabilities (Owen, 2001). In addition, confidential-ity can be a problem; although the participants should be randomly selected and thus unlikely to know each other, it is not uncommon for some of the participants to recognize each other in the group situation. Such an occurrence can be common if the participants are drawn from a relatively small initial universe of people. Finally, even if the individu-als have no prior knowledge of each other, they can develop personal perceptions of others based on the nature of the discussion. Conflicts and disagreements may become elevated from the discussion, reaching a point where participants criticize each other on personal levels.

Given all of these problems, it's not surprising that focus groups have their critics. Dionne (1991, p. 311), for example, complained that focus group research undermined our political system:

> The focus group may be the perfect symbol of what has happened to democ-racy in America. Insofar as "the people" are consulted by political leaders these days, their reactions are of interest not as a guide to policy but simply as a way of exploring the electorate's gut feelings, to see which kind of (usually divi-sive) message might move them the most. The approach to politics is not even Machiavellian; it is Pavlovian.

Participant-Observation Research

Participant-observation research is "a combination of a first-person and a second-person account, which takes place in a naturalistic setting, of the actions and behaviors of a specific group of people" (Hocking, Stacks, & McDermott, 2003, p. 195). This pro-cess is one in which the researcher examines communication activities as they occur naturally, looking at those activities from the perspective of both a participant and an observer (Spadley, 1980). Ideally, this research technique allows for both a subjective and an objective view of the topic or event. The goal of such an approach is ethnomethodology (Garfinkel, 1967), i.e., "how people make sense out of the situations in which they find themselves" (Hocking, Stacks, & McDermott, 2003, p. 197). The approach has been used for a variety of purposes that include such diverse topics as studying the social norms of southern rednecks (Roebuck & Hickson, 1982), nursing home residents (Brown, 1990), communication problems in a government bureaucracy (Powell & Hickson, 1977–78), urban neighborhoods (Phillipsen, 1975), organizational communication (Hickson, 1974), and political campaign strategies (Powell & Shelby, 1981).

Interviews conducted as part of a participant-observation study can be useful as a means of generating discussions on topics that are of interest to the researcher. However, such interviews face some obstacles that other forms of research do not have to face. Two problems in particular must be faced by participant-observation researchers who use interviews. First, the interviewer cannot do anything during the interview that disrupts the normal activities of the event being observed. Thus, if the interview itself is disruptive, that in itself may reduce the value of the data being obtained. Consequently, interviews for this type of research are usually conducted in informal situations. The interviewee, in fact, probably will not consciously realize they're being interviewed; instead, the topics to be discussed are elicited during an interaction that could be described as a typical conversation. Will the interviewer ask a lot of questions? Yes, but since their presence is often that of one who is new to the group or situation, those questions will not be typical of those asked by any newcomer.

Second, the researcher usually cannot record the interview. As Hocking, Stacks, and McDermott noted, there is often "a fine line between participant-observation and violating another person's right of privacy" (p. 201). While laws vary from state to state, most places require the consent of the second party before any interview can be recorded. To do so in a participant-observation study inherently disrupts the nature of the study. Even if the interview occurs in a state where such a recording is allowed, there is still the ethical question regarding a violation of the person's rights. Consequently, the general rule when conducting such research is that such conversations should not be recorded. Instead, participant-observation researchers rely on extensive note-taking (if they can do so without being noticed) or the use of a reflective log of observations. The latter format— the reflective log—is perhaps the most common, with most researchers recording their observations on a daily basis. Such a log usually incorporates the researcher's observations of the situation and the behavior of the participants, their interpretations of what happened, the typical and atypical elements of the event, an assessment of how the participants were influenced, and an assessment of how the researcher was influenced by the event. By recording such impressions on a daily basis, the researchers can gradually develop a database of impressions from which they can draw broader conclusions.

Participant-observation research is a tool that can be used to study some communication behaviors that can't be fully researched from other perspectives. Furthermore, while it takes some training, it still takes less training than most other forms of communication research. It requires a range of skills that are fully within reach of most undergraduate students (Hickson, 1977). Still, one obvious weakness of participant-observation research is that it is highly time consuming. Gathering and analyzing the data for such a project may take months or years to complete. Even then, the researcher may merely stop once they realize that the accumulated data is starting to become repetitive. In doing so, they may then miss subsequent changes in the way the group behaves and interacts. Still, through an extensive process of interacting and talking with individuals in the group, the researcher can develop an understanding of the participants in ways that would not occur in other forms of communication research.

Data Analysis

The interview is the means by which the researcher collects the research data. To be useful, however, that data must be subjected to some type of systematic analysis, with the interview questions serving as the "raw material" for the analysis (Krueger, 1998, p. 23). The most common means for this is some form of **content analysis**. In its purest form, content analysis involves "the systematic study and quantification of the content or meaning of communication messages" (Stacks & Hocking, 1999, p. 163). It is systematic in that the researcher analyzes the data in terms of categories related to the topic being studied. It involves quantification to the extent that instances of communication that fall within each category can be identified and counted. Krueger (1998) identified three key elements that have to be part of data analysis, i.e., that the analysis must be systematic, verifiable, and timely. The extent to which it is systematic usually depends on the categories used for the analysis. The extent to which it is verifiable depends on the researcher's ability to base their conclusions on specifics within the data. Timeliness refers to (a) having sufficient time to do a thorough analysis without (b) taking too much time and thus jeopardizing the validity of the conclusions.

When well done, the resulting data from the analysis can be used to give either a description of a particular communication event ("Among young adults, 56% said the political issue that concerned them the most was education"), an explanation for a communication behavior ("Sixty percent of the people who voted for Candidate A said they did so because they were dissatisfied with the incumbent"), or a comparison of opposing opinions ("Women in the group generally liked A, while men were more likely to support B"). The specific units used for a content analysis will vary, depending on the purpose of the research. Berelson (1952) identified five major units that serve as broad guidelines. Three of those units—words or symbols, themes, and time and/or space—are frequently used in the content analysis of interviews.

Words or symbols refer to analyses that only look at specific words within the interview, rather than the entire interview. Powell and Kitchens (1975), for example, studied student interviews with each other and coded the summaries of those interviews in terms of personal pronouns. The study found that women typically summarized their conversations with joint pronouns ("We talked about . . .") whereas men usually spoke in first- and third-person pronouns ("He said . . . and I answered . . .).

Themes refers to commonality of topics and ideas. Thematic analysis is a common approach for both in-depth interviews and focus groups. The research reviews the conversation to look for repetitive topics that are mentioned by more than one person. Furthermore, the analysis will include the responses of other people to that topic, i.e., do people agree or disagree when the topic of higher taxes is mentioned.

Time and/or space refers to quantitative measurements of discussion topics. Researchers may combine it as a content analysis technique for thematic analysis. Suppose, for example, that a researcher found that the interviewee made an equal number of references to education and to taxes during an in-depth interview. Which issue was of more concern to the individual? The thematic analysis wouldn't say, but the question could perhaps be answered by measuring how much time the person spent discussing each issue or how much space was devoted to each topic in the written transcript.

Other options for analysis are usually left open to the individual skills of the researcher. Typically, for example, the researcher will also look for internal consistencies or inconsistencies among the remarks. Thus, does one person say one thing that is inconsistent with another of their remarks? Or does one individual say something that is consistent with several other views that have been expressed? If so, how specific is their complaint or praise?

Krueger (1998) also recommends that the analysis include two other key elements. First, the researcher should look for unspoken ideas, i.e., "what was not said" (p. 37). Things that are not articulated can reflect common assumptions that all of the participants made about the topic or can identify taboo topics that they did not feel comfortable approaching. And finally, it is essential, as Krueger wrote, for the research to "find the big ideas" (p. 38). After the first analysis of the data is completed, the researcher must review that data again to look for overall ideas that represent the primary results of the groups' comments. Only then does the researcher have data that is useful in explaining the discussion.

Ethical Questions

The nature of qualitative research methodology has triggered at least two major ethical questions: (1) invasion of privacy/confidentiality and (2) audience pampering/manipulation. Confidentiality and privacy issues are a major concern in participant-observation research (Johannesen, 1990). To what extent should the subject of the research know that they are being investigated? The general guideline here is the concept of **informed consent**, i.e. that the participants should have a basic understanding of what the researcher is doing so that they could withdraw from the project "at any point in the study" (Hocking, Stacks, & McDermott, 2003, p. 58). Although some deception is often necessary (to ensure the validity of the data), no deception should be used that could cause any harm to the interviewee (Kelman, 1967).

Informed consent is a viable concept for focus group research and in-depth interviews, but it's not a realistic goal for a participant observation study conducted in a naturalistic setting. Even asking for informed consent could destroy the nature of the investigation. Instead, the ethical goal in this form of research is to *minimize invasiveness*. The research should do as little as possible to interfere with the participants or their environment. Whenever possible, this means gathering data in such a manner that the participants are relatively anonymous. In focus groups, for example, each participant is typically identified only by their first name. The identities of the individual participants, after all, is relatively unimportant. What is important is what they say and what they believe, not who they are.

Some forms of research require that both the interviewer and interviewee be identified. Still, identification of the individuals could potentially cause them problems. One author, for example, conducted interviews with academic personnel at an international university. One faculty member, though, was highly critical of the university's administration. Publication of that person's name would have caused potential harm to them and to their career. As a result, all responses in the final report were presented anonymously. In reality, the true level of privacy was that of confidentiality. The researcher knew the name of the respondent but did not divulge it to anyone else.

Focus groups have been criticized for their use in pandering to audiences and manipulating political behaviors and consumer buying habits. Marketing companies use focus groups to develop advertising campaigns for their products, campaigns that will enable them to tailor their appeal to the needs and desires of their target audience. Politicians use focus groups to examine audience attitudes on political issues, adjusting their persuasive appeals on the basis of the resulting data. At one extreme, such approaches can be accused of pandering to audiences instead of providing leadership on issues. At the other end, critics see marketers using focus group research for manipulative purposes. Dionne (1991), for example, complained that focus group research undermined our political system.

The focus group may be the perfect symbol of what has happened to democracy in America. Insofar as "the people" are consulted by political leaders these days, their reactions are of interest not as a guide to policy, but simply as a way of exploring the electorate's gut feelings, to see which kind of (usually divisive) message might move them the most.

Perhaps such ethical questions are inherently part of any form of audience analysis. Still, the extent to which interviewing techniques are being used to market and sell products and ideas in modern society warrants continued examination and scrutiny of the process.

Summary

In-depth interviews provide researchers with a chance to engage in extended conversations with individuals. Such interviews provide for insight into the lives of those individuals that allows for generalizations to be drawn regarding larger research issues. Retrospective interviews are a form of in-depth interviews that try to help individuals reconstruct events and circumstances in a chronological order by asking the interviewee to graph and discuss the changes that have occurred to them over time. The known associate interview is a technique in which the researcher interviews individuals who are known to be friends, family, and/or business associates of a particular person; the goal of this approach is to gain some insight of that person as part of a larger research project. Field interviewing is a semi-directed conversation in which the researcher seeks to elicit the participant's point of view on a topic; such interviews are often conducted in conjunction with participant-observation and ethnology research.

Focus groups allow the researcher to gather a small group of individuals to discuss a single topic and exchange opinions on that topic. Polls and surveys provide a means of gathering quantitative information about a topic, while focus groups provide qualitative data of those same groups. Polls answer the question "how many?" whereas focus groups tell the researcher "why?" In-depth, or extended, interviews offer researchers an alternative means of obtaining qualitative information on a topic. They have the added advantage of gathering that data without the potential influence of group opinions.

Participant-observation research is a way to conduct research in a naturalistic setting while gathering data from the perspective of both a participant and an observer. Interviews become useful in this research technique as a means of sparking discussions of topics that are important to the researcher.

The use of one form of interview does not exclude the use of others. Some researchers, in fact, use multiple methodologies to gather data for their research topic. McKinley and Jensen (2003), for example, used both in-depth interviews with radio staff members and focus groups with audience members to assess the impact of health programming on citizens in Peru. Regardless of the type of interview, though, the quality of the data is frequently dependent upon the skills of the researcher. Good interviews provide reliable data.

Discussion Questions

1. Develop a discussion guide for a focus group on the topic of your choice. How would you open the discussion so that everyone feels comfortable? How would you

lead in to the main topic of discussion? What would you do to ensure that everyone participates?

2. Take the same topic and divide it into smaller subtopics. For which of these subtopics would quantitative research methodologies be appropriate? Which ones would require another research approach?

3. Choose a commercial product and analyze its sales campaign. Can you identify any elements of that campaign, including slogans and sales pitches, that you believe may have been developed with the help of focus groups?

4. Assume that you wanted to investigate the communication behaviors of sales workers at a local retail outlet through the use of in-depth interviews. Construct an interview guide for those interviews. How many interviews with different people do you think would be necessary for you to fully understand this subject?

 Please see the companion website for additional resources at [www.routledge.com/cw/amsbary].

References

Adams, T., & Stalder, A. (2002). *Themes and connections from individual member interviews.* Paper presented at the annual meeting of the National Communication Association, New Orleans.

Allen, K. R., & Pickett, R. S. (1987). Forgotten streams in the family life course: Utilization of qualitative retrospective interview in the analysis of lifelong single women's family careers. *Journal of Marriage & the Family, 49,* 517–526.

Asai, A., Ohnishi, M., Nishigaki, E., Sekimoto, M., Fukuhara, S., & Fukui, T. (2004). Focus group interviews examining attitudes towards medical research among the Japanese: A qualitative study. *Bioethics, 18*(5), 448–470.

Bandy, J. (2004). Paradoxes of transnational civil societies under neoliberalism: The coalition for justice in the Maquiladoras. *Social Problems, 51,* 410–431.

Baxter, L. A. (2001). Communicatively remembering turning points of relational development in heterosexual romantic relationships. *Communication Reports, 14,* 1–17.

Baxter, L. A., Braithwaite, D. O., & Nicholson, J. (1999). Turning points in the development of blended family relationships. *Journal of Social and Personal Relationships, 16,* 291–313.

Baxter, L. A., & Bullis, C. (1986). Turning points in developing romantic relationships. *Human Communication Research, 12,* 469–493.

Berg, A. S. (1999). *Lindberg.* New York: Putnam.

Berger, A. A. (1998). *Media research techniques* (2nd ed.). Thousand Oaks, CA: Sage.

Betts, N. M., & Baranowski, T. (1996). Recommendations for planning and reporting focus group research. *Journal of Nutrition Education, 28*(5), 279–281.

Bifulco, A., Brown, G. W., & Harris, T. O. (1994). Childhood experience of care and abuse (CECA): A retrospective interview measure. *Journal of Child Psychology & Psychiatry & Allied Disciplines, 35,* 1419–1435.

Boose, L. E., & Flowers, B. S. (1989). *Daughters and fathers.* Baltimore, MD: John Hopkins University Press.

Brenner, M. (1985). Intensive interviewing. In M. Brenner, J. Brown, & D.V. Canter (Eds.), *The research interview: Uses and approaches* (pp. 147–161). London: Academic Press.

Brown, M. H. (1990). "Reading" an organization's culture: An examination of stories in nursing homes. *Journal of Applied Communication Research, 18,* 64–75.

Bullock, M., & Jones, J. (1999). Beyond surveys: Using focus groups to evaluate university career services. *Journal of Career Planning & Employment, 59*(4), 38–40.

Bushman, B. J., & Anderson, C. A. (1998). Methodology in the study of aggression: Integrating experimental and non-experimental findings. In R. G. Geen & E. Donnerstein (Eds.), *Human aggression: Theories, research, and implications for social policy* (pp. 23–48). New York: Academic.

Calderon, J. L., Baker, R. S., & Wolf, K. E. (2000). Focus groups: A qualitative method complementing quantitative research for studying culturally diverse groups. *Education for Health: Change in Learning & Practice, 13*(1), 91–95.

Carey, M. A. (1995). Comment: Concerns in the analysis of focus group data. *Qualitative Health Research, 5*, 487–495.

Carey, M. A., & Smith, M. W. (1994). Capturing the group effect in focus groups: A special concern in analysis. *Qualitative Health Research, 4*, 123–127.

Chen, G., & Chen, H. (2002). An examination of People's Republic of China business negotiating behaviors. *Communication Research Reports, 19*, 399–408.

Dionne, E. J., Jr. (1991). *Why Americans hate politics.* New York: Simon & Schuster.

Duggleby, W. (2004). Methodological issues in focus group data analysis. *Nursing & Health Sciences, 6*(2), 161.

Eklund, M., Rottpeter, J., & Vikstrom, F. (2003). The meaning of psychosocial occupational therapy in a life-story perspective: A long-term follow-up of three cases. *Occupational Therapy International, 10*(3), 185–205.

Erbert, L. A. (2000). Conflict and dialectics: Perceptions of dialectical contradictions in marital conflict. *Journal of Social & Personal Relationships, 17*, 638–659.

Garfinkel, H. (1967). *Studies in ethnomethodology.* Englewood Cliffs, NJ: Prentice-Hall.

Glick, J. A. (1999). Focus groups in political campaigns. In D. D. Perlmutter (Ed.), *The Manship School guide to political communication* (pp. 114–121). Baton Rouge, LA: Louisiana State University Press.

Golish, T. D. (2000). Changes in closeness between adult children and their parents: A turning point analysis. *Communication Reports, 13*, 79–97.

Graham, E. E. (1997). Turning points and commitment in post-divorce relationships. *Communication Monographs, 64*, 350–367.

Greenbaum, T. L. (1988). *The practical handbook and guide to focus group research.* Lexington, MA: D. C. Heath.

Gutgold, N. (2003). *Interviewing 'Ramrod and Rainbow' (Bob and Elizabeth Dole).* Paper presented at the annual convention of the Eastern Communication Association, Washington, DC.

Hansen, A., Cottle, S., Negrine, R. E., & Newbold, C. (1998). *Mass communication research methods.* Washington Square, NY: New York University Press.

Hickson, M., III (1974). Participant-observation technique in organizational research. *Journal of Business Communication, 11*, 37–42, 54.

Hickson, M., III (1977). Communication in natural settings: Research tools for undergraduates. *Communication Quarterly, 25*, 23–28.

Hocking, J. E., Stacks, D. W., & McDermott, S. T. (2003). *Communication research* (3rd ed.). Boston, MA: Allyn & Bacon.

Huer, M. B., & Saenz, T. I. (2003). Challenges and strategies for conducting survey and focus group research with culturally diverse groups. *American Journal of Speech-Language Pathology, 12*, 209–220.

Hunter, P. (2000, August). Using focus groups in campaigns: A caution. *Campaigns & Elections, 21*(7), 38–40.

Huston, T. L., Surra, C. A., Fitzgerald, N. M., & Cate, R. M. (1981). From courtship to marriage: Mate selection as an interpersonal process. In S. Duck & R. Gilmore (Eds.), *Personal relationships 2: Developing personal relationships* (pp. 53–90). New York: Academic Press.

Hyde, A. C., & Yi, H. U. (2000). Focus groups: It's not just for social research anymore? *Public Manager, 29*(3), 57–58.

Janesick, V. J. (1998). *"Stretching" exercises for qualitative researchers.* Thousand Oaks, CA: Sage.

Johannesen, R. L. (1990). *Ethics in human communication* (3rd ed.). Belmont, CA: Wadsworth.

Johnson, A. (1996). 'It's good to talk': The focus group and the sociological imagination. *Sociological Review, 44,* 517–538.

Kelman, H. (1967). Human use of human subjects: The problem of deception in social psychological experiments. *Psychological Bulletin, 67,* 1–11.

Keyton, J. (2001). *Communication research: Asking questions, finding answers.* Mountain View, CA: Mayfield.

Kitzinger, J. (1994). The methodology of focus groups: The importance of interaction between research participants. *Sociology of Health & Illness, 16,* 103–121.

Kotter, J. P., & Cohen, D. S. (2002). *The heart of change: Real-life stories of how people change their organization.* Boston, MA: Harvard Business School Press.

Krueger, R. A. (1998). *Analyzing and reporting focus group results.* Thousand Oaks, CA: Sage.

Lindsley, S. L. (1999). Communication and "the Mexican way": Stability and trust as core symbols in maquiladoras. *Western Journal of Communication, 63,* 1–31.

Loewenthal, K. M., MacLeod, A. K., Lee, M., Cook, S., & Goldblatt, V. (2002). Tolerance for depression: Are there cultural and gender differences? *Journal of Psychiatric & Mental Health Nursing, 9,* 681–688.

MacDougall, C. (2001). Planning and recruiting the sample for focus groups and in-depth interviews. *Qualitative Health Research, 11*(1), 117–126.

MacDougall, C., & Baum, F. (1997). The devil's advocate: A strategy to avoid groupthink and stimulate discussion in focus groups. *Qualitative Health Research, 7,* 532–540.

Mansell, I., Bennett, G., Northway, R., Mead, D., & Moseley, L. (2004). The learning curve: The advantages and disadvantages in the use of focus groups as a method of data collection. *Nurse Researcher, 11*(4), 79–88.

Markowitz, F. (2000). *Coming of age in post-Soviet Russia.* Chicago: University of Chicago Press.

McCracken, G. (1988). *The long interview.* Newbury Park, CA: Sage.

McKinley, M. A., & Jensen, L. O. (2003). In our own voices: Reproductive health radio programming in the Peruvian Amazon. *Critical Studies in Media Communication, 20,* 180–203.

McVeigh, J. A., Norris, S. A., & de Wet, T. (2004). The relationship between socio-economic status and physical activity patterns in South African children. *Acta Paediatrica, 93,* 982–988.

Moore, T. (2003). Promoting change through the African American church and social activism. *Journal of Psychology & Christianity, 22,* 357–362.

Morgan, D. L. (1995). Why things (sometimes) go wrong in focus groups. *Qualitative Health Research, 5,* 516–523.

Morgan, D. L. (1997). *Focus groups as qualitative research* (2nd ed.). Thousand Oaks, CA: Sage.

Morgan, D. L., & Krueger, R. A. (1993). When to use focus groups and why. In D. L. Morgan (Ed.), *Successful focus groups: Advancing the state of the art* (pp. 3–19). Newbury Park, CA: Sage.

Morrison, J. (2002). *Focus group themes and findings: The nature of intercultural communication contact from the group perspective.* Paper presented at the annual meeting of the National Communication Association, New Orleans.

Mullen, L. (2003). *Communication and community in Las Vegas: Interviews with political leaders past and present.* Paper presented at the annual convention of the Eastern Communication Association, Washington, DC.

Murdaugh, C., Russell, R. B., & Sowell, R. (2000). Using focus groups to develop a culturally sensitive videotape intervention for HIV-positive women. *Journal of Advanced Nursing, 32,* 1507–1513.

Murphy, J. T. (1980). *Getting the facts: The fieldwork guide for evaluators and policy analysts.* Santa Monica, CA: Goodyear.

Murray, P. J. (1997). Using virtual focus groups in qualitative research. *Qualitative Health Research, 7,* 542–549.

Nayyar, S. (2003, March). A window into what consumers think and feel. *American Demographics, 25*(2), 6.

Norby, C. J. (2002). Investigating teacher-student interactions that foster self-regulated learning. *Educational Psychologist, 37*(1), 5–15.

Olsen, D. (2003). *Interviewing National Endowment of the Arts players.* Paper presented at the annual convention of the Eastern Communication Association, Washington, DC.

Owen, S. (2001). The practical, methodological and ethical dilemmas of conducting focus groups with vulnerable clients. *Journal of Advanced Nursing, 36,* 652–658.

Peterson, T. R., Witte, K., Enkerlin-Hoeflich, E., Expericueta, L., Flora, J. T., Florey, N., Loughran, T., & Stuart, R. (1994). Using informant directed interviews to discover risk orientation: How formative evaluations based in interpretive analysis can improve persuasive safety campaigns. *Journal of Applied Communication Research, 22,* 199–213.

Phillipsen, G. (1975). Speaking "like a man" in Teamsterville: Culture patterns of role enactment in an urban neighborhood. *Quarterly Journal of Speech, 61,* 13–22.

Powell, L., & Amsbary, J. (2001a). Cardiovascular disease in rural Alabama. *Alabama's Health, 35*(4), 9, 11.

Powell, L., & Amsbary, J. (2001b). Barriers to WIC participation: A research note. *Alabama's Health, 35*(4), 10–11.

Powell, L., & Hickson, M. (1977–78). The influence of macrospace and job status on organizational communication. *Georgia Speech Communication Journal, 9,* 39–41.

Powell, L., & Kitchens, J. T. (1975). Elements of participant satisfaction in dyads. *Southern Speech Communication Journal, 41,* 59–68.

Powell, L., & Shelby, A. N. (1981). The strategy of assumed incumbency: A case study. *Southern Speech Communication Journal, 46,* 105–123.

Press, A. L., & Cole, E. R. (1995). Reconciling faith and fact: Pro-life women discuss media, science and the abortion debate. *Critical Studies in Mass Communication, 12,* 380–402.

Reed, J., & Roskell, V. (1997). Focus groups: Issues of analysis and interpretation. *Journal of Advanced Nursing, 26,* 765–771.

Reilly, J., Muldoon, O. T., & Byrne, C. (2004). Young men as victims and perpetrators of violence in Northern Ireland: A qualitative analysis. *Journal of Social Issues, 60,* 469–484.

Robinson, N. (1999). The use of focus group methodology—with selected examples from sexual health research. *Journal of Advanced Nursing, 29,* 905–913.

Roebuck, J. B., & Hickson, M., III (1982). *The southern redneck: A phenomenological case study.* New York: Praeger.

Schilder, K., Tomov, T., Mladenova, M., Mayeya, J., Jenkins, R., Gulbinat, W., Manderscheid, R., Baingana, F., Whiteford, H., Khandelval, S., Minoletti, A., Mubbashar, M. H., Murthy, R. S., Deva, M. P., Baba, A., Townsend, C., & Sakuta, T. (2004). The appropriateness and use of focus group methodology across international mental health communities. *International Review of Psychiatry, 16,* 24–30.

Schneider, S. J., Kerwin, J., Frechtling, J., & Vivari, B. A. (2002). Characteristics of the discussion in online and face-to-face focus groups. *Social Science Computer Review, 20*(1), 31–42.

Shoaf, E. C. (2003). Using a professional moderator in library focus group research. *College & Research Libraries, 64*(2), 124–132.

Sim, J. (1998). Collecting and analysing qualitative data: Issues raised by the focus group. *Journal of Advanced Nursing, 28,* 345–352.

Smith, M. K. (2000). Recovery from a severe psychiatric disability: Findings of a qualitative study. *Psychiatric Rehabilitation Journal, 24*(2), 149–158.

Spadley, J. P. (1980). *Participant observation.* New York: Holt, Rinehart and Winston.

Stacks, D. W., & Hocking, J. E. (1999). *Communication research* (2nd ed.). New York: Longman.

Stjerna, M., Lauritzen, S. O., & Tillgren, P. (2004). "Social thinking" and cultural images: Teenagers' notions of tobacco use. *Social Science & Medicine, 59,* 573–584.

Stockdale, M. S. (2002). Analyzing focus group data with spreadsheets. *American Journal of Health Studies, 18*(1), 55–69.

Swenson, J. D., & Griswold, W. F. (1992). Focus groups. *Small Group Research, 23*, 459–474.

Taylor, P. (1990). *See how they run: Electing the president in an age of mediaocracy.* New York: Alfred A. Knopf.

Tiberius, R. (2001, September). Making sense and making use of feedback from focus groups. *New Directions for Teaching & Learning, 87*, 63–75.

Traulsen, J. M., Almarsdottir, A. B., & Bjornsdottir, I. (2004). Interviewing the moderator: An ancillary method to focus groups. *Qualitative Health Research, 14*, 714–525.

Weinberger, M., Ferguson, J. A., Westmoreland, G., Mamlin, L. A., Segar, D. S., Eckert, G. J., Greene, J. Y., Martin, D. K., & Tierney, W. M. (1998). Can raters consistently evaluate the content of focus groups? *Social Science & Medicine, 46*, 929–933.

Wellner, A. S. (2003, March). The new science of focus groups. *American Demographics, 25*(2), 29–33.

Williams, A. (2004, August 22). The alchemy of a political slogan. *New York Times, 153*(52949), 9:1.

Wimmer, R. D., & Dominick, J. R. (1994). *Mass media research.* Belmont, CA: Wadsworth.

Wolf, M. E., Uyen, L., Hobart, M. A., & Kernic, M. A. (2003). Barriers to seeking police help for intimate partner violence. *Journal of Family Violence, 18*(2), 121–129.

10

QUANTITATIVE RESEARCH INTERVIEWS

A research group representing a politician conducts a political poll in the days before an election. A restaurant wonders if its customers like their new menu items and commissions a market survey to answer the question. A radio station tests a new format by gathering some of its listeners and asking them to rate a list of songs being considered for the playlist.

Each of these examples represents a form of research interview, i.e., interviews intended to gather data that can be used to draw conclusions and/or make decisions about some target audience. In other words, research interviews are a systematic form of audience analysis. The interviewer talks with people from a target audience for the purpose of understanding that group. While a number of different techniques can be used for this purpose, most fall within two distinct categories: (1) public opinion surveys and (2) convenience/intercept surveys.

Public Opinion Surveys

The use of surveys and polls to measure public opinion began in the late 1930s, a development that coincided with a nationwide increase in the use of scientific approaches on communication variables. By the 1970s, public opinion research was a staple tool of consumer market researchers and political campaigns. By the 1980s, it was a standard tool for media outlets who were covering political campaigns and other public opinion issues (Taylor, 1990, p. 261).

Although most people use the terms interchangeably, there is a technical difference between a poll and a survey. A poll is a relatively short questionnaire with a descriptive purpose; its intent is to describe attitudes and behavioral intentions, and it does so with relatively simple questions. A survey uses a longer questionnaire and seeks more in-depth information about voter attitudes and predispositions. Both approaches fall within a broader category of **cross-sectional** research, i.e., research that analyzes a cross-section of a population to study at *a given time* (Stacks & Hocking, 1998, p. 237). Though the term "pollster" is often synonymous with those who conduct polls for political campaigns, it is used here in the broader terms of anyone conducting survey interviews.

The Polling Process

Questionnaire Development

The process of political polling begins with the questionnaire development. Typically, the researcher and the client discuss the research questions and the issues and circumstances surrounding that issue. As a result of the discussion, the researcher develops a first draft of a questionnaire to test these relevant factors. This is followed by subsequent rounds of discussions and revisions until all parties are satisfied that the questionnaire will provide the information needed for campaign decisions. A researcher using surveys would use previous research and other printed sources to answer the same question.

Designing questionnaires requires that the pollster be careful in constructing and writing the questions. Questions need to be direct, clear, and unambiguous. Furthermore, unless there is a specific reason for testing audience biases, most questions should be phrased in an unbiased manner. This can be difficult, because many clients prefer only to phrase questions from their own perspective. Still, the researcher will be of little use to the client if the survey does not provide it with unbiased information.

Most quantitative researchers use some version of forced-choice options or Likert-type questions. Forced-choice are closed-ended questions that limit the respondents' options (e.g., "Yes" or "No."). Likert-type questions expand the options slightly, to cover a broader continuum of responses, but still offer limited options (e.g., "strongly agree, somewhat agree, undecided, somewhat disagree, or strongly disagree").

Sometimes, other techniques have been attempted, but with limited success. Some researchers have used a "Feeling Thermometer" in which respondents rate individuals or products on a scale ranging from 0 to 100. Generally, most individuals have trouble making such fine distinctions; in fact, research indicates that voters make their most optimum distinctions about candidates and issues if the options are limited to no more than nine intervals (Miller, 1956). Furthermore, some voters interpret the 0 to 100 scale differently; some view it as if it is an academic scale. As a result, the hypothetical mid-point of "50" (which should be an average rating) is considered a "failing grade" by some respondents.

Zaller and Feldman (1992) oppose both the Likert-type scales and alternative scales such as the Feeling Thermometer, arguing that attitudes on issues are particularly difficult to measure as precise preference points because such positions may be based on a number of considerations that might impel them toward various positions on that issue. These "considerations" are underlying arguments that are recalled from memory and may vary with time (Chong, 1993). Zaller (1990) also argues that responses to survey questions are influenced by the political sophistication of the respondents; when counted though, the responses of uninformed voters are weighted equally with those of political sophisticates. The only way to counter this, they argue, is to measure attitudes in terms of a range of possible responses that are either acceptable or not acceptable to the voter.

Several different types of survey questions are often employed. These include (1) the greeting, (2) the screen, (3) attitude questions, (3) projective questions, (4) open-ended questions, and (5) demographic questions.

The greeting is a brief statement that introduces the interviewer to the telephone respondent and leads to a question about their interest in responding to the survey. Typically, the greeting starts with (1) an introduction ("Hello, I'm John Doe") and (2) identification of the research unit ("and I'm calling from JLP Research"). As Stacks and Hocking (1998) noted, these two elements serve "as a credibility inducement and provides indication that the project is important" (p. 251).

Next is an explanation of the project ("We're conducting a public opinion survey on issues facing the state") coupled with a request for assistance ("Would you mind taking a few minutes to answer a few questions?"). Typically, before the person can answer "yes" or "no," an additional *inducement* is provided by mentioning (1) the short amount of time involved and (2) the importance of the call ("The questions will only take about five minutes, and your answers could help us understand the state better").

If the respondent agrees to participate, the next job for the interviewer is to determine if they qualify for the survey. This qualification element is operationally defined by the survey's screen, a question which verifies their eligibility. For marketing surveys, the screen often involves demographic descriptors of the target audience ("Are you at least 35 years old?"). For political polls, the minimal and most basic screening question is one which asks whether or not the respondent is a registered voter; if not, the phone call should be terminated.

Most pollsters add additional screens depending upon the nature and circumstances of the campaign. For example, political polls might include questions regarding whether the respondent plans to vote in the election, and the likelihood of their doing so. Due to the possibility of embarrassing someone who does not vote, these questions are often asked in a manner which makes it socially acceptable to say they will not vote. Thus, instead of asking, "Are you going to vote in the up-coming election," the screen is instead phrased, "As you know, the state will be holding its election for statewide offices in November. Do you currently plan to vote in that election, or do you expect that you will be unable to vote in that election?" If the person qualifies under the screen, and agrees to participate, then the rest of the survey can be completed.

The research questions comprise the bulk of the questionnaire. These are primarily closed-ended questions that represent those items to which the researcher is seeking answers.

From a structural view, the first questions on the survey should be relatively easy. If the respondents can answer the first few questions easily, then it tends to create inter-est in the survey and increases the chances that they will participate for the duration of the questionnaire (Wimmer & Dominick, 1994, p. 119). Conversely, if the survey starts off with questions that the respondent feels they cannot answer, they will often hang up.

Attitude questions are a specific form of research question that are often used in surveys. Attitude questions are intended to measure public reactions to statements that represent various views on public opinion. Although the formats for these questions vary considerably, the most common techniques for measuring issues are in terms of (1) support or opposition of an issue, (2) agreement or disagreement with a position, or (3) forced choices of major positions.

Support/opposition questions generally use a Likert-type approach such as, "Do you strongly support, somewhat support, somewhat oppose, or strongly oppose requiring a three-day waiting period for the purchase of handguns?"

Agree/disagree approaches identify an expressed position related to an issue to see if the public agrees with it. Again, it typically uses a Likert-type scaling technique, such as asking respondents if they "strongly agree, somewhat agree, somewhat disagree, or strongly disagree" with the statement: "Any attempt to limit handgun purchases inter-feres with the public's constitutional right to bear arms."

Forced-choice issue questions offer a variety of positions and ask the respondents to pick the one that is most closely aligned with their own. An example: "Do you support efforts to require a three-day waiting period for the purchase of handguns, or do you consider such efforts an infringement on the public's right to bear arms?"

Controversial issues are often difficult to test, particularly when it comes to measuring minority opinions. Noelle-Neuman's (1974) "spiral of silence" model hypothesized that people whose opinions are not congruent with the national majority may be reluctant to discuss those issues in public. Research has indicated that the premise is particularly true when talking with a stranger, such as someone conducting an interview over the telephone (Salmon & Neuwirth, 1990).

Projective questions are short "what-if" scenarios that are intended to give them some idea as to what reactions specific messages might create with the audience. Although this form of question is frequently used in public opinion research, the validity of its use is highly questionable. The respondents often don't know exactly how to answer such questions and provide a response only because they are required to do so. The past is more knowable than the future, and people are more likely to make judgments on retrospective information than prospective ones.

One problem with most survey questions is that the respondents can only answer what is asked. Because most questions use closed (or forced) options, the pollster has no way of analyzing what other issues or factors may be operating within the electorate. One way to counter this problem is with the use of open-ended questions that allow the respondents to express an opinion with no guidance from the pollster. The most common question to use this approach is the "Most Important Factor" question ("Overall, what do you think is the most important factor you consider when deciding to choose a restaurant for dining out?"). The open-ended format of this question allows for a range of responses that can go beyond the scope of the closed-ended questions in the survey.

Open-ended questions are also used as "probes" when more information is needed to explain responses to a forced-choice question. For example, market surveys may ask people to say whether their next automotive purchase is likely to be a car, an SUV, or a truck. When the respondent makes a choice, the interviewer may then probe with an open-ended question, "Why do you prefer an SUV?" to get more insight into the public's explanation for their decisions. The disadvantages of open-ended questions are that they generally provide less information than can be developed from structured questions, and the results are less reliable in assessing the impact of attitudes on campaigns (Rahn, Krosnik, & Breuning, 1994). Miller and Shanks (1996, p. 503) noted that structured survey questions provide a clearer picture of the sources of voters' preferences because they are not hampered by the ambiguity of open-ended questions and uneven or incomplete data that often results.

Demographic questions measure attributes of the respondents such as age, income, gender, and ethnic background. They are usually delayed until the end of the survey, and they serve three purposes. First, they allow the pollster to stratify the sample and verify its representativeness. Second, cross-tabulations of the results, by these demographic questions, are the primary statistical analysis for the survey. Third, the demographic breakdowns provide crucial targeting information.

Sampling

The accuracy of any poll or survey is dependent upon the extent to which the sample chosen by the pollster represents the actual voting turnout on election day. For that reason, the use of some means of random sampling is essential, and a variety of techniques have been developed for that purpose.

Random digit dialing involves the use of a computer to dial numbers using a random process. Researchers who lack a computer with this capability can substitute a *random numbers table* and achieve the same effect. This process has the advantages that the researcher cannot deliberately bias the sample in any manner and that households with unlisted numbers can be included in the sample. Its disadvantage is that many middle- and upper-income homes now have multiple phone lines coming into the house, while lower-income households only have one; this creates a risk of biasing the results against lower-income households.

Another common approach is the use of *computer-generated lists* of randomly selected telephone numbers. To increase efficiency, lists generated with this approach use some multiple (usually ranging from 10 to 20) of the projected sample size as the basis for the list generation. Thus, if the target sample size for the survey is 600 registered voters, then a list of 6,000 randomly selected telephone numbers (if a multiple of 10 is used) is generated. The multiple numbers allow for efficient calling, because many of the calls cannot be completed for a variety of reasons (no answers, phone machines answering, disconnected numbers, etc.). The disadvantage of this approach is that it does not reach unlisted numbers, creating a potential bias against lower-income households.

The most common approach, regardless of how the list is generated, is to use a process called *stratified random sampling*. In this approach, the pollster pre-determines how many people he/she needs to call in one identified demographic category (usually geography), and then respondents are randomly selected from within each of the subgroups of that category. This approach is the preferred choice of most professional pollsters because it guarantees that certain groups within the population will be sampled. Or, as Hansen et al. (1998, p. 241) noted, stratified random sampling "allows for the appropriate representation of different groups in the population" to ensure that the sample represents the population under study.

A variation of the stratified random sample is *cluster sampling*. Cluster sampling involves the development of computer-generated lists of "clusters" of people with similar demographic characteristics based on the stratification criteria. Thus, a pollster conducting a statewide survey of 600 registered voters would create a computer-generated list of 600 clusters of voters (with 10 to 25 names matched with phones per cluster), with those clusters corresponding to the stratification criteria of the survey. One name from each cluster would be interviewed for the survey.

Interviewing

Most political polling involves the use of telephone interviews and professional callers, and it is a crucial part of the process. Volunteers almost always bias the results in favor of the candidate they prefer, even when trained to do otherwise. Professional interviewers know to read the questions as they are written, know when to repeat questions that are not understood, and know to refrain from commenting or reacting nonverbally. Even then, there will be problems, because not everyone reached by telephone will agree to respond to the survey. Yu and Cooper (1983), in an analysis of surveys reported in academic journals, found that the average completion rate for telephone surveys was about 72 percent. Phone banks that specialize in political contacts often reach an 80 percent rate when dealing with lists of registered voters, but their success can drop if a general population list is used. The completion rate of the interview goes down as the length of the interview increases. Wimmer and Dominick (1994, p. 121) recommend that telephone surveys be limited to a maximum of 20 minutes in length, since there is a significant increase in the break-off rate (hang-ups) when interviews exceed that length. Electronic surveys have to be even shorter, since it is easier for people to hang up on a machine than on another human (Havice, 1990).

What Can Go Wrong?

Any number of things can confound the results and lead to unreliable poll numbers. The most common problems are (1) sampling errors, (2) question framing, (3) ordering effects, and (4) interviewer effects.

Sampling errors are perhaps the most common source of mistakes. If the sample in the survey is not representative of those voters **who will vote on election day**, then the survey is likely to be inaccurate. That can easily occur. In some instances, the respondent selection process was not truly random, leading to skewed results. Other times, the pollster may use a stratified random sample based on turnout patterns of previous elections; if those turnout patterns are altered in future elections, the survey will be inaccurate. And, the sample can be affected by the use of an improper screening questions. Some media surveys, for example, screen only for "head of household." Most political pollsters who are involved in the campaign believe that a more accurate sample is generated by what is known as a "tight" screen in which only "probable voters" are selected for the survey. Most market surveys would want to screen for the income level and demographic factors that reflect the target audience.

Question framing is another major factor that can affect the results of the survey (Hansen et al., 1998, pp. 244–246). Ideally, questions used in the survey should be clear and simple, requiring a minimum amount of effort on the respondent's part. Lengthy questions create confusion, with the respondent often forgetting the first few options by the time the last ones have been read (Wimmer & Dominick, 1994, p. 109).

Biased questions use words and phrases that have positive or negative connotations to the voters. For example, consider the question: "Do you favor or oppose spending more money on welfare?" That question often receives a majority of negative responses, due to the negative connotations that some people have of the word "welfare." Conversely, if that question is phrased with a positive connotation ("Do you favor or oppose providing more money to the poor and needy?"), it is likely to generate an undue number of positive responses. The goal of the pollster is to use neutral language to obtain an unbiased response ("Do you favor or oppose increasing the budget for health and human services").

Another question format that can influence survey results is the use of *leading questions*. Some leading questions may be based on a defined frame of reference, a process that will change the response. Kinder and Sanders (1990) noted that, in political polls, a person's response to a candidate can be altered by manipulating the priority that the respondents give to different arguments or considerations. Such processes frame political issues to the advantage of the candidate, creating favorable poll results that might be used in efforts to mobilize current constituencies (Jacobs & Shapiro, 1994). A similar bias can be created for any product or service, with the researcher framing the question in such a manner that it leads the respondent in a specific attitudinal direction.

In addition, *double-barreled questions* should be avoided. Double-barreled questions refers to questions that contain two parts, creating a situation in which the voter may respond to either or both ideas separately. For example, a question such as "Do you support the president's efforts at gun control and his attempts to fight crime?" is double-barreled. The voter might have different reactions to the president's efforts on gun control and his anti-crime program, even if one is part of the other. The result could be poll numbers that reflect some unknown combination of the two attitudes.

A third factor that can influence survey responses is an *ordering effect*. Ordering effects refer to the impact of question placement on voter response. As Hansen et al. (1998) noted, "where a question is placed both in a numerical sense but also in a contextual way, can impact on the meaning of the question and the results" (p. 246). Wimmer and Dominick (1994, p. 120) called this problem "question contamination," in reference to the impact that the presence of one question might have on subsequent questions. For example, suppose a survey included a series of questions aimed at voter attitudes toward education; if those questions were followed by another asking them which issue they considered to be the most important problem facing the state, an undue number would likely answer "education." Another example of an ordering effect was reported by Morrison (1986) in his study of public attitudes toward the BBC, in which response differences were attributable to the ordinal placement of the questions. As noted earlier, favorability ratings and test ballots are typically placed in an early ordering position on the questionnaire, to avoid the impact of any other questions on those results. Conversely, demographic data and personal/sensitive questions are generally placed near the end of the questionnaire; this allows time for the interviewer to establish a rapport with the respondent, and the other responses have already been obtained should the respondent choose not to answer those questions.

Interview effects refers to those responses that are produced as a result of the behaviors of the interviewer. Research has indicated that face-to-face interviews can be influenced by the type of clothing worn by the interviewer (Hickson & Stacks, 1992; McPeek & Edwards, 1975), and any other number of nonverbal cues (e.g., nodding, smiling, tone of voice) can influence responses.

Most market and political surveys are conducted by telephone. While telephone interviewing does not eliminate all interview effects, it does eliminate those that are related to the personal appearance of the interviewer. Additional control can be obtained by using professional interviewers who are not connected to the campaign. Preferably, the telephone personnel who are actually conducting the survey should not even be aware of which candidate is paying for the survey, thus limiting their ability to influence the results. Another technique for controlling this problem is to use callers who do not know any of the candidates. This is frequently done by subcontracting the phone calls to a phone bank in a state different from that of the campaign.

One common demonstration of how interviewer effects alter a poll can be seen with the use of "volunteer" polling. To save money, a new business may use their own staff to conduct their own in-house polling for the campaign. This approach invariably over-inflates support for that product or service. Even if extensive training is conducted for each worker, it is still impossible to eliminate all of the subtle cues that they will give to respondents. Consequently, the survey results will be altered.

Intercept Interviewing

One form of research interview that many people have experienced is the *intercept*. In this approach, the interviewer approaches people in a public area and asks them to participate in a research interview. Intercept interviews have several advantages. The major one is cost; intercept interviews offer a low-cost means of data gathering. The second major advantage is interviewer control (Hornik & Ellis, 1988). Conducting the interview in person rather than over the phone offers the interviewer more control. That control also increases flexibility, allowing the interview to incorporate experiments (such as "taste tests") into the research. There are, however, some obvious disadvantages. The first is the possibility of haphazard sampling (Hornik & Ellis, 1988), since selection of whom to interview is often the decision of the individual interviewer. Even if this is controlled, however, non-sampling errors are still major problems (Bush & Hair, 1985). Even though the intercept provides more interview control on the part of the interviewer, that is an advantage only if the researcher is doing their own interviewing. If professional interviewers are hired, the interviewer has less control on the potential impact of interviewer effects. Finally, intercept interviews are susceptible to high rates of non-response. Gates and Solomon (1982) estimated that 44 percent of all those approached refuse to participate in intercept interviews.

Mall Intercepts

The most common commercial form of an intercept interview is the **point-of-purchase** or **mall intercept** interview (Sudman, 1980; Gates & Solomon, 1982; Bush & Hair, 1985).

The name is derived from the fact that a number of research companies have offices located in major consumer malls. Their staff will conduct interviews with consumers at the mall, often testing products offered by one of the mall's retail outlets. Such interviews are used to gather data on consumers that include food products, tourism, and a variety of other products and services (e.g., Litvin & Kar, 2001; McCullum & Achterberg, 1997; Robinson, Smith, Murray, & Ennis, 2002). Intercepts have also been used occasionally in academic research, studying topics such as risk for HIV (Fernandez-Esquer & Krepcho,1997) and other sexually transmitted diseases (Baseman & Ross, 1999). Furthermore, they have become international in nature, with researchers in other countries employing the technique (Jaffe, Pasternak, & Grifel, 1983).

Mall intercepts have become one of the most popular forms of research interviews. Schleifer (1986) once reported that individuals reported that 33 percent of all American households had participated in a mall intercept—the most frequent form of research participation accounted for in the study. And, even with its disadvantages, it still produces better research data than comparable efforts to gather the information over the Internet (Litvin & Kar, 2001).

Exit Polling

Another form of intercept interviews, one frequently used by media outlets during political campaigns, is **exit polling**. Exit polling is sometimes used by media outlets as a means of making early projections about the winners of an election (Grossman, 2000). Exit polls consist of interviews that are conducted on site, on the day of the election, with voters as they leave the voting booth. The purpose of the interview is to identify (1) for whom they voted and (2) what factors influenced their voting decision. This data can be very useful to media outlets who are covering the election. It allows them to both project winners before the voting is completed and to provide some type of insight as to why one candidate won and another loss. Media outlets use it to shape election night coverage and as a means of managing technical resources.

Individuals who do exit interviews must be highly adept at (1) approaching strangers in a public environment, (2) quickly establishing rapport, and (3) asking political questions without offending the interviewee. Most interviews for exit polls are relatively short. The questionnaire is usually limited to one typed page, so that it fits easily on a single clipboard. The responses are recorded directly onto the questionnaire, so that results for each individual interview can be quickly recorded and added to the total database. Furthermore, research has indicated that the response rate for an exit interview increases if the interviewee is provided with a self-administered "secret ballot" questionnaire rather than having to answer questions in a face-to-face interview (Bishop & Fisher, 1995).

Some critics have argued that exit polls not only project winners, but they have the potential to actually influence the outcome of an election. In an ever-increasing effort to provide early election results, some media outlets use data from exit polls conducted early in the day to make projections about the entire election (Milavsky, 1985). The problem has been intensified by the presence of the Internet, through which the results of exit polls can be released while the election is still in process (Ledbetter, 2000). Critics have charged that such early projections may discourage supporters of the losing candidate who have yet to vote; assuming their candidate has already lost, they may simply not bother to vote. Such a scenario is potentially serious in presidential elections, where East Coast states may close their polling places hours before those on the West Coast. The problem has caused some to question the use of early exit polls to project elections (Thompson, 2004). The debate on this issue became a full-blown controversy in 1980 when Ronald Reagan claimed a landslide victory over Jimmy Carter (Grossman, 2000). Reagan's lead was so large that the national television networks projected Reagan's victory (and Carter conceded defeat) before the polls closed in the West. The same scenario was repeated in 1984 when the networks declared Reagan the winner over Walter Mondale, again before the polls closed in the Western states.

Granted, the possibility of a drop in turnout would not have altered the outcome in either of those elections. What concerns critics, however, is the possibility that it could influence other local elections. In particular, research has indicated that a drop in turnout ranging from 1 percent to 5 percent can occur (Sudman, 1986). Further, the dropoff is more likely to occur with voters who are Democrats; still, the resulting dropoff has a minimal effect on actual election outcomes (Citrin, Schickler, & Sides, 2003).

Another problem with early exit polls is that they can be inaccurate. Individuals who vote early in the day often represent different demographic and income groups as compared to those who vote later in the day; thus, exit polls based on interviews with early voters may not be representative of the entire universe of voters (Busch & Lieske, 1985). Indeed, the use of early exit polls to project winners has produced a number of embarrassing incidents for media outlets. The most famous, perhaps, are the mistakes made by the national television networks in projecting Al Gore as the winner of the presidential campaign in Florida in 2000 (Abramowitz, 2001). All of the major networks made the same mistake, which was an understandable problem when you realize that they were all sharing data from the same research organization—a joint effort known as the Voter News Network (Buell, 2001). Still, while the 2000 election may be the most famous exit poll blunder, it is far from the only one in American history. For example, in the 1989 gubernatorial campaign in Virginia, exit polling predicted that Gov. Douglas Wilder would win re-election by a ten-point margin—a number the state's media proudly touted; Wilder did win, but by a razor-thin margin of .2 percentage points (.002) (Traugott & Price, 1992).

Convenience Interviews

A variation of the intercept interview is the convenience interview. In this approach, the researcher identifies a group of people who will be gathered at one location and asks each of them to respond to the questionnaire. The most common use of this technique is in the academic setting. University professors frequently ask their students to help them with a research project by responding to a questionnaire. But a number of other research situations can find the technique useful. For example, an organization that has noticed a decrease in member satisfaction may use a meeting of that organization as a chance to measure satisfaction levels. A fast-food restaurant may ask its customers to give their opinion of a new menu item. Thus, the convenience interview may be used in a quantitative research model whenever a group that would make for an appropriate sample is gathered in one place.

Mystery Shoppers

Another variation of the intercept interview is the **mystery shopper**. The mystery shopper is something of a reverse intercept. Instead of selecting a location and interviewing those who approach the location, the mystery shopper visits the store being tested to see how sales personnel handle their interviews with customers (Lipke, 2000). In that sense, the mystery shopper is essentially an interview evaluator whose job is to assess employee behavior toward customers (Helliker, 1994). Mystery shoppers are used by a variety of retail outlets, including fast-food restaurants, banks, and the travel industry (Hudson, Snaith, Miller, & Hudson, 2001; Steinhauer, 1998). Several research companies have been established that focus primarily on the use of mystery shoppers (McDonough, 2004; Greco, 1994; Helliker, 1994; Brokaw, 1991).

In many cases, the use of mystery shoppers is an ongoing program that provides a company with a way of measuring customer service. Many organizations use the compiled responses as a way to reward employees and improve service. The shoppers themselves typically undergo a two- to three-hour training session before working their first assignment. Details of the training will vary, depending on the nature of the product or service, but two general rules typically apply. First, the shopper must limit their comments to things that they can observe. A mystery shopper at a restaurant, for example, could observe and report on the behavior of the servers and the quality of the food, but they would probably not be in a position to see what actually occurred in the kitchen during the preparation of the food. Second, the shopper must record their observations on the provided report form surreptitiously, so that the employees of the establishment won't realize that they're being evaluated. Should an employee ever spot a mystery shopper, they will give the shopper special treatment and thus destroy the intent of the research project.

The Ethics of Audience Analysis

Polls and surveys are essentially a sophisticated form of audience analysis—a way of measuring and identifying the public's perception toward any number of individuals, issues, products, and/or services. Still, several observers have criticized the polling process, particularly in terms of political polling, because of its potential impact on elections.

Many of the major critics of quantitative research do not attack its methodology, but rather its role in political campaigns and market research. Specifically, some people argue that such research has too much impact on campaigns and candidates. Taylor (1990) argues that polling has had a negative impact on the political process because "politicians have become increasingly dependent on the technologies of political market research . . . to guard against ever uttering an unpopular word in public" (p. 218). Taylor quotes Democratic pollster Stan Greenberg as saying, "The dialogue has become more sterile because the campaign ads are designed to repeat back to voters what they already know."

Such attitudes are not particularly new. Former President Harry Truman similarly lambasted the use of polls during his term in office:

> How far would Moses have gone if he had taken a poll in Egypt? What would Jesus Christ have preached if he had taken a poll in the land of Israel? What would have happened to the Reformation if Martin Luther had taken a poll? It isn't polls or public opinion of the moment that count. It's right and wrong and leadership.

Ryan and Wentworth (1999) argue that polling has had a negative impact on news coverage of political campaigns, with the media "focusing more on who is ahead and who is behind than the substance of political issues" (p. 81). One reason for this approach is that many reporters are not well informed on the issues themselves, and coverage of poll results is easier to do. Others argue that the public is also more interested in the ups and downs of political careers, or relative changes in candidate positions in the polls, than they are in specific issues. Regardless of the cause, though, today's media (newspapers and TV) do indeed have a strong focus on "horse-race" coverage. The trend has grown to such an extent that many media outlets now conduct their own surveys, in essence creating their own news to cover.

Former Democratic pollster Paul Maslin believes polling has contributed to the rise in negative campaigns. As quoted by Taylor (1990, p. 218), Maslin said, "It's like taking a shot, because you can see the way they [negative ads] move the numbers. The techniques have gotten so refined, the weapons so powerful, that if you don't use them, you'll lose."

Maslin's comment seems to echo the pragmatics of polling in modern political contests. They will be used. The ethical issue to be addressed is not whether to use them, but merely how to use them in an ethical manner. Polling is merely a sophisticated form of audience analysis—a basic skill taught in nearly all communication courses. If audience analysis is important for other forms of communication, then why not for political communication? Political candidates have a right and, ideally, an obligation to consider the beliefs and values of the people they represent. In a time when a single individual may represent thousands or millions of people, polling provides a means of assessing those beliefs and values.

One of the authors once met a local political activist who opened the conversation by saying, "I don't believe in polls." She then recounted a local tax referendum in which she had been involved, noting that she campaigned in the wealthy section of the community by talking of how the area would benefit from a better school system. When campaigning in the low-income areas, her message focused on the structure of the tax—one that would be paid by wealthy families. She summed up her story by smiling and saying, "We passed that without ever doing any polling."

No polling? Perhaps. But she did engage in audience analysis. With a small local electorate, one with which she was highly familiar, she was probably correct to reject formal polling. Her narrative indicated, however, that she did adjust her message to different target audiences based on her perceptions of those two audiences. Had she done a poll, the pollster would probably have recommended the same strategic approach that she used. She didn't need a poll, though, because she already understood her electorate well.

Candidates in major campaigns lack that capability. A person from a wealthy family from Texas may run for President, but it is unrealistic to expect that person to understand the problems faced by Hispanics in California, low-income white voters in Kentucky, or African American voters in Mississippi. Polling provides a way for the candidate to analyze large and diverse audiences within the electorate. Market researchers seem to receive less criticism, but they face some of the same issues, i.e., the extent to which they use market research information to influence cultural and consumer responses.

Pseudo-Polling

One particular form of polling that is sometimes used in an unethical manner are those that are known as "pseudo-polls" or "push polls." Push polls are not polls at all, but merely a questionable form of phone bank persuasion. This process takes advantage of the public's familiarity with the polling process by calling a respondent under the pretense of conducting a poll. Once the respondent agrees to participate, they are then read a list of questions that are designed to imply negative information about an opponent. Thus, instead of trying to elicit unbiased information from the respondents, the survey is merely used as a form of negative or smear campaigning.

A typical push poll was used in the 2000 South Carolina Republican presidential primary by George W. Bush. A phone bank in Houston, Texas, called Voter Consumer

Research called South Carolina voters and asked a series of carefully scripted questions. The initial questions were simple and straightforward—Will you participate in the Republican primary? How much attention have you paid to the Republican race? Are things better or worse in the country?—but the later questions were used as a means of providing negative information on Bush's competitor Sen. John McCain. The questions were not really questions, but merely messages disguised with a question format that attacked McCain's position on tax cuts, told the voters McCain had been reprimanded by the Senate Ethics Committee, and argued that his campaign finance plan would give more influence to unions and to the press (Yardley, 2000).

An earlier example emerged in a 1996 issue debate in Texas over the tobacco issue. A tobacco company (Phillip Morris) hired Public Opinion Strategies, an Alexandria, Virginia firm, to develop a push poll against the state's attorney general, Dan Morales, who was preparing to file a lawsuit against several tobacco companies. When the questionnaire was subsequently made available to Morales, the script "included more than a dozen negative statements about Mr. Morales record as attorney general," and the resulting information was used in an attempt to get him to drop the lawsuit (Van Natta, 2000).

Push polls are rarely used in market research, but some similar polling techniques used by market researchers are of dubious research value. One approach, for example, is to use a pseudo-poll for the purpose of identifying potential clients rather than to gain research information. Typical of this approach would be a market "survey" on household energy uses that includes questions regarding whether the respondents thought their utility bills were too high. Those who answer "yes" might find themselves contacted soon afterwards by a company offering to sell a product designed to reduce energy costs.

While push polls are generally identified with political communication, there are some parallels to market research. The most common form in the market arena is the use of a pseudo-poll for purposes of consumer targeting rather than to gather research information. For example, a household may be contacted one week and asked to respond to a survey about water quality issues. The survey might include some questions that ask them to rate the quality of their household drinking water. Those who give their water a negative rating might be called a week later by another person—someone trying to sell them a water purification system. Such a "coincidence" usually means that the real purpose of the first survey was to identify potential customers—not gather information.

Summary

Polling and survey research has become an integral part of modern public opinion research—both in market research and in the political arena. In its most essential form, polling is merely an extended form of audience analysis, providing the communicator with an understanding of the attitudes and values of the audience to be addressed. While its reliability rests on its statistical process, the validity of the process often lies within the interviews that are used to collect survey data. Good questions and good interviewers lead to good research results. Poor questions and biased interviewers, though, lead to unreliable and invalid research data.

Intercept interviews are another form of quantitative research interviews. These include point-of-purchase, or mall intercept interviews, exit interviews, convenience interviews, and mystery shoppers. Intercept interviews offer a low-cost means of conducting quantitative research, but they are sometimes susceptible to other errors.

The ethical questions surrounding quantitative research interviews are serious issues that must be addressed for each research project. The problem is intensified by those who use push polls for unethical purposes. It is also complicated by the frequent use by the media of pseudo-polls, which can cause the public to question the legitimacy of true research interviews.

Discussion Questions

1. The next time you get called and asked to participate in a public opinion survey, agree to do so. How do the questions progress? Is the order important? What options for answering were offered? Did you feel that they asked any questions that you did not understand? Did you feel that you knew the purpose of the survey once it was over?
2. Search your local newspaper for a published public opinion poll or survey. Analyze the quality of that poll based on the information provided in the story. What was its sample size? The margin of error? What screen was used to ensure that the poll was based on interviews with only those individuals who were appropriate for the study?

Please see the companion website for additional resources at [www.routledge.com/cw/ amsbary].

References

Abramowitz, A. (2001). The time for change model and the 2000 election. *American Politics Research, 29*, 279–262.

Baseman, J., & Ross, M. (1999). Sale of sex for drugs and drugs for sex: An economic context of sexual risk behavior for STDs. *Sexually Transmitted Diseases, 26*(8), 444–449.

Bishop, G. F., & Fisher, B. S. (1995). Secret ballots and self-reports in an exit-poll experiment. *Public Opinion Quarterly, 59*, 568–588.

Brokaw, L. (1991). The mystery-shopper questionnaire. *Inc., 13*(6), 94–96.

Buell, J. (2001). Media myopia and the future of democratic politics. *Humanist, 61*(1), 35–36.

Busch, R. J., & Lieske, J. A. (1985). Does time of voting affect exit poll results? *Public Opinion Quarterly, 49*, 94–104.

Bush, A. J., & Hair Jr., J. F. (1985). An assessment of the mall intercept as a data collection method. *Journal of Marketing Research, 12*, 158–167.

Chong, D. (1993). How people think, reason, and feel about rights and liberties. *American Journal of Political Science, 37*, 867–899.

Citrin, J., Schickler, E., & Sides, J. (2003). What if everyone voted? Simulating the impact of increased turnout in Senate elections. *American Journal of Political Science, 47*, 75–90.

Fernandez-Esquer, M. E., & Krepcho, M. A. (1997). Predictors of condom use among African American males at high risk for HIV. *Journal of Applied Social Psychology, 27*, 58–74.

Gates, R., & Solomon, P. J. (1982). Research using the mall intercept: State of the art. *Journal of Advertising Research, 22*, 43–50.

Greco, S. (1994). Keeping tabs on rivals. *Inc., 16*(9), 118.

Grossman, L. K. (2000). Exit polls, academy awards, and presidential elections. *Columbia Journalism Review, 39*(1), 70–71.

Hansen, A., Cottle, S., Negrine, R. E., & Newbold, C. (1998). *Mass communication research methods.* Washington Square, NY: New York University Press.

Havice, M. J. (1990). Measuring nonresponse and refusals to an electronic telephone survey. *Journalism Quarterly, 67*, 521–530.

Helliker, K. (1994, November 30). Smile: That cranky shopper may be a store spy. *Wall Street Journal, 224*(106), B1.

Hickson, M. L., & Stacks, D. W. (1992). *NVC: Nonverbal communication studies and applications* (3rd ed.). Dubuque, IA: Brown & Benchmark.

Hornik, J., & Ellis, S. (1988). Strategies to secure compliance for a mall intercept interview. *Public Opinion Quarterly, 52*, 539–551.

Hudson, S., Snaith, T., Miller, G. A., & Hudson, P. (2001). Distribution channels in the travel industry: Using mystery shoppers to understand the influence of travel agency recommendations. *Journal of Travel Research, 40*(2), 148–154.

Jacobs, L. R., & Shapiro, R. Y. (1994). Issues, candidate image, and priming: The use of private polls in Kennedy's 1960 presidential campaign. *American Political Science Review, 88*, 527–540.

Jaffe, E. D., Pasternak, H., & Grifel, A. (1983). Response results of lottery buyer behavior surveys: In-home vs. point-of-purchase interviews. *Public Opinion Quarterly, 47*, 419–426.

Kinder, D. R., & Sanders, L. M. (1990). Mimicking political debate with survey questions: The case of white opinion on affirmative action for blacks. *Social Cognition, 8*, 73–103.

Ledbetter, J. (2000). Should voter data be released? New media, old media disagree. *Columbia Journalism Review, 39*(1), 71–72.

Lipke, D. J. (2000). Mystery shoppers. *American Demographics, 22*(12), 41–43.

Litvin, S. W., & Kar, G. H. (2001). E-surveying for tourism research: Legitimate tool or a researcher's fantasy? *Journal of Travel Research, 39*, 308–314.

McCullum, C., & Achterberg, C. L. (1997). Food shopping and label use behavior among high school-aged adolescents. *Adolescence, 32*(125), 181–197.

McDonough, M. (2004). A sneak peek. *ABA Journal, 90*(5), 72.

McPeek, R. W., & Edwards, J. D. (1975). Expectancy disconformation and attitude change. *Journal of Social Psychology, 96*, 193–208.

Milavsky, R. (1985). Early calls of election results and exit polls: Pros, cons, and constitutional considerations. *Public Opinion Quarterly, 49*, 1–18.

Miller, G. A. (1956). The magic number seven, plus or minus two: Some limits on our capacity for processing information. *The Psychological Review, 63*, 81–97.

Miller, W. E., & Shanks, J. M. (1996). *The new American voter.* Cambridge, MA: Harvard University Press.

Morrison, D. E. (1986). *Invisible citizens: British public opinion and the future of broadcasting.* London: John Libbey.

Noelle-Neuman, E. (1974). The spiral of silence. *Journal of Communication, 24*, 43–51.

Rahn, W. M., Krosnik, J. A., & Breuning, M. (1994). Rationalization and derivations processes in survey studies of political candidate evaluation. *American Journal of Political Science, 32*, 582–600.

Robinson, R., Smith, C., Murray, H., & Ennis, J. (2002). Promotion of sustainably produced foods: Customer response in Minnesota grocery stores. *American Journal of Alternative Agriculture, 17*(2), 96–104.

Ryan, J., & Wentworth, W. M. (1999). *Media and society: The production of culture in the mass media.* Boston, MA: Allyn & Bacon.

Salmon, C. T., & Neuwirth, K. (1990). Perceptions of opinion 'climates' and willingness to discuss the issue of abortion. *Journalism Quarterly, 67*, 567–577.

Schleifer, S. (1986). Trends in attitudes toward and participation in survey research. *Public Opinion Quarterly, 50*, 17–26.

Stacks, D. W., & Hocking, J. E. (1998). *Communication research.* New York: Longman.

Steinhauer, J. (1998, February 4). The undercover shoppers. *New York Times, 147*(51058), p. D1.

Sudman, S. (1980). Improving the quality of shopping center sampling. *Journal of Marketing Research, 17*, 423–431.

Sudman, S. (1986). Do exit polls influence voting behavior? *Public Opinion Quarterly, 50*, 331–339.

Taylor, P. (1990). *See how they run: Electing the president in an age of mediaocracy.* New York: Alfred A. Knopf.

Thompson, D. F. (2004). Election time: Normative implications of temporal properties of the electoral process in the United States. *American Political Science Review, 98,* 51–64.

Traugott, M. W., & Price, V. (1992). The polls—a review: Exit polls in the 1989 Virginia gubernatorial race: Where did they go wrong? *Public Opinion Quarterly, 56,* 245–253.

Van Natta, Jr., D. (2000, February 15). Years ago, a Bush adviser helped draft a push poll against a Texas official. *New York Times,* p. A20.

Wimmer, R. D., & Dominick, J. R. (1994). *Mass media research.* Belmont, CA: Wadsworth.

Yardley, J. (2000, February 14). Calls to voters at center stage of G.O.P. race. *New York Times,* p. A1, A16.

Yu, J., & Cooper, H. (1983). A quantitative review of research design effects on response rates to questionnaires. *Journal of Marketing Research, 20,* 36–44.

Zaller, J. (1990). Political awareness, elite opinion leadership, and the mass survey response. *Social Cognition, 8,* 125–153.

Zaller, J., & Feldman, S. (1992). A simple theory of the survey response: Answering questions versus revealing preferences. *American Journal of Political Science, 36,* 579–616.

11

ORAL HISTORY INTERVIEWS

My grandfather used to tell stories of growing up in Oklahoma, losing his parents while he was still a teenager, and taking a stagecoach back to Alabama to live with relatives. Details of those narratives have been largely lost, though, because nobody ever recorded them. Such recollections came naturally to him. He was born in the nineteenth century and grew up in a world without television and radio. He grew up in a narrative tradition in which his family spent their spare time gathered around a fireplace exchanging stories.

That tradition is making a comeback in both the academic and family arenas. Academic disciplines have taken notice of the role of narrative traditions in modern life. The communication field, in particular, has looked at Fisher's narrative paradigm (1984, 1987) as a way of using stories to understand how people explain their lives. Meanwhile, as computers and the Internet have made genealogical information more accessible to family history researchers, an increasing number of genealogists have turned to oral history as a field that can flesh out the details of family traditions. There seems to be few limits to the possibilities. Pulitzer Prize–winning writer Rick Bragg (1997) has argued that every life has a dignity that makes its story worthwhile, regardless of how poor their health or their financial status in life. Best-selling author Studs Terkel agrees; one of his best works, indeed, is an oral history of working people in the U.S. (Terkel, 1997b). That view represents the goal of oral historians who attempt to record a wide range of lifestyles.

The primary research tool for an oral history is the interview. One or more individuals must sit down to record a one-on-one conversation with someone else. For the academic researcher, these conversations serve as primary data to record the history of a person or event. For genealogists, oral history records the traditions of a family by recording the stories of that family. That's why Jerome Bruner (1987) describes oral history as "life as narrative."

Oral history is not a new concept. Historians have used the approach for decades as a means of recording participants' views of historical events. Historian Cornelius Ryan, for example, made a career out of interviewing soldiers who participated in World War II battles and then reported on the war from their view. His resulting books included lengthy analyses of the Normandy Invasion on D-Day (*The Longest Day*, 1959), the Battle for Berlin (*The Last Battle*, 1961), and the ill-fated Allied offensive into The Netherlands (*A Bridge Too Far*, 1974). Similarly, historian Aaron Elson (1994, 1999, 2002; Elston & English, 1998) has done extensive work on oral histories among World War II veterans. Nor is the technique limited to military history, for oral history can provide insight into any number of different historical events. Oral history interviews can be used to study organizational culture, intercultural issues, and an entire host of other topics. Howell Raines (1983), for example, conducted a series of interviews with participants of the civil rights struggle in his recounting of those events. Similarly, oral histories have been used to record memories of former slaves (Hurmence, 1989), military heroes (Smith, Schwarzkopf, & Adams, 2003), World War II (Terkel, 1997a; Hoopes, 2002), the Vietnam War (Terry, 1989), the Great Depression (Terkel, 2000), and the 9/11 tragedy (Fink, 2002). For a lighter perspective, several authors have used the oral history approach to study the history of sports. Ballew (2002) used the oral history technique to look at Major League Baseball during the 1970s, while others have used oral history to study individual baseball teams (Golenbock, 2000a, 2000b; Eisenberg, 2001) and players (Powell, 2000). Oral history has also found some utility in counseling, particularly in the field of marriage counseling (Buehlman, Gottman, & Katz, 1992; Honeycutt, 1999). Furthermore, journalists routinely use oral history to illustrate news stories, supplementing their presentations of facts and figures with the stories of individuals affected by the story.

Public and university libraries have joined the movement, with many creating a wide range of oral history collections devoted to individuals or topics. These archives record oral history as source material for other researchers. The University of California at Berkeley, for example, has an extensive collection of interviews with people who knew and worked with former Chief Justice of the Supreme Court Earl Warren. The University of South Dakota has a collection of more than 5,000 interviews related to the history of Native Americans. Similarly, UCLA has a special collection devoted entirely to oral history. A number of professional organizations have similar collections related to their own fields of interest. The National Air and Space Museum has an oral history collection devoted to space, science, and technology. The Mississippi Humanities Council maintains a collection devoted to the Civil Rights era. The oral history collection of the U.S. Navy is an extensive group of interviews with veterans from all types of naval duty. Such collections serve as primary source material for other historians who are interested in studying such topics.

Oral history is also becoming increasingly popular as a means of recording the local history of a community. Typical of this approach is the work of the Pell City Oral History Committee in Pell City, Alabama. The project, sponsored by the local city government, conducted interviews with 30 older citizens in the community whom they identified as "historical treasures whose stories should be captured for future generations" (Ray, 2003, p. 20A). Interviewees included 94-year-old Jessie Armstrong, who talked about the city's first car and Franklin Roosevelt's 1934 visit to the city on a whistle-stop tour. Completed interviews were being transcribed and published either on CD or in manuscript form and made available to the public through the local library.

What makes modern oral history research different is its emphasis on popular use, i.e., the assumption that non-professional individuals can learn enough of the techniques so that recording their family's own oral traditions will bring them satisfaction. Indeed, oral history research is within the grasp of most people. Even those with little or no training in interviewing can find simple instructions to guide them in constructing an oral history of their own family. Still, even for the amateur, the process is more satisfying if proper procedures are used.

Elements of Oral History

Background Research

As with all other forms of interviewing, research should precede any significant amount of interviewing. Prior to asking any questions, the researcher must seek and discover as much information about the interviewee as possible. One of the authors of this book wrote an oral history on former baseball player Harry "The Hat" Walker (Powell, 2000). Before conducting any interviews, however, the author researched Walker's athletic career. Before any questions were asked, the interviewer knew that Walker was a former National League batting champion, had knocked in the winning run in the 1946 World Series, had a brother who also had a distinguished baseball career, and also had a successful career as a manager in the major leagues.

Such information can be critical in making the interview a success and in helping you get started (Krasner-Khait, 2002). Each research topic becomes a starting point for eliciting more information and for putting the person's story into context. In Walker's case, each reference triggered other memories while providing additional details to the original information. Furthermore, it allows the researcher to correct misinformation that may have become part of the public record. Many published accounts of Walker's game-winning hit in the 1946 World Series mention that he slashed a double to drive in that run. Actually, as he correctly noted, the hit was officially recorded as a single, with him going to second on an unsuccessful defensive throw to second base. A minor detail, perhaps, to most people, but a key point to baseball historians.

For public figures such as professional baseball players, written sources provide a means of doing preliminary research. The interviewer can consult old newspapers, magazines, books, or other publications for information related to the subject. These can then be compiled by topics, with those topics serving as the interview outline. For research into family histories, the interviewee often conducts preliminary interviews with other people, i.e., other family members or friends of the subject ("Has grandma ever told you anything about how her and granddad first met?"). These preliminary interviews can also be used to construct a topic list to guide the interview.

The important guideline here is that the interviewer should not conduct preliminary interviews with the person who is the subject of the research. Any attempt to do so will likely lead to a number of interesting stories, but none that will be recorded. Furthermore, once someone has told the story to the interviewer, they can rarely repeat it with the same enthusiasm and attention to detail that would have been captured in their first interview. Keep their story fresh, letting them tell it to you and to the tape recorder at the same time.

Technical Preparations

The primary tool of the oral historian is the tape recorder (Ives, 1980; Yow, 1994; Zimmerman, 1992). An oral history interview is ruined if the tape recorder doesn't work. It's the interviewer's responsibility to avoid that problem. That can be handled by advanced preparations that cover all of the potential technical disasters that might occur.

Practice with the recorder that you're planning to use. Learn how it operates, how it records, how it stops, and how it erases. The latter is particularly important, since it can prevent you from accidentally erasing hours of hard work.

The quality of the recording will be better if an external microphone is used, either a directional mike placed in front of the interviewee or an omni-directional lapel mike attached to their clothing.

Good batteries are essential. Generally, it's a good rule to put new batteries into the recorder for each major interview. Just in case, though, it's probably still wise to take an extension cord with you.

The tape itself is also important. If audio recording is used, most experts recommend using a high-quality 60-minute cassette tape. Shorter tapes don't have enough time on them for many interviews; longer tapes are more likely to break. Furthermore, be sure to take extra cassettes with you. You can never know how long the interview might last, and other people may happen by who can provide stories of their own. Each individual interview should be kept on its own individual tape. This makes it easier to catalog the collection and reduces the chances of accidentally taping over one interview with another.

The Oral Interview

After the initial round of gathering information and technical preparations, the researcher is ready for the first oral interview with the subject. The key term here is "first" interview, because a successful oral history often involves a series of interviews. The participant will rarely recall all of the key details of a story in one sitting. However, that initial interview should be the most productive of all of the interviews that might be conducted.

The interviewer should use an outline of questions that were prepared in advance. Samples of potential questions are presented elsewhere in this chapter, but each interview will have to have a progression of questions designed for that particular person, preferably with the questions arranged by keyword topics. If the interviewer is familiar with the individual, these keywords should be enough to guide the interview. Thus, the outline of questions should be a flexible guideline that ensures that all major topics are covered. Sometimes, if only one day is available for the major interview, that can be divided into morning and afternoon sessions, with both participants taking a lunch break together.

Don't wear the interviewee out. Plan for a maximum of two hours for each session, with at least one hour of recording time included in that session. Some researchers suggest limiting each session to 90 minutes of recording time.

The success of the oral history interview often hinges on the trust that is developed during the interactions between the interviewer and interviewee (McMahan & Rogers, 1994). McMahan (1989) described the effective oral history interview as one of cooperation and coherence in which the trust between the interviews leads to eliciting coherent narrative information. The process occurs, she said, as "a social event. As such it reflects the social relations of the moment—those between interviewer and interviewee—and those of the larger culture" (p. x). Consequently, like most interviews, the process begins prior to the actual recording of the conversation. The interviewer should chat with the interviewee while setting up the recording equipment and getting prepared for the interview. This offers an opportunity to establish some rapport before the questioning begins.

Once the interview starts, the first questions should be easy, open-ended inquiries that give the other person a chance to talk. The best oral history interviews are really a series of short monologues, rather than a series of questions and answers. The goal of the questions is to trigger a memory that will result in an extended narrative from the interviewee.

That entire process should be recorded. In the past, most such interviews were recorded on audio cassette tapes. These tapes are easily transportable and adaptable to a number of recording systems. More recently, the increased popularity of digital video cameras has led to their increased use for oral history interviews. The video image has the advantage of both recording the person's words while conveying the nonverbal expressions that accompany their stories.

The Written Transcript

In some ways, the term "oral" history is misleading. True, one goal of the research is to get participants to give an oral account of their lives or of some event in which they participated. To have its maximum effectiveness, though, that oral account must be transcribed into a written version. McMahan (1989) notes that the construction of a written text is inherent within the development of an oral history autobiography (p. x). Consequently, after the first interview has been conducted, the interviewer should return to their home or office and transcribe the interview into a written text. Three things are accomplished by doing this. First, it ensures that a written record of the interview is provided. Cassette tapes may be easy to make, but they are still awkward for others to use on an everyday basis. Other family members may become bored having to sit around and listen to a lengthy taped interview, but they would more willingly and more quickly scan a written text of that same interview. Second, the transcription provides the interviewer with an opportunity to review the entire interview. As the transcription is developed, the interviewer can identify those narratives in which more information is needed or in which more clarification is necessary.

The transcription is perhaps the single most time-consuming aspect of oral history research. While voice recognition software has made the job somewhat easier, that technological tool still needs improvements before most people can easily use it for their interviews. Most transcripts, unfortunately, are still done individually. Typically, one hour of tape-recorded interview equals about 50 pages of typed transcript and represents about eight hours of work. Some researchers choose to hire professional dictation stenographers to handle this job. Others only transcribe parts of the tape; they review each tape individually and use the digital counters on their recorders to identify those segments that they wish to transcribe. This latter approach, however, runs the risk of losing some key details that are important to the individual's story.

Back to the Library

Memories are faulty. Sometimes stories get ingrained into a family's narrative history, but they do so with such elaboration that some element of truth has been lost. The author once interviewed a relative of country music legend Hank Williams who recounted how Hank had written one of his hit songs while visiting her. It was a great story, but subsequent research revealed that Williams was not the person who wrote that song. She had confused a hit song that he didn't write with another song with a similar title that never received much radio play. Similarly, Harry Walker recounted a story in which Dizzy Dean struck out one player four times in a single game, with the last strikeout coming after Dizzy knocked down the catcher to keep him from catching a foul pop. When the researcher tracked down the game, though, he discovered that Dizzy did get the final strikeout following two foul balls by the batter, but neither of those fouls were playable by the catcher. Thus, the researcher has a responsibility to verify as much of the information obtained in the interview as possible. Discrepancies can become a topic for subsequent interviews, as the interviewer and interviewee work together to form a coherent account of the person's life.

More Interviews

The process of interview, research, and more interviews is repeated as often as necessary. More interviews provide more information. The questions differ, however. Most of the subsequent interviews focus on providing more details or filling in gaps created by the information in the first interview. As the questions are asked, other memories are frequently triggered that will, in turn, necessitate additional research by the interviewer. This may sometimes trigger entirely new lines of questioning on topics that had not initially been anticipated by the researcher. McMahan (1987) describes this process of exchanging and learning new information as "speech and counter speech," i.e., a give-and-take process in which language is used to elicit the details of a person's life. Similarly, Harris (1985) describes it as a process in which "memory, myth, ideology, language, and historical cognition interact in a dialectical transformation of the word into a historical artifact" (pp. 6–7).

Any discrepancies identified through research should be investigated more thoroughly with more questions that ask for specific details of the event. This process of probing is called **reality monitoring**. Reality monitoring works under the assumption that memories for real experiences are richer in sensory details and with contextual attributes than are memories for imagined events (Johnson & Raye, 1981; Johnson, 1988). Subsequent research on this topic has generally supported this theory (Anderson, 1984; Johnson, Foley, Suengas, & Raye, 1988, McGinnis & Roberts, 1996). The practical application of the research is to probe the topic, particularly those with potential discrepancies, for more details about how the person felt at the time and their memories of the context in which it occurred.

Editing the Narrative

The collection of interviews that comprise the oral history of any one individual will be a hodgepodge of stories that ramble in no particularly sequential order. All of the transcripts should be compiled and then edited into a coherent narrative form. The original transcripts should not be discarded; they should be retained in their original form for reference purposes. But, the final product itself must be an edited version.

The easiest way to do this editing is to order all topics by chronological, spatial, or topical sequence. If the oral history is on the life of an individual, the chronological organizational pattern usually works best. Divide the topics into early years, young adult, career, and elderly years. Under each topic area, appropriate subtopics can be developed. For example, a person's early years might include subtopics related to their parents, siblings, hometown, early schooling, and childhood activities. Each of the interview transcripts is scanned for material that would fall into each category, and then a cut-and-paste editing job is used to organize the various segments. From there, the narrative is edited further to ensure that the story is a coherent one, all the time taking care to tell the story in the words of the interviewee rather than the interviewer. It is, after all, their story—not yours.

Oral History for Academic Research

Oral history is perhaps the world's oldest academic discipline. Its role in society precedes that of a literate society. Before the development of written languages, people maintained their cultural identity through the telling and re-telling of oral histories. Over time, many of these stories became myths or legends that eventually found their way into our written culture. Was there a great flood that once covered massive parts of the earth? That story was apparently part of the oral tradition of several cultures, and it was eventually written down in a few. But verifying its accuracy is difficult, since it existed only as an oral tradition for centuries.

In modern academic communities, oral history first found its home in the discipline of history. Historians found that extensive use of oral history could provide details and insight into an historical event. A written record might provide an objective account of an event, but personal impressions provided an understanding of that event. As mentioned earlier, Cornelius Ryan (1959, 1961, 1974) recorded the oral histories of combat veterans for his historical account of three World War II battles. Similarly, a number of researchers have used oral history methodology to examine historical events related to the civil rights movement of the 1960s. Diane McWhorter (2001) won a Pulitzer Prize for her account of the civil rights battles in Birmingham, Alabama, during the1960s. Culpepper Clark (1995) narrowed his topic to a single event—Governor George Wallace standing in the school-house door at the University of Alabama—and examined it through oral history interviews.

As illustrated by these examples, the most common use of oral history in academic research is to examine one event or topic from the perspective of its participants. From the communication perspective, this line of research is a subcategory of a specific form of communication research—critical events analysis. The focus of critical events analysis is the study of major discrete events that test the relationship between media and politics (Kraus, Davis, Lang, & Lang, 1976). A number of research studies have used the approach, with many looking at high-profile political debates (Kraus, 1962) or provocative events such as the assassination of President John F. Kennedy (Greenberg, 1964; Mendelsohn, 1964) and the attempts on the lives of candidate George Wallace (Steinfatt, Gantz, Siebold, & Miller, 1973) and President Ronald Reagan (Gantz, 1983; Weaver-Lariscy, Sweeney, & Steinfatt, 1984).

Oral history differs from pure critical event analysis by its focus on the interview technique. For purposes of a broad study of a critical event, a variety of research methodologies would be used. Interviews with participants would be one of the methods used, but only one of several. Typically, critical events analysis might also include survey data, analysis of media output, and analysis of general public opinion responses. Oral history is content to offer an in-depth view of the event with one methodology—the in-depth focused interview.

Still, as with any form of interview, advanced preparation is essential. The researcher must become thoroughly familiar with the event before any interviews are conducted. The uninformed interviewer will be dismissed by the participants if a lack of knowledge is demonstrated during the interview. Once the interviewer loses credibility, it can be difficult to re-establish.

Oral History as a Narrative of Family History

Don't let the use of oral history for academic research scare you from using the technique for personal reasons. A nationwide interest in family history research has also led to a wider interest in oral history interviews as a way for an individual to record portions of their family's personal history. The desire to engage in an oral history project immediately shows the subject of your interview that you care about them and their topic (Zimmerman, 1992). This approach provides the individual with a different way of understanding their family's past. It can also fill in gaps that might not be revealed by documents that merely record births, weddings, and deaths. As Linda Spence (1997, pp. 3–4) noted,

> As we move through our lives, we carry with us the stories of our childhood. We may change them, forget or deny them, smile or cry over them, but, like charms or spells, they bring back a sense of who we were and how we came to be the people we've become.

For a really effective family history, rule number one is to start early. Genealogists recommend that the interview should not wait until the last minute or insist that everything be perfect to begin the project (Xiong, 2002). Every day lost is another potential memory that will never be recorded. Start by asking the oldest members of the family—grandparents, great aunts and uncles—to talk about their lives. Family gatherings such as birthdays, holidays, or anniversaries are particularly good times to do the first interviews. Such events trigger a number of memories, and such gatherings typically involve children. Seniors generally find it easier to talk to children than to adults.

A number of published and online guides are available to the novice. Typical of these are some sample questions included within this chapter. The specific questions may vary in detail. Spence (1997), for example, includes nearly 400 possible questions that can be used to trigger a person's memory, but don't feel that you have to record everything in one sitting. That attitude will produce frustration for both the interviewer and the interviewee. Instead, be prepared to conduct at least one more interview using a different topic to prompt more stories.

One option is to schedule your interviews around major topics. In practice, the interviewer will not be able to stick entirely to that schedule. Any question can prompt memories from multiple stages of the interviewee's life. Still, some broad areas can serve as a general outline for the interviews. Spence (1997) recommends organizing the interviews around nine different topics:

1. *Beginnings and childhood.* This starts with having the person list as many names as possible from their family tree, telling what they know about those ancestors. It can move from there to where they were born, their earliest memories, descriptions of their childhood home, pets, games they played, where they started school, weekend activities, holiday rituals, childhood chores, heroes, adults around them, and family rules.

2. *Adolescence.* This is a key phase in identity development, one that many people remember vividly. Set the scene in terms of where they lived and went to school and what they did at school. Remember the activities that made them proud and those that caused them to stumble. What about the person's relationship with their parents during these times? And, what did they do that got them in trouble or involved risky behavior (remember, teenagers do both).

3. *Early adult years.* Those first steps into the real world can be memorable. What were the significant milestones in the person's early career? What was happening with their family during this time? How did their values change during this part of their life?

4. *Marriage.* Not everyone in modern society includes this stage in their own personal life, but marriage still plays a major role in the lives of most people. The key here is getting the individual to talk of how they were attracted to their partner, how they met, and how their courtship progressed. How about details of the wedding? What obstacles did they have to overcome in the early years of the marriage, including those of their careers? And, try to recall some of the good times and bad times of those early years together.

5. *Being a parent.* Children change the dynamics of family life as both parents have to adjust their lives for the new members in the group. Start with the basics—name, date, and place of birth of each child—and move on to the feelings, dreams, and behaviors of the child and those around them. How did they react to parenthood? What memories do they have of the children's childhood? What activities did they share with their children? How did their relationship with the child vary as the child grew older?

6. *Middle adult years.* Spence (1997) notes that one's middle years are those where "we see the results of the time and energy we've given to our family, work, community,

self" (p. 101). This stage in one's life provides an opportunity for assessing everything that came before and preparing for what will come later. What was their family like during this time? What did they do during a typical workday? Who were their friends? What did they do in terms of community involvement? What was the most difficult part of these years? What was the best part?

7. *Being a grandparent.* Grandparents often have special relationships with their grandchildren. Getting grandparents to talk about this stage of their life is usually easy, particularly when they talk about their grandchildren. The interviewer, though, should also get them to talk about their role as grandparents and how they felt about that role.

8. *Later adult years.* Individuals who are in their eighties or nineties can aptly be described as "today's pioneers" (Spence, 1997, p. 119), but their memories are often overlooked. Questions from any previous stage in their life can be used here, but these individuals can also provide insights that younger interviewees don't have. They can compare the modern world with the one in which they were born and lived. They can recall how lifestyles, means of transportation, and our methods of communication have varied. And, they can often speak passionately about changes in values and culture. Each of these ideas provides insights into the person and their times.

9. *Reflections.* Spence (1997) lists this category as a distinctly different topic, but it could also easily fit as a subcategory or topic for "later adult years." It simply refers to a specific type of question in which the interviewee is encouraged to recall critical phases of their life and to make comparisons about their past life and modern life. Is life harder or easier for today's children? What did you learn from life that was important? What were the fears and uncertainties that you had to face? Were there any lost opportunities?

By using this nine-step process, the interviewer—over time and through the use of multiple interviews—will be able to elicit some extended narrative stories that will provide insight into the individual's life. Both the interviewer and the interviewee are likely to enjoy and be surprised by what they discover.

Things to Consider

Oral history interviews have one major weaknesses—reliability. Memories are notoriously faulty. As time passes, people forget some details, others are accentuated, and new—and inaccurate—data may become part of the story as it gets embellished. That's why the interviewer must verify as much as possible. Not only does that increase the accuracy of the final text, but that research can also produce written records that can reinforce or corroborate the narrative, and perhaps trigger additional memories.

Other important issues revolve around the ethical and legal considerations of the interview. It is important that the interviewee is a willing participant in the process. Getting them to sign a release form before asking any questions is a simple means of verifying this permission. It provides both persons with legal protection.

Confidentiality is another issue. As the interview progresses, the interviewee may comment freely on a number of personal events in their lives and in the lives of other people. Before the finished transcript is compiled, the interviewee should have a chance to review it for accuracy and confidentiality. For example, during an interview with one of the authors, one interviewee voiced the opinion that the death of one associate—ruled a suicide by the police—was more likely to have been a murder. When the participant reviewed the transcript, though, he chose to delete that statement from the final version. His justification was that the idea was merely speculation on his part, and he had no evidence to support the idea. Making such a claim with no evidence could put an undue burden on the victim's family.

Oral histories can also be time consuming. Rick Bragg (2002) spent three years working on an oral history of his grandfather. A. Scott Berg (2003) spent 20 years interviewing actress Katherine Hepburn before the publication of his memoir about her. Although not all oral histories require such a lengthy involvement of time, they are all substantially more time-consuming than other forms of interviewing. Thus, the person who embarks on one must be committed to seeing it through. If not, both the interviewer and the interviewee will be disappointed.

Summary

Oral history interviews offer a rich opportunity for both the academic and popular communities. For academicians, oral history provides a means of viewing history from the perspective of the participants. Battles are studied in terms of their human turmoil and suffering, rather than as strategic activities. Social history is viewed by those who lived it rather than as a summation of demographic descriptors.

At the popular and personal level, family oral histories provide individuals with a chance to learn more about themselves and their families. Recording such an oral history helps to bridge the gap between generations as the stories of one generation are passed on to another. Furthermore, these oral histories provide a lasting record of the lives of older Americans, one that can be passed on to future generations.

As such, oral history interviews have the capability of making major contributions to both the academic community and to the lives of individuals. All it requires is a tape recorder, a little patience, and a desire to record someone's story so that others can know what they experienced.

Discussion Questions

1. Choose an oral history topic that interests you. Read a book on that topic that uses the oral history technique. What questions were asked? How were the interviews used to develop the topic?
2. Design an interview guide for an oral history project. Who would be the subject of your interview? What initial research work would be necessary? What questions would you ask?

Please see the companion website for additional resources at [www.routledge.com/cw/amsbary].

References

Anderson, R. E. (1984). Did I do it or did I only imagine doing it? *Journal of Experimental Psychology: General, 113*, 594–613.

Ballew, B. (2002). *The pastime in the seventies: Oral histories of 16 major leaguers.* Jefferson, NC: McFarland.

Berg, A. S. (2003). *Kate remembered.* New York: Putnam.

Bragg, R. (1997). *All over but the shoutin.* New York: Random House.

Bragg, R. (2002). *Ava's man.* New York: Random House.

Bruner, J. (1987). Life as narrative. *Social Research, 54*, 11–32.

Buehlman, K., Gottman, J. M., & Katz, L. (1992). How a couple views their past predicts their future: Predicting divorce from an oral history interview. *Journal of Family Psychology, 5*, 295–318.

Clark, E. C. (1995). *The schoolhouse door: Segregation's last stand at the University of Alabama.* New York: Oxford University Press.

Eisenberg, J. (2001). *From 33rd Street to Camden Yards: An oral history of the Baltimore Orioles.* New York: McGraw-Hill.

Elson, A. (1994). *They were all young kids.* Maywood, NJ: Chi Chi Press.

Elson, A. (1999). *9 lives: An oral history.* Maywood, NJ: Chi Chi Press.

Elson, A. (2002). *Tanks for the memories.* Maywood, NJ: Chi Chi Press.

Elson, A., & English, S. (1998). *A mile in their shoes: Conversations with veterans.* Maywood, NJ: Chi Chi Press.

Fink, M. (2002). *Never forget: An oral history of September 11, 2001.* New York: Regan Books.

Fisher, W. R. (1984). Narration as human communication paradigm. *Communication Monographs, 52*, 1–22.

Fisher, W. R. (1987). *Human communication as narration: Toward a philosophy of reason, value, and action.* Columbia, SC: University of South Carolina Press.

Gantz, W. (1983). The diffusion of news about the attempted Reagan assassination. *Journal of Communication, 33*, 56–66.

Golenbock, P. (2000a). *Bums: An oral history of the Brooklyn Dodgers.* New York: McGraw-Hill.

Golenbock, P. (2000b). *The spirit of St. Louis: A history of the St. Louis Cardinals and Browns.* New York: Avon.

Greenberg, B. S. (1964). Diffusion of news of the Kennedy assassination. *Public Opinion* Quarterly, *28*, 225–232.

Harris, A. K. (1985). Introduction. In R. J. Grele (Ed.), *Envelopes of sound: The art of oral history.* Chicago: Precedent Publishing.

Honeycutt, J. M. (1999). Typological differences in predicting marital happiness from oral history behaviors and imagined interactions. *Communication Monographs, 66*, 276–291.

Hoopes, R. (Ed.). (2002). *Americans remember the home front: An oral narrative of the World War II years in America.* New York: Berkeley.

Hurmence, B. (1989). *Before freedom, when I just can remember: Twenty-seven oral histories for former South Carolina slaves.* Winston-Salem, NC: John F. Blair Publishing.

Ives, E. D. (1980). *The tape-recorded interview: A manual for field workers in folklore and oral history.* Knoxville, TN: University of Tennessee Press.

Johnson, M. K. (1988). Reality monitoring: An experimental phenomenological approach. *Journal of Experimental Psychology: General, 117*, 390–394.

Johnson, M. K., Foley, M. A., Suengas, A. G., & Raye, C. L. (1988). Phenomenal characteristics of memories for perceived and imagined autobiographical events. *Journal of Experimental Psychology: General, 117*, 371–376.

Johnson, M. K., & Raye, C. L. (1981). Reality monitoring. *Psychological Review, 88*, 67–85.

Krasner-Khait, B. (2002, December). How to write an intriguing family history. *The Writer*, 34–37.

Kraus, S. (1962). *The great debates.* Bloomington, IN: Indiana University Press.

Kraus, S., Davis, D., Lang, G. E., & Lang, K. (1976). Critical events analysis. In S. H. Chaffee (Ed.), *Political communication: Issues and strategies for research* (pp. 195–216). Beverly Hills, CA: Sage.

McGinnis, D., & Roberts, P. (1996). Qualitative characteristics of vivid memories attributed to real and imagined experiences. *American Journal of Psychology, 109*, 59–77.

McMahan, E. M. (1987). Speech and counter speech: Language-in-use in oral history fieldwork. *Oral History Review, 15*, 185–208.

McMahan, E. M. (1989). *Elite oral history discourse: A study of cooperation and coherence.* Tuscaloosa, AL: University of Alabama Press.

McMahan, E. M., & Rogers, K. L. (Eds.). (1994). *Interactive oral history interviewing*. Mahwah, NJ: Lawrence Erlbaum.

McWhorter, D. (2001). *Carry me home: Birmingham, Alabama: The climactic battle of the civil rights movement*. New York: Simon & Schuster.

Mendelsohn, H. (1964). Broadcast vs. personal sources of information in emergent public crises: The presidential assassination. *Journal of Broadcasting, 8*, 147–156.

Powell, L. (2000). *Bottom of the ninth: An oral history on the life of Harry "The Hat" Walker*. San Diego, CA: Writer's Showcase.

Raines, H. (1983). *My soul is rested: Movement days in the deep South remembered*. New York: Viking Press.

Ray, D. (2003, July 27). Living history: Pell City project captures residents' fading memories of past. *Birmingham News*, p. 20A.

Ryan, C. (1959). *The longest day: June 6, 1944*. New York: Simon & Schuster.

Ryan, C. (1961). *The last battle*. New York: Simon & Schuster.

Ryan, C. (1974). *A bridge too far*. New York: Simon & Schuster.

Smith, L., Schwarzkopf, H. N., & Adams, E. (2003). *Beyond glory: Medal of Honor heroes in their own voices*. New York: W. W. Norton.

Spence, L. (1997). *Legacy: A step-by-step guide to writing personal history*. Athens, OH: Swallow Press/Ohio University Press.

Steinfatt, T. M., Gantz, W., Siebold, D. R., & Miller, L. D. (1973). News diffusion of the Wallace shooting: The apparent lack of interpersonal communication as an artifact of delayed measurement. *Quarterly Journal of Speech, 59*, 401–412.

Terkel, S. (1997a). *The good war: An oral history of World War Two*. New York: New Press.

Terkel, S. (1997b). *Working: People talk about what they do all day and how they feel about what they do*. New York: New Press.

Terkel, S. (2000). *Hard times: An oral history of the Great Depression*. New York: New Press.

Terry, W. (1989). *Bloods: An oral history of the Vietnam War by black veterans*. New York: Ballantine.

Weaver-Lariscy, R. A., Sweeney, B., & Steinfatt, T. (1984). Communication during assassination attempts: Diffusion of information in attacks on President Reagan and the Pope. *Southern Speech Communication Journal, 49*, 258–276.

Xiong, N. (2002, January 29). Words of remembrance: Families capture past on tape with oral histories. *Birmingham Post Herald*, p. C4.

Yow, V. R. (1994). *Recording oral history: A practical guide for social scientists*. Thousand Oaks, CA: Sage.

Zimmerman, W. (1992). *Instant oral biographies: How to interview people & tape the stories of their lives*. New York: Guarionex Press.

12

INTERVIEWS IN CONTEXT

As discussed in the beginning of this text, interviewing is an everyday occurrence. Though most people think of it primarily in terms of employment and media, there are many contexts, both formal and informal, in which interviewing takes place. Although many of these contexts do not dramatically impact the fundamental nature of the interviewing dynamic, two should be discussed—both because they have a significant impact on the dynamic itself and because the consequences of failure in the interview can literally mean the difference between life and death. For this reason, this chapter will explore interviewing in the forensic and medical fields.

Forensic Interviewing

It is hard to watch the news today without hearing news of a traffic stop or police encounter turning violent. More and more attention is being placed on how police and citizens are interacting with each other, and interactions can escalate tensions and deescalate tensions. Furthermore, an understanding of how investigators and lawyers use interviews in their day-to-day jobs can help us understand how to make their jobs more effective. Forensic interviews are those that take place within the legal system, specifically how police officers and lawyers use them in their daily routines.

Police Interviews

Within the U.S. legal system, (1) police officers patrol their beats for the purpose of reducing crime and apprehending those that they catch in the act of committing such crimes (Langworthy & Travis, 1994); (2) felony cases require the involvement of detectives who use sophisticated interrogation methods to gather information; (3) lawyers for both sides use a structured form of interview known as the deposition to gather information from the other side; and (4) the courtroom environment lends itself to interviews by prosecution lawyers, defense lawyers, and the judge.

An understanding of police interviewing techniques is important for the police force, those involved in the judicial process, and reporters who cover the process. Research indicates that the most important factor influencing whether or not a case is solved is the information obtained by the patrol officer who initially responds to a complaint. Initial interviews at the scene with victims, witnesses, and suspects help the investigators to determine which crime has been committed and to identify possible suspects (e.g., Smith, Moracco, & Butts, 1998). Sometimes an arrest can be made immediately; other times, the information from those initial interviews is broadcast to other officers who can watch out for suspects or suspicious vehicles (Gaines, Kappeler, & Vaughn, 1997, p. 169). Regardless, if the patrol officer can identify witnesses or suspects who can be interviewed, the case is likely to be solved (Greenberg, Elliot, Kraft, & Procter, 1975). In fact, about 80 percent of all cases can be traced back to information obtained in these initial interviews (Greenwood, Chaiken, & Petersilia, 1977). What is often overlooked is that many of the techniques taught in typical university interviewing classes simply don't apply to the legal environment. Consider these differences:

- *Most interview situations place a value on openness and a willingness to communicate about one's self; in a legal interview, such actions could send you to jail.* Criminal suspects have constitutional protection against self-incrimination. If they don't want to answer questions, they don't have to do so.
- *Most interview training stresses the need for honesty and integrity; in a police interrogation, it's considered ethical for the police to lie in order to gather information related to a crime.* As of this writing, the Supreme Court has placed few limits on the use of deception in the interrogation room. As a result, it remains a major tool used by police for interrogation purposes (Skolnick & Leo, 1992) and has created a situation in which police often treat the interrogation as a "confidence game" in which they seek to trick the suspect into confessing (Leo, 1996b, p. 259). The officers may use a variety of techniques that include misrepresenting the seriousness of the offense or presenting fabricated evidence to elicit a confession (Skolnick & Leo, 1992). Magid (2001) has argued that virtually all successful interrogations involve some deception.
- The effectiveness of most interviews is enhanced when the participants adopt a collaborative style in which they seek to help each other; in a police interrogation, there is a clear adversarial relationship between the police and the suspect. The police want a confession from a guilty suspect, or at least information that would incriminate the suspect. The suspect, though, wants to stay out of jail.
- *Police interviews can be highly stressful on those police officers who conduct the interviews.* The nature of their job can place high levels of stress on individual police officers. The norms of their profession require that they remain calm and in control, constantly guarding their emotions, as they conduct interviews to gather evidence and interrogate suspects. The result can be repressed feelings that build up over time. Research indicates that the stress of the job is enormous. Furthermore, regardless of what kind of stress management technique may be used to combat stress, the emotional strain and tragedy associated with the job takes an emotional toll on police officers (Pogrebin & Poole, 1995).
- *Police interviews may involve complex intercultural interactions.* Police often work among and with diverse cultural groups. To be effective in that situation, effective police work requires a recognition and understanding of intercultural communication (Cornett-DeVito & McGlone, 2000).

The general rule is that you toss most of your interviewing rules out the window. Whereas most interview formats emphasize the need to be open and trusting, police officers are more likely to be suspicious, less trusting, aloof, and secretive (Westley, 1970). The attitudes of the investigators can have a direct impact on the behavior of the police officers when interacting with individuals at a crime scene (Black & Reiss, 1967). People who are interviewed by the police, including average citizens with nothing to hide, may find that they are uncomfortable and that their resulting interactions are somewhat unnatural (Piliavin, 1973). To learn interviewing from a legal perspective, you'll need to start all over. We'll do that by dividing the topic into two sections—interviews by police and interviews in the courtroom. Interviews by police fall into two broad categories—interviews of witnesses and interrogations of suspects.

Interviewing Witnesses

Witnesses to a crime tend to fall into three distinct categories: victims, eyewitnesses, and others with information related to the crime. Typically, the police use different interview techniques with each one.

Interviewing 911 Callers. The initial citizen-police contact on crime reports often comes through emergency 911 calls in which someone calls to report a crime. The call-taker's job is to get essential information from the caller that can be used to direct a police response to the emergency (Zimmerman, 1984, 1992). In many places, automated 911 allows the call-taker to identify the location from which the call is made, but additional information is still needed (Whalen, Whalen, & Zimmerman, 1990). The problem, to the dismay of many 911 workers, is that the person reporting the crime often resists answering questions (Tracy, 2002). In particular, Tracy found that call-takers often posed questions is such a manner that the callers thought the call-taker was questioning their trustworthiness, their intelligence, and their moral character. When this was combined with a need to feel unimpeded, they resisted further questioning from the 911 workers. Furthermore, Tracy noted that "callers occasionally have trouble answering open-ended questions such as 'Which way did the suspect go?'" (p. 153), but they generally do better if call-takers use only short closed-ended questions. Tracy also recommends that call-takers use polite language when phrasing questions, using embedded questions such as "Can you tell me if . . ." rather than "Tell me if. . . ." Such wording is less threatening to the caller. Another technique is to preface the question with a statement indicating urgency, such as "We need a description of the suspect so the police can identify the assailant." While that wording takes slightly longer than a direct question, it allows a distraught caller motivation for calming down and answering the question.

Interviewing Victims. Interviewing victims requires a high level of tact and skill. Talking to them as quickly after the crime as possible ensures a more vivid recollection of the event (Cordner, Greene, & Bynum, 1983). At the same time, the trauma of the event may still have them in such a state of shock that the interviewer has to go slowly and carefully. Research on attribution theory has demonstrated that, as time passes, witnesses rely less upon what they saw and heard during an event while relying more upon their "attributions," i.e., their theory of what must have occurred. Thus, talking to the victims as soon as possible allows the interviewer to gather more accurate data. Later, even though the victim doesn't mean to do so, they may unwittingly point the police in the wrong direction.

Interviewing Witnesses. The key to building a case is gathering evidence. The second level of evidence, after the victims themselves, are those witnesses who have information relevant to a case, particularly eyewitnesses. Eyewitness testimony must be carefully approached. Investigators must gather information that can be used in court without doing anything that would prohibit the introduction of that evidence. That's not always easy to do. Witnesses are notoriously inaccurate in providing testimony, since they may describe what they *thought* they saw rather than what actually happened (Stephen, Allen, Chan & Dahl, 2004). In addition, several demographic variables can affect the accuracy of witness testimony, including age (Memon, Bartlett, Rose, & Gray, 2003), gender (Butts & Mixon, 1995), and ethnic background (Natarajan, 2003). Furthermore, their first reaction may be to describe their holistic impression of the event ("Everything was crazy!") rather than what happened ("I heard an explosion and turned around to see a dozen people running toward me"). The police investigators must frame their questions and their interviewing techniques in such a manner as to move the witnesses toward the latter type of information.

One approach used with multiple witnesses is called **social remembering**. Social remembering is a process of interviewing witnesses in dyads or groups. Thus, instead of treating recall as an intrapersonal phenomenon, this approach considers the recall process to be one that is enhanced by multiple cues. In the group interview, the investigator relies on cues from the responses of one person to trigger additional recall elements for another person. Research has generally found that this approach creates more accurate recall of events, but may also lead to overconfidence in inaccurate elements of those memories (Clark & Stephenson, 1990).

One common approach for doing this is the **cognitive interview technique** (Geiselman, Fisher, MacKinnon, & Holland, 1985; Geiselman, Fisher, MacKinnon, & Holland, 1986; Fisher, Geiselman, Raymond, Jurkevich, & Warhagtig, 1987; Fisher & Geiselman, 1992; Memon & Wark, 1997). The approach uses context restatement and social techniques for increasing rapport in order to enhance witness recall. The primary approach is context restatement, probing for more specificity. When a witness says, "I saw a man with a hat," the investigator follows up with "What color was the hat?" "Did you see his face?" "What was he doing?" etc. Each question is intended to spark more memories of the event. The technique is remarkably effective at increasing witness recall. Unfortunately, it can sometimes be too effective. It may trigger inaccurate memories. A number of studies demonstrated that extensive probing can produce errors in witnesses' statements (Memon & Wark, 1997). The problem seems to be particularly acute when the witness is a child.

Interrogation of Suspects

There was a time during the first half of the twentieth century when police would frequently use questionable techniques to induce confessions from suspects. One early study (Hopkins, 1931) found that more than 20 percent of all suspects had suffered some abuse at the hands of police—a finding that led one authority to describe the interrogation techniques of the time as the "detective as inquisitor" (Gaines, Kappeler, & Vaughn, 1997, p. 166). Fortunately, that trend has changed—fueled by laws that protect the rights of suspects and growing accountability requirements within police departments.

Still, the key to solving many crimes is the interrogation of the key suspects. Inbau (1999) calls the interrogation process a "practical necessity" in modern police work (p. 1403). Indeed, without the information gained from the interrogation, many cases would be difficult to solve. Leo (1996a) noted that the strength of the evidence prior to the interrogation was the key factor leading to a successful interrogation in one-third of the cases he studied.

Interrogations differ in format from other forms of interviews in that there is a definite adversarial relationship between the interviewer and the interviewee. The reason for the antagonistic situation is that the interviewee is also a suspect in a crime. As such, there is an imperative facing the interviewer to either confirm or disconfirm the investigator's suspicion. If their suspicions are confirmed, then the interviewer tries to go one step further—obtaining a confession. As Dillingham (1995a) noted, "A confession is the biggest hurdle a defense attorney must jump when trying to absolve his client" (p. 8). Getting a confession may not be easy, though. Like any good interview, an interrogation takes preparation, skill, and (usually) establishing rapport with the suspect.

Professional police interrogators usually approach the interrogation as a developmental process in which their actions and their goals change as the interrogation progresses. It is, as such, a multi-stage process. The goal of each process must be met before the interrogation can productively progress to the next level.

Establishing Rapport. Like any good interview, the first goal sought by the interviewer is to establish a positive relationship with the person being interviewed. In the interrogation, this goal is somewhat more complicated. Both participants recognize that the interrogation is an adversarial situation, and the interviewee will be understandably skeptical of any efforts to establish such a relationship. Still, some degree of rapport can be developed by a skillful investigator. When rapport is achieved, the suspect will find it harder to tell a lie.

The techniques for doing this fall within two broad categories—verbal and nonverbal. The most common verbal technique is to start the conversation on a topic unrelated to the crime. Any topic might be appropriate, but the one most frequently used in actual police interrogations is the criminal history of the suspect. Police Departments will have extensive information about any past crimes the suspect has committed. Furthermore, the suspect knows that these crimes are part of his or her criminal record. In many cases, they have already gone to jail for these crimes. As a result, they frequently discuss their past crimes freely and openly, particularly when talking to the police. There is, after all, no obvious penalty for telling the truth and no way to effectively deceive an officer who has a copy of the record. So why discuss such topics anyway? Because "once a suspect begins talking to you about one subject . . . it is more difficult for him to not talk about other subjects. This includes crime the suspect has committed" (Dillingham, 1995a, p. 9). Such discussions create a momentum of truth that benefits the investigator.

The nonverbal aspects of establishing rapport are traditional techniques—using open positions and gestures, smiling, and leaning toward the suspect. These behaviors convey an openness on the part of the investigator that simultaneously indicates that the interviewer is not a threat to the suspect, but is interested in hearing their side of the story. The suspect's response to such behavior is typically a relaxing of their own defensive posture. As this relaxation occurs, the interrogator typically moves closer as the interview progresses. The use of nonverbal cues to determine truthfulness is often misleading, and its validity as a means of determining truth from lying is becoming more suspect.

Verbal cues can often be more illuminating, because liars tend to use vague language when answering questions. When asked if he had been drinking, Jack gave the answer of a guilty person. Perhaps, subconsciously, he felt guilty for having "a few beers" even if he wasn't drunk. The guilty response in this instance is the vague response—"a few beers." In a similar situation, an innocent sober person would say "I had two beers" or "three beers." That is, the innocent person gives a precise answer. The guilty person gives a vague answer. Jack's vague response of "a few beers" was enough to make the policeman suspicious.

Such an incident reflects the importance of *key questions* during the interrogation. Key questions are those questions that are typically answered by innocent people differently than by those who are guilty, or at least those who are being deceptive. Unlike interviews for witnesses, which often use closed-ended questions, key questions are more frequently open-ended in nature. Their purpose is to help in identifying deception, and it's easier for a suspect to lie when answering a closed-ended question. Open-ended questions require longer answers and offer more opportunity for the investigator to identify deceptive responses.

Police interviews differ from others in that they fall into two distinct categories. Interviewing of witnesses typically involves talking with people who have information about the crime. Since they are not suspects, many of them will try to be helpful, even if their memories of the event are foggy. When the interview shifts to the interrogation of suspects, though, there is also a major shift in the adversarial nature of the interaction. The skillful interviewer must establish rapport with a person whose crime may be repulsive, but such rapport may be crucial to gaining a confession. There is, then, an element of duplicity and deception in police interrogations. The police may engage in deceptive behavior in order to get a deceptive person to tell the truth. As a result, the interrogator must always be alert to the possibility that they can elicit a false confession from a vulnerable suspect.

Interviews for Lawyers

From the viewpoint of the police, interrogation of suspects is an adversarial relationship that requires an aggressive interviewing technique. When interviewing witnesses, though, the police generally take a gentler approach that relies on building rapport with witnesses and stimulating their memory. Interviewing witnesses, at least, is not an adversarial interview situation.

Not so, though, for the courtroom. Anyone who testifies in a courtroom, either for the defense or the prosecution is likely to be subjected to both a supportive and an adversarial interview. The side for which the witness presents evidence will interview them politely and confidently. The opposition side will then do its best to discredit the testimony or to at least limit its credibility. Serving as a witness in a court case, then, is essentially a high-stress situation in which the interviewee is almost certain to face an adversarial interview.

The legal profession assumes that communication is a key attribute that influences success within the profession. Matlon (1988) views the legal interview as a form of dyadic communication that operates according to force field theory. The attorneys are agents of change who seek to use the judicial process to effect change on behalf of their client or the state. The interviews that occur within that process are forces that can either hurt or help their case. To be effective in that situation, the attorney must be an effective communicator who can show empathy, listen, and provide advice to clients. The structure for doing that follows two steps of the classic three-step approach. The first two stages—establishing rapport and gathering information—are consistent with most interviewing situations. The difference for the legal interview is that those first two stages are then used for a different purpose—either to provide advice to the client or to use the information for the client's benefit.

Understanding interviews in the courtroom thus requires an understanding of the role of the interview in that setting. Typically, such interviews are divided into six distinct categories: (1) client interviews, (2) witness interviews, (3) depositions, (4) jury selection interviews, (5) direct examinations, and (6) cross-examinations. We shall look at each of those situations individually.

Client Interviews

Client interviews are those conversations that attorneys have in their office with clients or potential clients (Bailey, 1985; Delia, 1980; Fahrenz & Preiser, 1980; Goldsmith, 1980; Thompson & Insalata, 1964). Those interviews can cover a range of topics that include criminal matters, real estate, divorce, domestic violence, or estate planning (Perkins, 1981; Greenwood, 1986; Custureri, 1989; Goldstein, 1992; Lehrman, 1995). Regardless of the topic, individuals who need legal services come to the lawyer to ask for advice (Meyerowitz, 1996). Edelstein (1992) noted that this initial contact is critical to the success of the attorney-client relationship. The attorney speaks with clients, gathering information about their case, and advises them on possible courses of legal action (Perkins, 1981; Greenwood, 1986). As such, the purposes of such interviews are three-fold—to gather information, to provide legal advice, and for the lawyer to decide whether to consider taking the case (Baum, 1983; Herman, 1995; Sugarman & Yarashus, 1995). The attorney's ability to handle those initial interviews can be critical in determining the success of the attorney's legal practice (Lezin, 1987).

Those goals may be simple, but an effective attorney must wade through a multitude of barriers that are not always present in other interview situations. People who need to talk with an attorney bring a variety of backgrounds and emotions to the interview environment. Potential clients are often from a different social class than that of the attorney; this class distinction can inhibit their disclosure, making it harder for the attorney to gather the information needed. They will come from a variety of educational backgrounds, a factor that will require the attorney to converse well with clients regardless of whether they possess a Ph.D. or have less than a junior high level of education (Matlon, 1988). Overcoming such barriers requires active listening skills on the attorney's part (Barkai, 1984; Jenkins, 1990; Lidman, 1998; Keeva, 1999).

The client's need to talk with an attorney may be triggered by a traumatic event within their lives, one that often triggers the expression of a variety of emotions. They may have been arrested for a crime, something that can trigger both embarrassment and guilt. They may have suffered a major problem—something that can cause pain and embarrassment. Lehrman (1995) noted that the attorney may be the first person to hear the whole story from the client, since the pain and embarrassment of their problem has inhibited full expression to other people. Such factors can inhibit their willingness to communicate. Still, if the attorney is to help them, such information must be elicited (Reuben, 1987). Thus, the attorney must assure them that all information within the story will remain confidential due to the attorney-client privilege (Lehrman, 1995).

All of these factors can be exacerbated by environmental factors at the attorney's office. If clients have to wait long, their concern about the approaching interview can intensify. Once the interview begins, anything that interrupts the discussion can also disrupt their disclosures. Thus, most attorney-client interviews occur within an area that maintains privacy for both parties, while the rest of the attorney's staff is instructed to minimize or eliminate disruptions such as telephone calls.

Witness Interviews

To prepare for a trial, an attorney will typically interview a number of witnesses who can provide information about the case—some of which will support his side while others may benefit the opposition (Harrigan, 1986; Reuben, 1987; McElhaney, 1997). Background research for such interviews will include reviewing police files on the case and identifying those people who could provide relevant information. Even then, though, care must be taken to ascertain the reliability of the information. People may withhold information because of a reluctance to get involved. Others may interpret events in light of their particular biases in the case. And some people will simple not remember things accurately. As a result, Frank (1973) estimated that witnesses are probably correct only half of the time. Schum (2001) goes even further, arguing that nearly all such evidence is inconclusive, imprecise, and vague.

Matlon (1988) noted that witnesses tend to remember four things well: (1) events that have been frequently observed, (2) intense events, (3) recent events, and (4) events that evoke experiences of pleasure or pain (pp. 63–65). The combination of these factors make it important for the attorney to interview witnesses as soon as possible, when they are still eager to talk about it and their memories are better. The attorney must use questions that help jog the witnesses' memory (Cope, 1989), with many attorneys using a variation of the cognitive interviewing process used by police investigators for this purpose (Fisher & Geiselman, 1986; Geiselman & Padilla, 1988). Matlon (1988) also notes that there is a psychological advantage to being the first attorney to interview witnesses, because "they tend to remain more loyal to the first party who interviews them" (p. 60).

The location for the interview should be comfortable and isolated. Others should not be present, or they might influence the witnesses' responses. The attorney should, of course, be polite. Special care should also be taken to use simple language that minimizes the use of legal jargon. As with most interviews, establishing rapport must be an early goal, but the focus for doing so is often to increase rapport for the victim rather than the attorney. People are often reluctant to reveal much information to an attorney unless they are sympathetic toward one of the parties in the dispute (Keeton, 1973, p. 311).

The attorney should also be prepared to ask useful questions (Powell, 1991). While that will include reviewing all elements of the case prior to conducting the interview, particular importance should be placed on visiting the scene. As Matlon (1988) noted, "Familiarity with the scene makes it easier to determine accuracy of accounts and lets the attorney help a witness remember some details" (p. 63).

As the interview progresses, the attorney must do two things—assess the value of the information and evaluate the potential impression that the witness will have for a jury. The credibility of the witness may be influenced by any number of factors—their training, appearance, nonverbal behavior, and/or verbal skills. The attorney can do some things to enhance some elements, such as making suggestions regarding how to dress. McElhaney (1993) suggests that the attorney consider a full range of options if a witness needs rehabilitation, including re-direct examination, asking simple questions, reminding them not to bluff, and the calling of corroboration witnesses. Still, some personality elements can still influence the jury's perceptions, with the witness's demeanor being a factor that the jury will weigh when considering the testimony (Imwinkelried, 1985).

A bigger concern may be memory problems (Cope, 1989). The testimony of most eyewitnesses is limited by the impact of the selectivity process. *The selectivity hypothesis* provides an explanation for how distortion, inaccuracy, and incompleteness creeps into a person's perceptions of events. Specifically, it attributes memory distortions to a combination of four effects: (1) selective exposure, (2) selective attention, (3) selective perception, and (4) selective retention.

Selective exposure refers to the idea that people tend to choose from a variety of perceptual stimuli at any given time. Even if a witness was on the scene of a crime or accident, they may not have been looking at the event when it occurred. *Selective attention* assumes that people only pay attention to some of the perceptual stimuli to which they are exposed. Information theorists note that the eye can process about five million bits of data per second, but the brain is capable of only processing about 500 bits during the same time. Given that disparity, only a portion of the available data is actually processed by an individual into any long-term memory bank (Egeth, 1967). In that situation, the selectivity hypothesis argues that even if they saw a two-car accident, they may have been paying attention to only one of the cars. Furthermore, they can easily be distracted by noise or other stimuli in their perceptual field (Smith, 1991).

But what if they had a good view and paid close attention to the entire accident? Their impression of the event can still be distorted through the process of *selective perception*. A person's past experiences, attitudes, and expectations will influence their view of any event. Finally, even if they perceive the event accurately, there is no guarantee that they will remember it for any extended period of time. The principle of *selective retention* states that a person more accurately remembers messages that are favorable to their self-image than messages that are unfavorable (Levine & Murphy, 1943). Thus, the overall impact of the selectivity process is to distort any witnesses' reports of any event.

Inaccurate eyewitness identification is not always intentional. Sometimes ethnic factors may interfere with the identification process, because members of one race often have trouble identifying members from another race (Malpass & Kravitz, 1969). Identification will also be compromised if someone else gives them information about the case, particularly if the information is incorrect. Mudd and Govern (2004), testing viewer memories of incidents on the television series *Cops*, found that misinformation provided by a confederate became incorporated into the memories of the other individuals viewing the show in a group setting. Furthermore, this effect increased over time, with individuals becoming more confident in those false memories over a two-week delay.

Depositions

Depositions are a particular form of pre-trial legal interviews that are used to gather information as part of the pre-trial preparation. It is an adversarial interview in which a potential witness for one side of the case is interviewed prior to the trial by the attorney for the opposing side (Blumenkopf, 1981; Harrigan, 1986; McElhaney, 1997). Ruvoldt (2001) described the deposition as the key to an effective cross-examination. Matlon (1988, pp. 70–71) identified four reasons for using a deposition:

- To assist the attorney in investigation and preparation for a case
- To evaluate a case for possible settlement
- To gain information to use in impeaching a witness during cross examination
- To appraise the performance of the opposition's witness

Although the deposition is not typically conducted in a courtroom, it is part of the court's legal record. Depositions are conducted under oath and are subject to the same rules of perjury. Those being deposed are required to tell the truth. Anything said during a deposition must be consistent with later testimony in court, or the individual could be subject to perjury prosecution. Furthermore, any questions that trigger an angry or evasive response during a deposition may warrant further inquiry during the cross-examination.

Jury Selection Interviews

The judicial name for jury selection interviews is *voir dire*. Matlon (1988) defines the term as "the oral face-to-face questioning of prospective jurors by judges and lawyers for the purpose of determining the jurors' competence to serve" (p. 114). In theory, the goal of the voir dire process is to seat a jury that will be impartial and objective. In reality, attorneys for both sides try to use the interviews to enhance their chances of getting a jury that will be favorable toward their side of the case (Sannito & McGovern, 1999). Their goals are threefold: (1) to get a jury that will be favorable toward their side of the case, (2) to establish credibility with the jury, and (3) to sensitize the jury toward their side of the case (Matlon, 1988, pp. 114–115). Those goals are actually presented in reverse order. Broeder (1965) found that most of the attorney's time during voir dire was spent on the sensitization goal, with the selection of favorable juries ranking last. The credibility goal seems to take up about 40 percent of the jury selection process (Balch et al., 1976).

Generally, attorneys can have some impact on choosing a favorable jury, but ultimately that impact is limited by the sample of jurors chosen for their case. Still, since a favorable or unfavorable attitude on the part of one juror can impact the process, some questions nearly always focus on this area. Mauet (1988) recommends outlining open-ended background questions in advance, with probes added to identify specific attitudes that may be related to the case. If a bias against the attorney's case can be identified, the attorney can challenge the right of the prospective juror to sit on the panel. Questions often used for this purpose are those asking if there is anything that would prevent the juror from being impartial; whether they know the judge, the lawyers, or any of the parties; if they've had prior jury duty (if so, what kind of case); whether they've ever been sued; and if they've ever been the victim of crime. Attitudes toward capital punishment are relevant on murder cases, for example. If the case is a civil case, whether they work for an insurance company and questions about willingness to compensate a plaintiff are acceptable.

The credibility component is achieved by being friendly and conveying a sense of professionalism. Typically, the attorney makes an effort to use clear and simple language that will not intimidate the juror. The attorney must also be careful to do nothing that would make the juror dislike him or her. As Mauet (1988) wrote, "Never embarrass a juror. Make sure you never force a juror to reveal anything about his job, family, home, education, or background that may embarrass him" (p. 34). Attorneys also seem to use some personality variables in their selection of ideal jurors. Individuals who get excused from jury duty by attorneys tend to have higher levels of verbal aggressiveness, dominance, and contentiousness than do empaneled jurors (Wigley, 1999). Thus, a potential juror who leaves a favorable impression with an attorney is more likely to be selected for the jury.

Most of the attorney's focus is typically on jury sensitization or, as Holdway (1968) defined it, indoctrination. From this perspective, questions asked of the jury are asked more for the educational statements that they make than to gather real information from the jurors. As Mauet (1988) noted, the questions should familiarize the jury with legal and factual concepts that are related to the attorney's side of the case (p. 36). At the same time, the jurors' responses to the questions will help the attorney assess the likelihood that they will accept arguments based on those principles. These questions often fall within the category of *leading questions*, i.e., questions that provide cues of what answer the interviewer is expecting (McElhaney, 1989). As a result, little true information is obtained. But, as Mauet (1988) noted, "they serve a valuable purpose by introducing the jurors to legal and factual concepts pertinent to case" (p. 37).

Direct Examinations

Direct examinations refer to those questions that an attorney asks of their own witnesses during the presentation of their case in court (Packel, 1982; Rubinowitz & Torgan, 2002). Matlon (1988) defines it as oral testimony that "is given when witnesses are brought to court in person to present information" (p. 60).

Mauet (1988) argues that witness preparation "involves both evidence selection and testimony preparation" (p. 11). He recommends the following rules for ensuring that each witness receives sufficient preparation:

1. *Prepare witnesses individually.* Mauet goes even further, noting that each witness should receive individual planning by the attorney. The questions the attorney plans to ask should be outlined on a separate sheet for each witness, and those "witness

sheets should reflect what exhibits the witness will qualify and the location of all prior statements" (p. 11).

2. *Review all previous testimony by the witness.* This usually means a review of the depositions given earlier in the case. It is essential that the testimony in court is consistent with the previous testimony in the deposition. Consistency is important to the attorney's case. Inconsistency could result in a charge of perjury against the witness.

3. *Review all exhibits with the witness.* The witness needs to know which of the exhibits the attorney will ask him/her to identify and discuss. Furthermore, the attorney should explain to the witness how this exhibit fits the overall strategy for the case.

4. *Review probable testimony of other witnesses.* The attorney focuses on potential inconsistencies, identifying anything in this witness's testimony that may be contrary to what someone else will say in court.

5. *Prepare and review direct examination.* Using their outline of questions, the attorney will review each question and the order in which they will be presented in court. The goal here is to make the witness comfortable with the process and confident about how to handle each question. However, the attorney typically does not show the actual written questions to the witness. The opposing attorney may specifically ask if such an exchange occurred and use the response to imply that the attorney attempted to influence the witness's testimony (Mauet, 1988, p. 13).

6. *Anticipate cross-examination.* The techniques of cross-examination will be discussed in the next section. However, the attorney typically tries to anticipate what the opposing attorney will ask the witness during that session, helping to prepare them to handle those questions better. The specific elements involved in this process will be discussed in the section on cross-examinations.

Advising the Witness. In addition to the preparation time spent with each witness, the attorney will also often work with each witness to provide suggestions for enhancing the impact of their testimony with the jury. The following suggestions are often included in this advice:

1. *Pay attention to courtroom appearance.* One of the basic principles of interviewing is that the nonverbal impression of the interviewee can have an impact on their credibility. To handle this, the attorney typically advises the witness on how they should dress for the court appearance. Sometimes the advice will be more specific, such as advising the witness to get a haircut or to trim a beard.

2. *Remind the witness to tell the truth.* Telling a lie is a questionable moral behavior in the real world. In the courtroom, it's a crime called perjury. Furthermore, any witness who is caught lying will hurt the attorney's case. It is essential that each witness tell the truth (McElhaney, 2003). As defense attorney Leslie Abramson noted, "It's so much more dangerous for the defense to put on a witness who lies than for the prosecution to do it. . . . It will be the excuse to convict, because no matter what the rules say, the impulse is to convict" (Abramson & Flaste, 1997, p. 107).

3. *Emphasize the importance of listening.* The most effective witnesses listen to every question and answer only that question. They don't ramble on to other issues or topics, or volunteer information that is not requested.

4. *Be polite.* Juries are more responsive to witnesses who are polite to the attorneys, to the jurors, and to the judge. A rude response may be rejected, even if it is accurate.

5. *Ask the lawyers to rephrase any question this is not understood.* During the cross-examination, the opposing lawyer may ask complicated questions. Asking the attorney to simplify such a question is both acceptable and recommended.

6. *Don't speculate.* A witness can testify only to what they personally did, saw, or heard. Even the latter may not be allowed if it is from a secondary source, i.e., someone else tells you what a third party said. Such comments are considered hearsay evidence and are usually not accepted as evidence in court.

7. *If either attorney makes an objection, wait for the judge to rule.* If the objection is sustained by the judge, then it officially was never asked. There is then no need for an answer. Furthermore, the witness who answers too soon may say something prejudicial to one side or the other. That could lead to a mistrial.

Selection and Order of Witnesses. Part of the attorney's preparation for trial includes who to ask and in what order to present the evidence (Maggiano, 1998). That requires decisions about which witnesses to present in court and in what order the information should be presented to the jury. The general rule here, as described by Mauet (1988), is "Don't overprove your case" (p. 17). When several witnesses will testify to the same thing, not all of them are needed. The attorney will typically choose only one or two of them—those who will make the best impression—to get that information into the trial. Other witnesses may have information that is irrelevant to the attorney's theory of the case. In those instances, the attorney must remember that they're "not required to prove everything, only the elements of your claim or your defenses" (p. 17).

The order of the witnesses will be based on three principles: (1) start with a strong and important witness; (2) present the case in a manner that discusses the evidence in a chronological or logical manner; and (3) finish with a strong witness. Mauet (1988) argued that "effective direct examinations that clearly, logically, and forcefully present the facts of the case will usually have a decisive effect on the outcome of the trial" (p. 75). The first and last witnesses emphasize the concepts of primacy and recency— factors that have received a great deal of attention in communication research. Audience members, whether they are jurors or television viewers, often pay close attention to the first and last segments of any message. Strong introductions and strong conclusions enhance the impact of any message. If the case is a lengthy one that covers several days, the attorney will typically space out witnesses so that each morning and afternoon session begins with a strong witness. Weak or adverse witnesses are usually called during the middle of the case. Technical information is also usually done in the middle of the case, calling several successive witnesses if it's necessary to explain and simplify the information. Corroboration witnesses, i.e., those that testify to the same thing and support each other, are called in succession, with the second witness immediately adding credence to what the first witness said.

Conducting a Direct Examination. In court, the attorney will follow a few general principles for conducting the direct examination interview (Paine, 2000; McElhaney, 2003). Some specific variations will also be used, depending on the particular type of witness being addressed. Most attorneys use the *witness narrative method,* in which broad questions are used that allow the witness to tell their story. The general rule here is that "the witness is star," so the attorney uses open-ended questions that allow them to be the center of attention (Matlon, 1988, p. 224). The attorney guides the process by eliciting "from the witness, in a clear and logical progression, the observations and activities of the witness so that each of the jurors understands, accepts, and remembers his testimony" (Mauet, 1988, p. 75). For each witness, questions have to be crafted that elicit relevant information and evidence that is beneficial to the client's case (Stuart, 1999). Some witnesses will be used to establish facts in the case (Bossart, 1998), whereas others may be asked to provide expert testimony (Malone, 1988; Lubet, 1993; Parker, Mills, & Patel, 2001). The attorney has to do all of this while using no leading questions, since leading questions are usually not allowed in direct examination. Mauet (1988) describes the resulting interview as "a creative art, one which allows you to tell a story to the jury in a way that is most advantageous to your party" (p. 76).

The principles for direct examination are as follows:

Step 1: Putting the witness at ease. Most witnesses experiences at least some mild form of anxiety when they first step into the courtroom. The attorney's first job is to calm them down. This is typically done by opening the interview with preliminary questions that are nonthreatening, such as asking them their name and background (Matlon, 1988, p. 224).

Step 2: Establishing witness credibility. When the preliminary questions have been covered, the attorney typically moves on to a series of questions that establish the witness's credibility on the topic. This may include an extension of background questions, particularly for expert witnesses, and other questions that explain to the jury why this witness is qualified to provide evidence on this case. Mauet (1988) noted that "Witness credibility is determined by who the witness is (background), what he says (content), and how he says it (demeanor)" (p. 75). The attorney's job is to ask preliminary questions that enhance the witness's credibility on each item. This is achieved by asking questions that tell the jury why the witness is there and shows them why the witness should be believed. Exhibits may be necessary at this point to help orient the jury. Meanwhile, the attorney must be a good listener who pays attention to the witness's responses. Not only does this ensure that all vital information is covered, but it also monitors the interview for unexpected answers while increasing the witness's credibility. Some members of the jury will be looking at the attorney to be sure the attorney is interested in the testimony.

Step 3: The key question. Typically, each witness is brought to court to testify to one key question related to the case. Once the witness's credibility on that question has been established, the attorney is poised to ask that key question. To emphasize its importance, though, Matlon (1988) recommends that the question be preceded by a "punch line" so the jury will know the focus of the testimony is about to come (p. 225). That punch line may be a preliminary question that emphasizes the importance of the approaching testimony ("Did you see anything unusual at that time?"), followed by the key question presented in an open-ended narrative format ("Could you tell us what that was?"). Mauet (1988) calls these punch lines "orientation questions" that let the jury know what to expect, noting that they are technically leading questions that are permitted by the court because of their preliminary nature. Mauet (1988) also recommends dividing the key question into two subtopics: scene description and action description. The ideal action questions elicit flowing descriptions in which the witnesses "paint a picture that the jury can actually visualize" (p. 86). Either way, the open-ended format is critical. Research has demonstrated that the use of closed-ended questions with specific answers triggers more errors by the witness than does the request for an open-ended narrative (Cady, 1924). Furthermore, the narrative approach increases the witness's credibility with the jury; the more complete and detailed the story, the more believable it is (Loftus, Goodman, & Nagatkin, 1983). Conversely, the use of closed-ended questions during the direct examination hurts the attorney's credibility (O'Barr & Conley, 1976).

Stage 4: Inoculation questions. There are no perfect witnesses and no perfect cases. As Mauet (1988) noted, perfect cases are settled in advance and rarely go to trial (p. 213). Each witness will have some weakness in their testimony. Most attorneys prefer to bring out those weaknesses in their direct examination and present them in a favorable light so that the witness's credibility will not be damaged during the cross-examination.

Mauet (1988) recommends doing this but to "bury" the relevant questions during the middle of the direct examination (p. 86).

Cross-Examinations

The opposing attorneys have just finished their direct examination of a key witness. It's now your turn as the trial moves to that stage known as cross-examination. Cross-examinations are those follow-up witness interviews in which the witness for one side of the case is interviewed by the attorney of the opposing side (Stuart, 1999; Ruvoldt, 2001; Valdespino, 2004). Such interrogations typically serve three purposes: (1) to clarify direct testimony, (2) to elicit more testimony, or (3) to weaken or impeach the direct testimony (Matlon, 1988, p. 214).

The nature of cross-examinations may vary depending on which set of legal rules apply to the court in question (Mauet, 1988, p. 232). The *English Rule* of cross-examination allows the attorney to address any issue that is relevant to the case. The *American Rule* is stricter, limiting all cross-examination questions to those facts and circumstances that were covered in the direct examination. A compromise approach is the *Michigan Rule*, in which the opposing attorney can ask questions related to burden of proof but cannot raise new questions that are only related to their theory of the case. Typically, the attorney can try to achieve one of three different goals during any individual cross-examination: (1) eliciting information that is favorable to their case, (2) creating doubt about the facts in the witness's testimony, or (3) impeaching the witness's credibility.

Eliciting favorable testimony. Often the credibility of the witness is so high that the attorney will be unable to discredit their testimony. In those instances, the attorney will typically examine the witness's testimony for anything that could be used to bolster their own theory of the case. When that occurs, the cross-examination typically ignores all of the other facts presented during the direct examination and instead focuses on getting the witness to agree with those facts that help their side of the case.

Hinck and Hinck's (2000) politeness theory argues that violating expectations of politeness can have a negative effect on persuasive efforts. Their approach expands on the work of Brown and Levinson (1987), who argued that politeness is a universal value that operates across cultures. It certainly appears to operate in the courtroom, particularly when trying to elicit favorable testimony on cross-examination. Eliciting favorable testimony requires that the attorney be pleasant and courteous to the witness. They must take this approach in a natural and relaxed manner, because as Hamlin (1985a) noted, "The jury has a nose for phony friendliness" (p. 244). The technique is relatively simple. Instead of reviewing the entire direct examination, the attorney simply identifies those elements of the testimony that were favorable to his/her side. The questions asked are those that simply get the witness to repeat those portions of their testimony. The approach can be used even if the material is not mentioned during the direct examination. If the witness said something during earlier depositions or other prior statements that would be favorable, the attorney can get them to go over that portion of their previous testimony. The technique can be effective even if the witness doesn't fully admit what the attorney is seeking. As Matlon (1988) noted, "If the witness does not admit what you believe he should, the testimony will probably not be accepted by the jury either" (p. 225).

Another possibility, if the witness is a friendly one, is to use leading questions that may stimulate a memory or fact (Taylor, Buchanan & Strawn, 1984, p. 87). Such an approach can elicit information that is useful to the attorney, but it will only be solicited if the attorney politely asks for the information. Conversely, the attorney who is viewed as rude or who engages in impolite behavior is likely to diminish any chance of a positive response from the jury. Conley, O'Barr, and Lind (1978), for example, have noted that attorneys should avoid the temptation to interrupt a witness. The attorney may be tempted to do so if the testimony wanders away from its intended direction, but such interruptions are likely to hurt the attorney's credibility.

Creating doubts about the facts of the witness's testimony. This form of cross-examination does not seek to destroy the witness's credibility, but it does seek to create sufficient doubts about the testimony that the jury will either dismiss it or minimize its effect. Matlon (1988) describes this approach as having the goal "to demonstrate or suggest that the testimony is less probably true than appeared at the end of the direct examination" (p. 225). Thus, the emphasis of this approach is not on "destroying the witness" but on demonstrating that "the person may have colored their testimony by injecting their own attitudes and perspectives" (p. 225). Again, though, politeness theory comes into play; the attorney who seeks to discredit such testimony cannot make the cross-examination "a direct assault on the witness's integrity, because the jury will resent and reject this tactic" (p. 226). Instead, the attorney assumes that the witness is honest, but the cross-examination seeks to suggest that other factors could have adversely influenced the testimony. This might include raising doubts about the ability of the witness to be certain of their facts due to (1) deficient perception, (2) deficient memory, or (3) their ability to accurately communicate their testimony. The first area relates to physical problems (poor eyesight, hearing loss?) or the potential for confusion ("There were two dozen other people there as bystanders—could the defendant have been one of them?"). The second approach attempts to raise doubts about the witness's ability to remember what happened at that time. The third simply questions their ability to recall and relate the event accurately. Put another way, this approach questions the witness's ability to communicate and testify in a logical manner ("When you say it was a tall, dark-haired man, aren't you saying you're not sure who it was?"). Any of these approaches, when successful, can be used to trigger doubt about the accuracy of the testimony.

Impeaching the witness's credibility. This form of a cross-examination is often viewed as a "destructive" cross-exam, since its goal is to discredit the witness so the jury will minimize or disregard them. Matlon (1988) noted that this approach should be used only when the attorney has a sound basis for doing so. "Unsuccessful attempts are worse than mere failures," he wrote. "An impeachment attempt that fails causes opposing counsel's witnesses to look stronger than when they began" (p. 238). Mauet (1988) also notes that such decisions "invariably involve calculated risks" (p. 213) for the attorney, and that the wrong decision can backfire. Still, if the decision is made to use the destructive approach, it should begin quickly since the witness is likely to be more nervous at that time. Attorneys usually open their cross-exam with a question that is unrelated to where the direct examination ended. The direct examination ended on a strong point for the opposition, and the witness will feel somewhat comfortable with that position. So, attorneys usually open with a question about a topic on which the witness feels less confident. The first questions are used to lay a foundation for a specific objective, with the discrediting question coming only after that foundation has been established. Bergman's (1979) "Safety Model" is the safer the cross-exam, the more likely an attorney is to accomplish the intended purpose. The maxim for the Safety Model is simple: "Do not ask a question that you do not know the answer to" (p. 185). McElhaney (2000) expanded the concept somewhat, arguing that the attorney should never ask a question unless: "a) You know the answer; b) The answer doesn't matter; c) Any 'bad' answer would be absurd; or d) You can prove the 'bad' answer is wrong" (p. 69). The attorney should be able to anticipate the probable response from the witness based on their preparation and prior depositions. If the answer cannot be anticipated, they generally prefer not to ask the question.

The second general guideline for an impeachment cross-exam is to not ask the witness to repeat any aspect of their direct testimony (Mauet, 1988, p. 234). Furthermore, most attorneys specifically avoid using the same organizational pattern or chronology that was used by the opposing attorney during the direct examination. The witness will feel relatively comfortable if the questioning picks up where the direct examination left off, or if they can anticipate the flow of future questions; as their comfort level increases, impeachment becomes harder to achieve. The one exception to this rule involves instances in which the attorney suspects that a witness has memorized their testimony. In that instance, an effective technique can be to ask some of the same questions that were asked in the direct examination. If the witness has memorized their story, they are likely to repeat their answers in the same manner this second time. As Mauet (1988) noted, "Once this has been demonstrated, you should inquire whom the witness talked to before testifying, to uncover the origins of the memorization" (p. 263).

The third general rule for an impeachment cross-exam is to ask short, clear, closed-ended leading questions and to do so in a rapid manner. Closed-ended questions are used to keep control of the process. As Matlon (1998) noted, open-ended questions are dangerous because "hostile witnesses are always looking for an opening to slip in a damaging answer" (p. 216). The fast pace is used because, as veteran trial lawyer Melvin Belli (1976) once wrote, "A witness answering rapidly is more likely to contradict himself" (p. 172). Leading questions provide the attorney with a better chance of reducing witness credibility (Wells, Lindsay, & Ferguson, 1979). The general formula is to (1) make a statement of fact and have the witness agree with it, and (2) to gradually establish the information that will be used for the impeachment question. The use of short questions will assist in keeping the jury's attention. Asking them in a rapid manner keeps the witness uncomfortable and avoids long pauses that might be interpreted by the jury as doubt.

One approach to this form of impeachment is to use a series of small questions, the totality of which is intended to convey a narrative that is favorable (Hobbs, 2003). Each question is used as a point-by-point critique of the narrative provided by the witness during the direct examination, with the intent to provide an alternative interpretation to the narrative and the conclusion offered by the witness. Such an approach has the advantage of allowing the attorney to introduce a different interpretation that explains the event.

The fourth general rule is to end on a strong note. Matlon (1988) calls this the "stop when finished" principle, noting that "cross-examination continuously tempts you to keep going on. There is always one more question you could ask" (p. 219). Similarly, Mauet (1988) warns against proceeding "past a climax." Continuing past that high point could backfire, triggering what Matlon called "the one-question-too-many" (p. 218), which hurts the case. Primacy and recency both play a role in the effectiveness of the cross-exam. The attorney should begin with the intention of seeking only two or three main points from the witness, with one point identified early and the other at the end of the cross-examination.

The fifth general rule regarding impeachment of witnesses is which approach to take. Generally, two options are available: (1) internal contradictions and (2) a reputation for not telling the truth. Under the first option, the attorney structures the questions around apparent contradictions in one of three situations: (a) statements that are inconsistent with previous statements, (b) statements that contradict known facts, or (3) statements that are inconsistent with the witness's behavior (Brewer & Hupfeld, 2004). In any approach, the questioning begins with the attorney laying a foundation by establishing the inconsistent statement. This statement may be uncovered from prior testimony, written materials authored by the witness, or other legal pleadings. Regardless, a foundation is laid by quoting the exact language of the statement and asking the witness whether they said that. The goal is to get the witness to commit to the statement, build up that commitment, and then contrast it with an impeachment question, i.e., another statement from the same witness that is inconsistent ("Which of these is the truth—the first statement or the last?"). Option B—statements that contradict known facts—are approached in the same manner, with the impeachment question focusing on the inconsistency of the response and other known facts ("How could you have seen him do that—the defendant was 30 miles away at the time?"). Option C—inconsistent behavior—uses a similar approach, with the impeachment question focusing on behavior ("If that's what you saw, why didn't you run to help?").

Interviews within the legal system can occur outside of the courtroom or inside the courtroom. The initial interviews between an attorney and a client occur outside the courtroom; those interviews are important in allowing the attorney to gather the basic facts of the case, make a decision regarding whether to pursue the case, and offer initial advice and counsel to the client. That interview may be followed by witness interviews in which the attorney seeks additional information that may be useful to the case.

Interviews inside the courtroom fall within three broad categories: (1) voir dire, (2) direct examinations, and (3) cross-examinations. Voir dire refers to the process when the members of the jury are selected. Attorneys from each side will interview the prospective jurors to see if any of them might have a bias that could affect the jury's decision. The direct examination is an interview within the courtroom in which an attorney interviews a witness for their side of the case, using the question-and-answer format to introduce evidence that will be beneficial to the case. The cross-examination is a follow-up interview to a direct examination; it is conducted by the attorney for the opposing side with the intent to weaken the evidence presented during the direct examination.

Thus, the interviewing process plays a vital role in the legal system. It is the process through which attorneys gather information, present their case, and attempt to refute the case of the opposing side. Understanding this role can make both the attorneys and the witnesses more effective at presenting their positions.

Medical Interviews

Medical interviews are of interest because American medicine has traditionally embraced the "medical model" of disease, an approach that defined disease in biological terms and pays little attention to social concerns except as they relate to genetics (e.g., African Americans who contract sickle cell anemia). In that model, a patient's attitudes toward his or her health, well-being, or health-care provider was not always a major concern in this model. Modern medicine has, however, been embracing a more patient-centered approach to the diagnosis and treatment of disease. Weston and Brown (1989) argue that patients' attitudes about their conditions play a critical role in identifying and implementing effective treatments. These attitudes include: expectations toward the physician and health-care system, personal meaning and restrictions about their conditions, moral meaning ascribed to their conditions, and attitudes toward lifestyle changes. They argue that "Physicians who ignore these dimensions of sickness overlook a powerful source of information and potent tool for healing" (p. 77). The information-centered model claims that better healing is achieved when the doctors and patients achieve a consensus of understanding on the problems leading to the patient's condition, the goals of health-care treatment, and the roles taken by the patient and the caregiver. In short, every step in the wellness process is predicated on a clear understanding of patients' attitudes.

Functions of Medical Interviews

Perhaps the most vital role of medical interviews is to gather information about the patient that will assist the doctor in making a treatment decision (Roter & Frankel, 1992). A variety of technical information must be gathered—patient history, symptoms, allergies, and current medications, to name a few. Even more important, this information must be accurate. The presence of any inaccurate information can invalidate the suggested treatment and, in some cases, lead to the patient's death.

Marlow (1997, p. 55) describes the medical interview process as one of "data collection" that uses observational and communication skills. That data, in turn, is used to assess the patient's conditions and problem. "In reality, assessment can begin while information is being gathered," Marlow noted. "It differs from data collection in that judgments are made about the information that has been collected" (p. 57).

The medical interview is a two-way exchange of information that leads to the development of a relationship between a physician and a patient (Cegala, 2002). Pragmatically, most of the responsibility for achieving that relationship rests with the doctor (Cegala, Socha-McGee, & McNeilis, 1996; McNeilis, 2001, 2002), since the patient rarely initiates such communication. That relationship is commonly manifested in terms of the doctor's "bedside manner" and plays a vital role in the development of a doctor-patient relationship—one that can potentially have a positive or negative effect on the patient's prognosis. A positive result leads to an empathic relationship in which the patient perceives the physician as understanding their problem (Makoul, 2002) and increasing the likelihood that the patient will follow the suggested medical regimen to ensure good health (Clowers, 2002). The interview is an important tool in developing that relationship. The key, from the perspective of the medical professional, is to provide useful information. The doctor's messages for the patient are more likely to be effective if those messages provide explicit information while providing an implied message of concern (Cegala, 1997; Levinson, Roter, Mullooly, Dull, & Frankel, 1997).

For the doctor to be most effective, the patient must trust the doctor's expertise. Given that the patient is often relatively uninformed on medical or anatomical matters, much of that trust will be based on the patient's perceptions of the doctor's skills. Granted, the medical degree itself will bestow a great deal of credibility on the doctor, but that's often not enough. The patient will fine-tune their evaluation of the doctor based on their doctor-patient interview. Indeed, research has found that the physician's communication skills influence patient perceptions of the doctor's credibility in terms of competence, trustworthiness, and caring for the patient (Richmond, Smith, Heisel, & McCroskey, 2002). Doctors who rush through the interview will leave a patient feeling frustrated and cheated (O'Hair, 1989). Doctors who ask good questions are doctors who seem to know what they're doing. The patients who are treated by such doctors are more likely to be satisfied with the care they receive (Wanzer, Gruber, & Booth-Butterfield, 2002; Richmond, Smith, Heisel, & McCroskey, 2002).

Barriers to Effective Medical Interviews

Despite the need to gather accurate information in medical interviews, several barriers can develop that inhibit the exchange of such information. These generally can be attributed to barriers created by (1) the patient, (2) the doctor, (3) medical jargon, and (4) the situation.

Patient-based barriers generally fall into four broad categories: (1) a reluctance to share personal information, (2) a lack of understanding of medical terminology, (3) an inability to objectify symptoms, and (4) an inability to articulate symptoms.

Many medical problems are of a personal nature that require individuals to talk about their body in terms that they rarely discuss with others. Patients rarely seek information when talking with doctors (Cegala, 1997) and ask considerably fewer questions than doctors (Roter, Hall, & Katz, 1988), even though they express a desire for more information (Waitzkin, 1985). When they do seek information, they often do not ask for information directly (Beisecker & Beisecker, 1990), preferring instead to use indirect methods to approach a topic. Patients can be particularly reticent when it involves verbalizing their emotional state. The result is that the physician often ignores those concerns (Suchman, Markakis, Beckman, & Frankel, 1997). Sometimes even the most verbose patient becomes remarkably shy when asked to discuss their medical problems (Torres et al., 2002). This tendency is most pronounced regarding sexually related disorders, and the effect can be multiplied when the doctor and patient are of different genders (Hirschmann, 2002). A male with erectile dysfunction, for example, will often feel uncomfortable discussing the problem with a female nurse or doctor. But patient reticence can also extend into a myriad of other medical situations—the athlete who is reluctant to admit pain for fear of being released from the team; the factory worker who is reluctant to admit vision problems for fear of being transferred or fired; or a middle-aged man who fears that the pains in his chest are signs of his own mortality. The medical interviewer must gradually break through such reluctance to gain an accurate picture of the person's symptoms.

Charlotte is a nurse with extensive experience working in an office with surgeons. She is particularly adept at pre-interviewing patients and translating their symptoms into medical terminology that is relevant to the doctor's diagnosis. She is so good, in fact, that doctors frequently ask her to sit in on their interviews with patients so that she can explain what symptom the patient is trying to describe. Those skills become relatively useless to her, though, when she is placed in the role of the patient herself. When a nurse or doctor asks for her symptoms, she frequently finds herself making vague references to aches and pains without being able to identify the specific source of the complaint.

Such problems are common. Many patients, when placed under the duress of pain and discomfort, are unable to objectify their symptoms in such a manner as to give a precise description of them to the doctor or nurse. Others engage in lifestyle activities that accentuate the symptoms that are unrelated to medical problems (Meredith, Stewart, & Brown, 2001; Street & Millay, 2001). The medical personnel who interview the patient must verbally probe for finer and more distinct explanations of the patient's problem.

Johnny was admitted to the hospital for surgery to remove a kidney stone. By then, he had been in pain for a considerable amount of time, and his family doctor had administered pain relievers to help with the discomfort. Admission to the hospital, though, required the completion of a pre-admission interview—one in which he was not able to participate. That incident illustrates those instances in which the medical condition of the patient interferes with their ability to communicate. Such situations can exist due to the physical or mental condition of the patient (Jackson & Kroenke, 1999). Sometimes an injury or disease can have such a strong impact on the patient that they are physically unable to describe their symptoms to the medical practitioner. When that occurs, the physician has to rely more heavily on direct observation of physical cues (e.g., blood pressure, pulse rate, temperature), and the interview has to be conducted with a person who is familiar with the patient's symptoms—either a family member or witness.

Not all barriers to effective medical interviews reside with the patient. At times, the behavior and personality of the medical personnel conducting the interview can create problems. As one group of researchers noted, "It is well established that most medical interviews in primary care are characterized by a scarcity of patient-centered interventions" (Del Piccolo, Mazzi, Saltini, & Zimmermann, 2002, p. 1871). Several behaviors can contribute to this problem.

An overworked admissions clerk must deal with dozens of patients and their families every day. The clerk's job is to process information that will ensure treatment for the patient and payment for the medical personnel. It is, essentially, a process of transferring information to forms that serve as medical records. Over time, a clerk may increasingly focus on obtaining the needed information while showing less concern for the patients and their families. Nor is the clerk the only medical personnel subject to such problems. In a time when the medical profession has an increased reliance on insurance forms and government reimbursements, it is relatively easy for all practitioners—including doctors and nurses—to burn out and have moments of insensitivity toward their patients. Doctors can also be guilty of insensitivity. They often interrupt their patients' responses (Frankel, 1984), change topics (Frankel & Beckman, 1989), and put off answering a patient's questions (Cegala, 1997).

The opposite of insensitivity is immediacy or empathy, i.e., the ability to relate to the immediate needs of the other person on an interpersonal basis (Suchman et al., 1997). Research has shown that patients who perceive medical personnel as engaging in immediacy behaviors also are more satisfied with the medical service they receive (Richmond, Smith, Heisel, & McCroskey, 2001). Furthermore, immediacy is a major factor in patient reaction regardless of whether the medical personnel involved in the interaction is a doctor (Richmond, Smith, Heisel, & McCroskey, 2001) or a nurse (Adkins & De Witt, 2000).

A bigger problem, at least from the medical perspective, is the possibility that medical personnel will pre-judge a condition and—as a result—not conduct a thorough interview with a patient. Although such problems can occur at any time, they seem to be frequent during periods in which doctors see a number of patients with similar symptoms. An outbreak of a new flu virus, for example, will result in dozens of patients visiting the doctor with flu-like symptoms. Most of those will have the new virus, but some are likely to have different (and possibly more serious) problems. The medical personnel must avoid the temptation to think, "Here's another one."

Bernstein and Bernstein (1980, p. 78) point out that "Health care professionals do not share a common vocabulary with most patients." Indeed, the medical community uses a very precise form of jargon that is unique to those who work within the field. Proficiency with the jargon tends to increase over time so that experienced medical personnel find that using technical language is done almost subconsciously. In many ways, that is an asset because of the resulting precision in communication. One advantage of the medical language is its preciseness; each word in the medical vocabulary has a precise definition, and that connotative meaning is shared with other medical practitioners. That precision of word usage allows for an accurate exchange of information in doctor-to-doctor, nurse-to-nurse, or doctor-to-nurse interactions. It is not, however, conducive to effective communication between a medical practitioner and a patient. Words that easily and quickly roll off the tongue of a doctor or nurse may sound like a strange, multi-syllable foreign language to the medically naive patient.

The problem may be particularly acute when dealing with patients who are children. They frequently have little exposure to medical jargon, and many of the words used by the medical practitioner will be strange to them. Furthermore, the euphemisms for bodily functions that they use at home are likely to be different from the euphemisms used by medical personnel. Medical personnel, for example, often use the euphemism "BM" to refer to solid body waste excretions. That term itself is an abbreviation for "bowel move-ment." But the medical practitioner who asks a child if they've had a "BM" or "bowel movement" in the past 24 hours is likely to be met by a blank stare. That question has to be phrased with a different euphemism, one that conveys the question without embar-rassing or confusing the patient ("Have you been to the bathroom today?"). Or, the physician must work with the parents to obtain an accurate assessment of the child's symptoms and establish a positive relationship for the care (Wanzer, Gruber, & Booth-Butterfield, 2002).

The problem is also a major concern with patients from a diverse cultural background. Although a large percentage of medical doctors are white, their patients are growing increasingly more culturally diverse in terms of age, education level, ethnic background, and language. Communicating with people from such diverse backgrounds is a growing problem for the profession (Du Pre, 2002). Age can be a major factor, with some older patients less active in the interview process (Hines, Moss, & Badzek, 1997). Language is another barrier, both in terms of language skills and education level. The physician, in particular, has to be tolerant of patients who mispronounce medical terminology or risk alienating the patient. Furthermore, patients with lower levels of formal education are often less active in providing information to the doctor (Hines, Moss, & Badzek, 1997), a factor that may require more probing on the part of the medical personnel.

Some factors unrelated to both the doctor and the patient can adversely affect the medical interview. The two most common of these are (1) the location and physical environment in which the interview occurs and (2) the presence of other people during the interview.

Joe was involved in a traffic accident in which an automobile struck a motorcycle. The bike rider was thrown 15 feet by the impact of the collision and suffered major injuries; the emergency personnel who soon arrived quickly treated the victim, stabilized his condition, and had him transported to a nearby hospital before turning their attention to the occupants of the car. One child was spotted who was sitting in an uncomfortable manner. When the EMTs asked if he was in pain, the child admitted that both feet were hurting. The EMTs quickly rolled up his pants and carefully cut away his shoes to get a better look at the injury. As the shoes were removed, the boy sighed and said, "That's better. I tried to tell them those shoes were too small." The point, of course, is that the location of the interview created expectations about the nature of the patient's com-plaint. Those expectations are not always accurate, and medical practitioners have to be ready to adjust for those situations.

Locations can also cause medical personnel to alter their interview style, based on their assessments of the seriousness of the problem. Hospitals sometimes run out of emergency room space during accidents that generate injuries to a large number of people, and some of the injured may end up on cots in the hallway while waiting for an open room. In such situations, some personnel may assume that the hallway patients are not as badly injured as those already in treatment rooms. That assumption is not always correct. And patients who are strapped to a hospital cot may also assume that their injuries are more severe than they would if they were standing or sitting while responding to the interview.

Sometimes the presence of a third person (e.g., a spouse, a nurse) during the interview can alter the patient's responses—sometimes enhancing and sometimes detracting from the medical experience (Schilling et al., 2002). Some men may be reluctant to discuss sexual problems in front of a female nurse, or women may be reluctant to speak of pregnancy problems in the presence of a male nurse. Similarly, a husband may be reluctant to discuss symptoms related to sexually transmitted diseases with a doctor if the husband's spouse is present during the interview. During such situations, it is the medical practitioner's job to be sensitive to possible reticence created by the presence of the third person. When such reticence is identified, the medical personnel need to change the situation so that the third person leaves the room.

Types of Medical Interviews

Northouse and Northouse (1985) identified two distinct types of interviews in healthcare settings. These two types—the information-sharing interview and the therapeutic interview—are distinguished by the goals and approaches.

Information-sharing interviews are those that place an emphasis on content. These include admissions interviews, health history interviews, and interviews aimed at symptom identification. These interviews can vary dramatically in terms of (1) the level of information needed and (2) the expertise required to conduct the interview. Admissions interviews, for example, are typically collected by clerical staff workers who gather biographical, demographic, and financial information. Health history interviews may be conducted by nurses who greet and meet a patient before they are seen by a doctor. Information about symptoms may be gathered by the doctor prior to making a diagnosis and a recommendation for treatment.

Although there are several alternative techniques for conducting an information-sharing interview (Rimal, 2001), such interviews are usually divided into at least three distinct stages: (1) a medical history, (2) a physical examination, and (3) a conclusion that includes explanations and treatment plans (Billings & Stoeckle, 1998; Shaikh, Knobloch, & Stiles, 2001). That structure is particularly applicable to the initial interview, where the primary goal is to gather information that can assist in the screening out of some medical factors. That structure typically varies somewhat on subsequent return visits; the doctor will spend less time on the medical history and physical examination, but spends more time emphasizing health behaviors and the active involvement of the patient in their treatment (Bertakis, Azari, Callahan, Robbins, & Helms, 1999).

The primary purpose of a therapeutic interview is to establish a supportive relationship that will help patients identify and work through personal issues, concerns, and problems. Benjamin (1981) called such interviews "helping interviews," and they may arise as a result of a number of situations and may be conducted by social workers, nurses, doctors, chaplains, or psychologists.

Therapeutic interviews tend to fall into two distinctive variations. *Directive interviews* are those in which the medical personnel direct and guide the discussion for the purpose of providing prescribed solutions. *Non-directive interviews* use an open-ended technique in which the medical personnel use questions that encourage the patient to examine their own situation to find comfort and possible solutions. The directive technique is more likely to be used in those situations that lend themselves to prescribed solutions. Thus, a person who has just been told that they have cancer will need some time to adjust to the information; still, during the subsequent interview about their intentions, the medical personnel can guide them to a series of options that have worked for others in their situation.

The non-directive technique is more likely to be used in emotionally charged situations, such as the death of a loved one. At those times, a chaplain may use the non-directive method as a means of getting the individual to express and confront their grief.

The Reverse Interview: What the Patient Should Ask the Doctor

A patient bears some responsibility for a successful medical interview (Street & Millay, 2001). Unfortunately, that doesn't always occur. Patients often do not directly ask for information (Beisecker & Beisecker, 1990). Frankel (1984) argued that patients' questions use a *dispreference* process when talking with the doctor, by tagging indirect questions to answers that they provide to a doctor's question. Such reticence inhibits the patient's ability or willingness to express their real concerns about their medical condition (West & Frankel, 1991).

The prudent patient avoids that problem and prepares to get maximum advantage from a visit with a doctor (Post, Cegala, & Miser, 2002). Patients who ask more questions are more likely to recall the information offered by the doctor (Socha-McGee & Cegala, 1998). The result of patient involvement also pays off for the doctor, because the doctor will find that patients who have been trained in health communication have a higher compliance rate, are more likely to have a successful treatment outcome (Cegala, Marinelli, & Post, 2002), and are more likely to have their needs immediately addressed (Roter et al., 1997). To optimize that effect, the patient should be prepared to do the following:

- *Provide a complete medical history and a thorough list of medications.* You're not going to shock or embarrass the doctor with your problems. The doctors have seen it all (or at least most of it) before. Furthermore, providing this information shows the doctor that you're committed to the process, something that encourages him or her to be more active in your treatment (Walker, Arnold, Miller-Day, & Webb, 2001). A complete medical history is particularly important in dealing with negative medical problems, because it increases the chances of the doctor effectively solving the problem (Ptacek, Ptacek, & Ellison, 2001).
- *Identify your major problem and express it early in the interview.* Reticence can compel some patients to withhold discussing their real problem until they must, but don't wait until the doctor is ready to leave the room to tell them why you're really there. They may be resentful that you've wasted so much of their time or—even worse— may assume that it's a minor problem since you waited so long to bring it up.
- *Be specific about your symptoms.* You don't have to be an expert in medical terms to identify the source of your pain or discomfort and do so as specifically as possible. Developing a basic understanding of medical terminology will help you to be more specific (Du Pre, 2002). Vague complaints can generate multiple interpretations by the doctor, and that could potentially lead to an improper diagnosis.
- *Before you leave, be sure to ask what you should do when you get home.* Remember, you were feeling bad—that's why you went to the doctor in the first place. But your discomfort can (and probably will) interfere with your processing of the doctor's instructions. Before you leave, ask one final question about what specific instructions she or he has given for your return home. Pay particular attention to instructions related to prescription drugs (Parrott, 1994; Smith, 1998). If you don't get the first thing right, you probably won't get any of the other instructions right either.
- *Ask specific questions.* Patients are often tempted to embed a question into a longer statement, a communication tactic that is often used in informal communication

interactions. However, the intent is likely to be lost when that occurs. Research has shown that doctors generally don't respond to embedded questions as questions and thus are not likely to provide the information requested (McNeilis, 2002).

The reverse interview should become a focal point of the doctor-patient relationship if surgery is a possibility. When the doctor recommends surgery, the interview roles between the doctor and patient are reversed. It becomes, for practical purposes, a job interview. The doctor seeks a job assignment from the patient, while the patient has to decide whether (1) the job is necessary and (2) if this is the person they wish to hire for that job. When that occurs, the patient should be prepared to ask several questions of the doctor. These include:

- *Why do I need this surgery?* If the explanation is not adequate, wait awhile before making a final decision.
- *Is this surgery the typical treatment for this problem? What other alternatives are available?* Surgeons are more likely to recommend surgical treatments that represent their expertise. That particular treatment may or may not be the one most frequently advocated for your problem.
- *How many similar surgeries have you done?* One of the author's friends frequently says that he wants his surgeon to have some gray in his or her hair, because he assumes that means the doctor has more experience. While that oversimplifies the concept, it does represent the idea that a surgeon should be an expert in the particular procedure that's being recommended for you.
- *What's the success rate? What can go wrong?* The sad fact is that not all surgeries are successful, and some types of surgeries are less successful than others. Side effects from surgery can range from temporary discomfort to death. The patient should know those odds before making a decision.
- *What type of anesthesia will be used?* Despite the routine nature of most surgeries, there is some danger involved every time anesthesia is used. The doctor should discuss which ones will be used and what possible effect they may have on you.
- *How long will it take me to recover from the operation?* Different surgeries can keep a person down for differing lengths of time. The athlete who has ligament surgery will find themselves sidelined longer than someone who has cataract surgery. Knowing the length of the recovery time can help you adjust better psychologically to the recovery.
- *Can this procedure be done on an outpatient basis?* Modern medical technology has resulted in an increased number of operations that can be conducted on an outpatient basis. Knowing you won't have to spend an extended amount of time in the hospital might have some weight on your decision to have the surgery. But, not all patients should opt for an outpatient procedure. Because of the risk of complications, some patients, particularly the elderly, may want a brief hospital stay for even simple surgeries to ensure that nothing goes wrong.

Summary

Forensic and medical interviews represent, perhaps, the most demanding contexts in which interviewing takes place. There are many constraints placed on the interviewer, and the interviewee's life may literally be at stake in the interaction. It is likely that most of the students reading this text will not be lawyers, police officers, or doctors. It is, however, likely that they will encounter these individuals throughout their lives.

An understanding of how and why these interviews are conducted will likely serve to increase their satisfaction with these interactions.

Discussion Questions

1. Do you believe that you control your behaviors or that outside forces control them? Pick a behavior that you engage in that you would like to change (e.g., getting more exercise or eating a healthier diet). Identify those reasons you believe prevent you from making these lifestyle changes (e.g., "I live in the dorm and they serve fatty foods there"). Which of these things can you change and which are beyond your control?
2. Analyze the interview behavior of attorneys on a television drama such as *Law and Order*. To what extent do their actions in a direct examination reflect the principles mentioned in this book? What about their actions during cross-examination?
3. Visit a real courtroom and observe the behaviors of the attorneys in those cases. Are they similar or different from what you observed for the television attorneys? What was similar? What was different? Why?

 Please see the companion website for additional resources at [www.routledge.com/cw/amsbary].

References

Abramson, L., & Flaste, R. (1997). *The defense is ready: Life in the trenches of criminal law*. New York: Simon & Schuster.

Adkins, A. D., & De Witt, S. (2000). *Nurse-patient relationships: The function of social support and immediacy in a hospice setting*. Paper presented at the annual meeting of the Southern States Communication Association, New Orleans.

Bailey, W. S. (1985). The attorney /client relationship: The hidden dimension of advocacy. *Trial Diplomacy Journal, 8*(3), 17–20.

Balch, R. W., et al. (1976). The socialization of jurors: The voir dire as a rite of passage. *Southern California Law Review, 4*, 271.

Barkai, J. L. (1984). Active listening: One way to be a better advocate, counselor, and business person. *Trial, 20*(8), 66–69.

Baum, D. B. (1983). *The art of advocacy*. New York: Matthew Bender.

Beisecker, A. E., & Beisecker, T. D. (1990). Patient information-seeking behaviors when communicating with physicians. *Medical Care, 28*, 19–28.

Belli, M. (1976). *My life on trial: An autobiography*. New York: William Morrow.

Benjamin, A. (1981). *The helping interview*. Boston: Houghton Mifflin.

Bergman, P. (1979). *Trial advocacy in a nutshell*. St. Paul, MN: West Publishing.

Bernstein, L., & Bernstein, R. (1980). *Interviewing: A guide for health professionals*. New York: Appleton-Century-Croft.

Bertakis, K. D., Azari, R., Callahan, E. J., Robbins, J. A., & Helms, L. J. (1999). Comparison of primary care resident physicians' practice styles during initial and return patient visits. *Journal of General Internal Medicine, 14*(8), 495–498.

Billings, J. A., & Stoeckle, J. D. (1998). *The clinical encounter: A guide to the medical interview* (2nd ed.). St. Louis, MO: Mosby.

Black, D., & Reiss, A. (1967). Patterns of behavior in police and citizen transactions. In D.J. Black & A.J. Reiss (Eds.), *Studies in crime and law enforcement in major metropolitan areas* (pp. 1–139). Washington, DC: U.S. Government Printing Office.

Blumenkopf, J. S. (1981). Deposition strategy and tactics. *American Journal of Trial Advocacy, 5*, 231–251.

Bossart, D. R. (1998). Direct examination of fact witnesses. *Trial Lawyer, 21*(5), 200–204.

Brewer, N., & Hupfeld, R. M. (2004). Effects of testimonial inconsistencies and witness group identity on mock-juror judgments. *Journal of Applied Social Psychology, 34*, 493–513.

Broeder, D. W. (1965). Voir dire examinations: An empirical study. *Southern California Law Review, 38*, 503–528.

Brown, P., & Levinson, S. C. (1987). *Politeness: Some universal in language usage.* New York: Cambridge University Press.

Butts, S. J., & Mixon, K. D. (1995). Gender differences in eyewitness testimony. *Perceptual & Motor Skills, 80*, 59–63.

Cady, H. M. (1924). On the psychology of testimony. *American Journal of Psychology, 35*, 110–112.

Cegala, D. J. (1997). A study of doctors' and patients' patterns of information exchange and relational communication during a primary medical consultation. *Journal of Health Communication, 2*, 169–194.

Cegala, D. J. (2002). *Physicians' and patients' perceptions of patients communication competency in a primary care medical interview.* Paper presented at the annual meeting of the National Communication Association, New Orleans.

Cegala, D. J., Marinelli, T., & Post, D. (2002). The effects of patient communication skills training compliance. *Archives of Family Medicine, 9*, 57–64.

Cegala, D. J., Socha-McGee, D. S., & McNeilis, K. S. (1996). Components of patients' and doctors' perceptions of communication competence during a primary care medical interview. *Health Communication, 8*, 1–28.

Clark, N. K., & Stephenson, G. M. (1990). Social remembering: Quantitative aspects of individual and collaborative remembering by police officers and students. *British Journal of Psychology, 81*(1), 73–94.

Clowers, M. (2002). Young women describe the ideal physician. *Adolescence, 37*(148), 695–794.

Cope, V. (1989). Interview techniques help jog witnesses' memories. *Trial, 25*(3), 95.

Cordner, G., Greene, J., & Bynum, T. (1983). The sooner the better: Some effects of police response time. In R. Bennett (Ed.), *Police at work: Policy issues and analysis* (pp. 145–164). Beverly Hills, CA: Sage.

Cornett-DeVito, M. M., & McGlone, E. L. (2000). Multicultural communication training for law enforcement officers: A case study. *Criminal Justice Policy Review, 11*, 234–253.

Custureri, R. D. (1989). The initial interview in a dissolution of marriage proceeding. *Florida Bar Journal, 63*(3), 37–40.

Del Piccolo, L., Mazzi, M., Saltini, A., & Zimmermann, C. (2002). Inter and intra individual variations in physicians' verbal behaviour during primary care consultations. *Social Science & Medicine, 55*, 1871–1885.

Delia, J. G. (1980). The initial attorney client consultation: A comment. *Southern Speech Communication Journal, 45*, 408–410.

Dillingham, C. (1995a, May/June). Confessions 101. *Police and Security News, 11*(3), 8–11.

Dillingham, C. (1995b, September/October). Confessions 101: Part III—Enhancing interviews with databasing. *Police and Security News, 11*(5), 33–36.

Du Pre, A. (2002). Accomplishing the impossible: Talking about body and soul and mind during a medical visit. *Health Communication, 14*(1), 1–21.

Edelstein, S. I. (1992). Well begun is half done: Initial client meeting. *Trial, 28*(12), 28–32.

Egeth, J. (1967). Selective attention. *Psychological Bulletin, 67*, 41–57.

Enelow, A. J., & Swisher, S. N. (1979). *Interviewing and patient care.* New York: Oxford University Press.

Fahrenz, F. D., & Preiser, M. L. (1980). The initial client interview: A critical prelude to every criminal case. *Trial, 16*(10), 26–29.

Fisher, R. P., & Geiselman, R. E. (1986). Client memory enhancement with the cognitive interview. *Florida Bar Journal, 7*(8), 27–31.

Fisher, R. P., & Geiselman, R. E. (1992). *Memory enhancing techniques for investigative interviewing: The cognitive interview.* Springfield, IL: Thomas.

Fisher, R. P., Geiselman, R. E., Raymond, D. S., Jurkevich, L. M., & Warhagtig, M. L. (1987). Enhancing eyewitness memory: Refining the cognitive interview. *Journal of Police Science and Administration, 15,* 291–297.

Frank, J. (1973). *Courts on trial.* Princeton, NJ: Princeton University Press.

Frankel, R. M. (1984). From sentence to sequence: Understanding the medical encounter from microinteractional analysis. *Discourse Processes, 7,* 135–170.

Frankel, R. M., & Beckman, H. B. (1989). Evaluating the patient's primary problem(s). In M. Stewart & D. Roter (Eds.), *Communicating with medical patients* (pp. 86–98). Newbury Park, CA: Sage.

Gaines, L.K., Kappeler, V.E., Vaughn, J.B. (1997). *Policing in America* (2nd ed.). Cincinnati, OH: Anderson Publishing.

Geiselman, R. E, Fisher, R. P., MacKinnon, D. P., & Holland, H. L. (1985). Eyewitness memory enhancement in the police interview: Cognitive retrieval mnemonics versus hypnosis. *Journal of Applied Psychology, 70,* 401–412.

Geiselman, R. E., Fisher, R. P., MacKinnon, D. P., & Holland, H. L. (1986). Eyewitness memory enhancement in the cognitive interview. *American Journal of Psychology, 99,* 385–401.

Geiselman, R. E., & Padilla, J. (1988). Cognitive interviewing with child witnesses. *Journal of Police Science and Administration, 16*(4), 236–242.

Goldsmith, J. D. (1980). The initial attorney/client relationship: A case history. *Southern Speech Communication Journal, 45,* 394–407.

Goldstein, B. H. (1992). Professional responsibility and the introductory interview. *The Practical Real Estate Lawyer, 8*(2), 11–12.

Greenberg, B., Elliot, C., Kraft, L., & Procter, H. (1975). *Felony investigation decision model: An analysis of investigative elements of information.* Washington, DC: Department of Justice.

Greenwood, D. (1986). The first interview. *Family Law, 16,* 143.

Greenwood, P., Chaiken, J., & Petersilia, J. (1977). *The investigative process.* Lexington, MA: Lexington Books.

Hamlin, S. (1985a). *What makes juries listen.* New York: Harcourt Brace Jovanovich.

Hamlin, S. (1985b). Preparing a witness to testify. *ABA Journal, 71,* 80–84.

Harrigan, K. L. (1986). Deposing the plaintiff's expert witness. *For the Defense, 28*(5), 12–18.

Herman, R. M. (1995). Stop . . . look . . . listen: Interviewing and choosing clients. *Trial, 31*(6), 48–56.

Hinck, E. A., & Hinck, S. S. (2000). Politeness theory and political debates. In D. Bystrom, D. B. Carlin, L. L. Kaid, M. Kern, & M. S. McKinney (Eds.), *Communicating politics: Engaging the public in Campaign 2000 and beyond* (pp. 124–130). Washington, DC: National Communication Association Summer Conference.

Hines, S. C., Moss, A. H., & Badzek, L. (1997). Being involved or just being informed: Communication preferences of seriously ill, older adults. *Communication Quarterly, 45,* 268–281.

Hirschmann, K. M. (2002). Risk and pleasure: How physicians narrate sex differently for females and males. Paper presented at the annual meeting of the National Communication Association, New Orleans, LA.

Hobbs, P. (2003). 'You must say it for him': Reformulating a witness' testimony on cross-examination at trial. *Text, 23,* 477–511.

Holdway, R. M. (1968). Voir dire: A neglected tool of the art of advocacy. *Military Law Review, 40,* 1–6.

Hopkins, E. (1931). *Our lawless police.* New York: Viking.

Imwinkelried, E. J. (1985). Demeanor impeachment: Law and tactics. *American Journal of Trial Advocacy, 9*(2), 183–235.

Inbau, F. E. (1999). Police interrogation—a practical necessity. *Journal of Criminal Law & Criminology, 89*, 1403–1412.

Jackson, J. L., & Kroenke, K. (1999). Difficult patient encounters in the ambulatory clinic. *Archives of Internal Medicine, 159*, 1069–1075.

Jenkins, T. (1990). The overlooked communication skill. *Law Practice Management, 16*(7), 34–37.

Keeton, R. (1973). *Trial tactics and methods.* Boston, MA: Little, Brown.

Keeva, S. (1999). Beyond words: Understanding what your client is really saying makes for successful lawyering. *ABA Journal, 85*(1), 60–63.

Langworthy, R. H., & Travis, L. F., III (1994). *Policing in America: A balance of forces.* New York: Macmillan.

Lehrman, F. L. (1995). Strategies for interviewing domestic violence clients. *Trial, 31*(2), 38–42.

Leo, R. A. (1996a). Inside the interrogation room. *Journal of Criminal Law & Criminology, 86*(2), 266–303.

Leo, R. A. (1996b). Miranda's revenge: Police interrogation as a confidence game. *Law & Society Review, 30*(2), 259–288.

Levine, J. M., & Murphy, G. (1943). The learning and forgetting of controversial statements. *Journal of Abnormal and Social Psychology, 38*, 507–517.

Levinson, W., Roter, D. L., Mulloolly, J. P., Dull, U. T., & Frankel, R. M. (1997). Physician-patient communication: The relationship with malpractice claims among primary care physicians and surgeons. *JAMA, 277*, 553–559.

Lezin, V. (1987). Can we talk? The first interview with potential clients can make or break your practice. *California Lawyer, 7*(8), 27–31.

Lidman, R. C. (1998). The power of narrative: Listening to the initial client interview. *Seattle University Law Review, 22*(1), 17–29.

Loftus, E. F., Goodman, J., & Nagatkin, C. (1983). Examining witnesses: Good advice and bad. In R. J. Matlon & R. J. Crawford (Eds.), *Communication strategies in the practice of lawyering* (pp. 299–302). Annadale, VA: Speech Communication Association.

Lubet, S. (1993). Expert testimony. *American Journal of Trial Advocacy, 17*(2), 399–442.

Maggiano, M. (1998). Evidence with impact. *Trial Lawyer, 21*(5), 300–308.

Magid, L. (2001). Deceptive police interrogation practices: How far is too far? *Michigan Law Review, 99*(5), 1168–1210.

Makoul, G. (2002). *Empathic communication in the physician-patient encounter.* Paper presented at the annual meeting of the National Communication Association, New Orleans.

Malone, D. M. (1988). Direct examination of experts. *Trial, 24*(4), 42–49.

Malpass, R. S., & Kravitz, J. (1969). Recognition for faces of own and other race. *Journal of Personality and Social Psychology, 13*, 330–334.

Malton, R. J. (1988). *Communication in the legal process.* New York: Holt, Rinehart and Winston.

Marlow, D. R. (1997). *Textbook of pediatric nursing.* Philadelphia, PA: W.B. Saunders.

Matlon, R. J. (1988). *Communication in the legal process.* New York: Holt, Rinehart and Winston.

Mauet, T. A. (1988). *Fundamentals of trial techniques* (2nd ed.). Boston, MA: Little, Brown.

McElhaney, J. W. (1989). Leading questions. *ABA Journal, 75*(10), 104–106.

McElhaney, J. W. (1993). Helping the witness: Techniques for keeping witnesses out of trouble. *ABA Journal, 79*(8), 85–86.

McElhaney, J. W. (1997). Exposing fatal flaws: Deposition is the time to find weaknesses in witnesses. *ABA Journal, 83*(4), 78–79.

McElhaney, J. W. (2000). The cross-exam minefield. *ABA Journal, 86*(12), 68–69.

McElhaney, J. W. (2003). Take a good look at direct. *ABA Journal, 89*(10), 38–39.

McNeilis, K. S. (2001). Analyzing communication competence in medical consultations. *Health Communication, 13*, 5–18.

McNeilis, K. S. (2002). Assessing communication competence in the primary care medical interview. *Communication Studies, 53*, 400–428.

Memon, A., Bartlett, J., Rose, R., & Gray, C. (2003). The aging eyewitness: Effects of age on face, delay, and source-memory ability. *Journals of Gerontology Series B: Psychological Sciences & Social Sciences, 58B*(6), 338–344.

Memon, A., & Wark, L. (1997). Isolating the effects of the cognitive interview technique. *British Journal of Psychology, 88*(2), 179–197.

Meredith, L. L., Stewart, M., & Brown, J. B. (2001). Patient-centered communication scoring method on nine coded interviews. *Health Communication, 13*(1), 19–31.

Meyerowitz, S. A. (1996). The 'first contact': When the client phones. *New York Law Journal, 216*(126), 5.

Mudd, K., & Govern, J. M. (2004). Conformity to misinformation and time delay negatively affect eyewitness confidence and accuracy. *North American Journal of Psychology, 6,* 227–238.

Natarajan, R. (2003). Racialized memory and reliability: Due process applied to cross-racial eyewitness identification. *New York University Law Review, 78,* 1821–1858.

Northouse, P. G., & Northouse, L. L. (1985). *Health communication: A handbook for health professionals.* Englewood Cliffs, NJ: Prentice-Hall.

O'Barr, W. O., & Conley, J. M. (1976, Summer). Language use in the courtroom: Vehicle or obstacle. *Barrister,* 1–9.

O'Hair, D. (1989). Dimensions of relational communication and control during physician-patient interactions. *Health Communication, 1,* 97–115.

Packel, L. (1982). How to prepare and conduct a direct examination of witness. *Practical Lawyer, 28*(1), 63–74.

Paine, D. G. (2000). The ten commandments of direct examination. *Tennessee Bar Journal, 36*(3), 20–23.

Parker, D. B., Mills, W. K., & Patel, J. (2001). Expert grilling. *Los Angeles Lawyer, 24*(8), 41–46.

Parrott, R. (1994). Exploring family practitioners' and patients' information exchange about prescribed medication: Implications for practitioners' interviewing and patients' understanding. *Health Communication, 6*(4), 267–280.

Perkins, J. H. (1981). How to prepare for the first interview with a client, and what it should cover. *Estate Planning, 8*(2), 92–99.

Piliavin, I. (1973). *Police-community alienation: Its structural roots and a proposed remedy.* Andover, MA: Warner Modular Publications.

Pogrebin, M. R., & Poole, E. D. (1995). Emotional management: A study of police response to tragic events. *Social Perspectives on Emotion, 3,* 149–168.

Post, D. M., Cegala, D. J., & Miser, W. F. (2002). The other half of the whole: Teaching patients to communicate with physicians. *Family Medicine, 34,* 344–352.

Powell, G. R. (1991). Take control: The right question gets the right answer. *Barrister, 21*(1), 17–20.

Ptacek, J. T., Ptacek, J. J., & Ellison, N. M. (2001). "I'm sorry to tell you . . ." Physicians' reports of breaking bad news. *Journal of Behavioral Medicine, 24*(2), 205–217.

Reuben, D. H. (1987). Getting the truth from the client. *Litigation, 14*(1), 11–13.

Richmond, V. P., Smith, R. S., Heisel, A. D., & McCroskey, J. C. (2001). Nonverbal immediacy in the physician/patient relationship. *Communication Research Reports, 18,* 211–216.

Richmond, V. P., Smith, R. S., Heisel, A. D., & McCroskey, J. C. (2002). The association of physician socio-communicative style with physician credibility and patient satisfaction. *Communication Research Reports, 19,* 207–215.

Rimal, R. N. (2001). Analyzing the physician-patient interaction: An overview of six methods and future research directions. *Health Communication, 13,* 89–99.

Roter, D., & Frankel, R. (1992). Quantitative and qualitative approaches to the evaluation of the medical dialogue. *Social Science and Medicine, 34,* 1097–1103.

Roter, D. L., Hall, J. A., & Katz, N. R. (1988). Patient-physician communication: A descriptive summary of the literature. *Patient Education and Counseling, 12,* 99–119.

Roter, D., Stewart, M., Putnam, S. M., Lipkin, M. F., Stiles, W., & Inui, T. S. (1997). Communication patterns of primary care physicians, *JAMA, 277*, 350–357.

Rubinowitz, B., & Torgan, E. (2002). Direct examination: The basics. *New York Law Journal, 228*(3), 3.

Ruvoldt, H. (2001, December 3). Key to perfect cross lies in deposition. *New York Law Journal, 226*, L6.

Sannito, T., & McGovern, P. (1999). Jury selection: The winning edge. *Trial Lawyer, 22*(5), 341–352.

Schilling, L. M., Scatena, L., Steiner, J. F., Albertson, G. A. Lin, C. T., Cyran, L. Ware, L., & Anderson, R. J. (2002). The third person in the room: Frequency role and influence of companions during primary care medical encounters. *Journal of Family Practice, 51*, 685–690.

Schum, D. A. (2001). *The evidential foundations of probabilistic reasoning.* Chicago: Northwestern University Press.

Shaikh, A., Knobloch, L. M., & Stiles, W. B. (2001). The use of verbal response mode coding system in determining patient and physician roles in medical interviews. *Health Communication, 13*, 49–60.

Skolnick, J. H., & Leo, R. A. (1992). The ethics of deceptive interrogation. *Criminal Justice Ethics, 11*(1), 3–12.

Smith, A. P. (1991). Noise and aspects of attention. *British Journal of Psychology, 82*, 313–324.

Smith, D. H. (1998). Interviews with elderly patients about side effects. *Health Communication, 10*(3), 199–209.

Smith, P. H., Moracco, K. E., & Butts, J. D. (1998). Partner homicide in context. *Homicide Studies, 2*(4), 400–421.

Socha-McGee, D., & Cegala, D. L. (1998). Patient communication skills training for improved communication competence in the primary medical care interview. *Journal of Applied Communication Research, 26*, 412–430.

Stephen, L. D., Allen, B. P., Chan, J. C. K., & Dahl, L. C. (2004). Eyewitness suggestibility and source similarity: Intrusions of details from one event into memory reports of another event. *Journal of Memory & Language, 50*, 96–111.

Stile, W. B., Putman, S. M., James, S. A., & Wolf, M. D. (1997). Dimensions of patient and physician roles in medical screening interviews. *Social Science and Medicine*, 13A, 335–341.

Street, R. L., Jr., & Millay, B. (2001). Analyzing patient participation in medical encounters. *Health Communication, 10*(3), 199–209.

Stuart, P. B. (1999). The basics of direct and cross-examination of a fact witness. *Trial, 35*(1), 74.

Suchman, A. L., Markakis, K., Beckman, H., & Frankel, R. (1997). A model of empathic communication in the medical interview. *JAMA, 277*, 678–682.

Sugarman, N., & Yarashus, V. A. (1995). Case selection: Resolving the threshold question. *Trial, 31*(4), 66–69.

Taylor, P., Buchanan, R. W., & Strawn, D. U. (1984). *Communication strategies for trial attorneys.* Glenview, IL: Scott Foresman & Co.

Thompson, W. N., & Insalata, S. J. (1964). Communication from attorney to client. *Journal of Communication, 14*, 22–33.

Torres, M. G., Rao, N., Lee, S., Pant, S., Beckett, C. S., & Rupert, D. (2002). *Disclosure, truths, and half-truths in physician-patient communication: An exploration and comparison among Argentina, Brazil, India, and the U.S.* Paper presented at the annual meeting of the National Communication Association, New Orleans.

Tracy, S. J. (2002). When questioning turns to face threat: An interactional sensitivity in 911 call-taking. *Western Journal of Communication, 66*, 129–157.

Valdespino, J. M. (2004). Cross-examination: The rules of the game. *American Journal of Family Law, 18*(2), 87–92.

Waitzkin, H. (1985). Information giving in medical care. *Journal of Health and Social Behavior, 26*, 81–101.

Walker, K. L., Arnold, C. L., Miller-Day, M., & Webb, L. M. (2001). Investigating the physician-patient relationship: Examining emerging themes. *Health Communication, 14*(1), 45–68.

Wanzer, M. B., Gruber, K., & Booth-Butterfield, M. (2002). *Parent perceptions of health-care providers' communication practices: The relationship between patient-centered communication and satisfaction with communication and care.* Paper presented at the annual meeting of the National Communication Association, New Orleans.

Wells, G. L., Lindsay, R. C. L., & Ferguson, T. J. (1979). Accuracy, confidence and juror perceptions in eyewitness identification. *Journal of Applied Psychology, 64,* 440–448.

West, C., & Frankel, R. (1991). Miscommunication in medicine. In N. Coupland, H. Giles, & J. Wiemann (Eds.), *Miscommunication and problematic talk* (pp. 166–194). Newbury, CA: Sage.

Westley, W. (1970). *Violence and the police.* Cambridge, MA: MIT Press.

Weston, W., & Brown, J. (1989). The importance of patients' beliefs. In M. Stewart & D. Roter (Eds.), *Communicating with medical patients* (pp. 73–86). Newbury Park, CA: Sage.

Whalen, M. R., Whalen, J., & Zimmerman, D. H. (1990). Describing trouble: Practical epistemology in citizen calls to the police. *Language in Society, 19,* 465–492.

Wigley, C. J., III (1999). Verbal aggressiveness and communicator style characteristics of summoned jurors as predictors of actual jury selection. *Communication Monographs, 66,* 266–275.

Zimmerman, D. H. (1984). Talk and its occasion: The case of calling the police. In D. Schiffrin (Ed.), *Meaning, form, and use in context* (pp. 210–228). Washington, DC: Georgetown University Press.

Zimmerman, D. H. (1992). Achieving context: Openings in emergency calls. In G. Watson & R. M. Seiler (Eds.), *Text in context: Contributions to ethnomethodology* (pp. 35–51). Newbury Park, CA: Sage.

INDEX

INDEX

interview, quantitative research: ethical
questions 148–149; intercept interviewing
145–148; introduction 139; polling process
139–145; probe questions 124–125, 142;
projective questions 140–142; pseudo-
polling 149–150; summary of themes
150–151
interview, radio and television 88–99;
checkbook journalism 98–99; discussion
questions 99; FACE formula 88; feedback
93, 98; interview tools 92–96; open-
ended questions 95–96; other side of the
microphone 96–98; political interviews
105–107; soundbites 88–89; summary
of themes 99; Sunday news shows
109–110; telephone interviews 98; types
of 89–92
interview, research: interviews in context
166–190; oral history 154–163; qualitative
type 123–134; quantitative type 139–151
interview, screening: in medical context
187; of potential hires 24–25, 51–52; in
research 125, 141, 144
interview, spot 90–91; see also interview,
radio and television
interview, surprise question 95–96; see also
interview, radio and television
interview, techniques: closed-ended
questions 8–10, 18; feedback 11, 15,
18; funnel sequence questioning 7, 9,
18; improper questions 9–10; interview
structure 11–12; inverted funnel sequence
questioning 7, 9, 18; monitoring 10–11;
open-ended questions 8–12, 18; probe
questions 8, 18; projective questions
8; question phrasing 8–9; question
sequences 7; third-person questions 8, 18,
131; tunnel sequence questioning 7, 18;
verbal tools 7–8
interview, therapeutic 187–188; see also
interview, medical
interview, witnesses: categories of witness
168–169; closed-ended questions 168,
178, 181; cognitive interview technique
169; establishing credibility 178; by lawyer
172–174; leading questions 177–179,
181; open-ended questions 168, 177–178,
181; by police 168–169; probe questions
115; selectivity hypothesis 173–174; social
remembering 169; suspect interrogation
169–171; things most remembered
172–173; witness court preparation
175–177
interview, workplace 4–5

interview effect 145; see also polling process
interviewer/interviewee relationship 12–13
interviews in context 166–190; forensic
interviews 166–182; lawyer interviews
171–182; medical interviews 182–189;
police interviews 166–171
interview structure 11–12
intrarater reliability 61; see also appraisal/
performance interview; interview, appraisal/
performance
inverted funnel sequence questioning 7, 9, 18;
see also interview, techniques
Ivins, Molly 91

job interview see interview, employment
Jones, C. 97
journalistic interview types 81–83
Jud, Brian 96, 98
jury selection 174–175; goal of 174; jury
sensitization 175; leading questions 175;
probe questions 174
jury sensitization 175; see also jury selection

key questions: direct examination 170–171;
suspect interrogation 170–171
key word question list 92
known associate interview 124; see also
qualitative research, in-depth interviews
Koppel, Ted 92–93

lawyer interview 171–182; client interview
171–172; cross-examinations 179–182;
depositions 174; direct examinations
175–179; interview locations 171, 182;
jury selection 174–175; witness interview
172–174
leading questions: direct examination
177–179, 181; interview, quantitative
research 144; interview, radio and
television 95; interview techniques 9,
18; jury selection 175; see also improper
questions; polling process
legal issues, appraisal/performance
60–61
legislative hearings: interview types 114–115;
purpose of 113–114
listening, the act of 93–94; see also interview,
radio and television
live interview 89–90; see also interview, radio
and television
loaded questions 8, 18; see also improper
questions
low individual interest 13; see also interviewer/
interviewee relationship

201